THE SIR JOHN T. GILBERT
COMMEMORATIVE LECTURES
1998—2007

The Sir John T. Gilbert Commemorative Lectures

1998—2007

DUBLIN CITY PUBLIC LIBRARIES

2009

This collection first published 2009 by
Dublin City Public Libraries,
138 – 144 Pearse Street, Dublin 2, Ireland.
© Dublin City Public Libraries

Compiled and edited by Máire Kennedy and Alastair Smeaton
Designed and typeset by David Cooke
Index compiled by Emily Odlum
Printed by Grafo, Bilbao

ISBN: 978-0-946841-98-1

Dublin City Public Libraries
Celebrating 125 years of service
1884–2009

Foreword 1998

As Dublin City Librarian I am pleased to inaugurate this series of publications based on the annual lectures given to commemorate the work of John T. Gilbert in documenting the history of Dublin and Dubliners. A distinguished panel of speakers has been invited to illuminate particular aspects of Dublin's history and to bring these insights to a modern audience. With the publication of the lectures they will now reach a larger and more widespread public.

Dublin City Public Libraries has a number of interconnecting objectives in relation to its research collections. The first is to assemble a broadly-based collection of materials on Dublin and Ireland of which the capital city and its citizens can be proud, developing a research collection of world significance. Secondly a duty of care in maintaining the collections is vital for the preservation of Dublin's printed heritage for future generations. The most important objective, perhaps, is to make the collections known and accessible locally through lectures and publications and to make them available to the world-wide community of researchers through the catalogue on the web. Ultimately, through the process of digitisation it is also intended to make remote access to the materials possible.

This series will continue, with the annual lectures held in the newly refurbished Pearse Street library. In restoring and developing Pearse Street Library and Archive, thereby creating a worthy home for the Dublin City Archives and Special Collections, the City Council has shown its ongoing commitment to the preservation of Dublin's cultural heritage.

Introduction

by **Dublin City Librarian, Deirdre Ellis-King**

The Sir John T. Gilbert Lecture series was initiated in 1998 both to commemorate and to build on the work of one of Dublin's most eminent bibliophiles and historians. A primary objective was to encourage interest in the history of Dublin and to make that history accessible to new audiences. Over a decade, ten eminent speakers have brought to life the Dublin of our ancestors, raising new questions in our minds about the city in which we live. Each has offered a personal insight into the historical, architectural and indeed, cultural and social fabric which has shaped the lives of those Dubliners who form either the primary focus of discussion and analysis, or, who act as shadows to the evolving physical fabric of city development. We are indebted to those speakers whose scholarly research and analysis casts new light on the stones of Dublin alleyways and buildings, on its people, its culture, and on the early visitors who sailed up the river, pausing to reflect on the setting as a place in which to build a future, and paving the way to a Dublin whose people can consider and value the evolving story of a great city.

Dublin City Libraries and Archives is publishing the ten lectures delivered to date within the series in single volume form, because, while each lecture is unique, together they offer the reader a convenient interacting perspective on varying aspects of extreme change in the story of Dublin's growing urbanisation. Publication of individual lectures will continue annually with a second series in single volume form to be published at the end of the next decade.

The first six lectures were held in the Oak Room of Dublin's Mansion House, and are now delivered, as was my expressed intention, in the restored Dublin City Library and Archive building in Pearse Street. In 2009, as we celebrate the centenary of the Pearse Street Public Library building and the 125th anniversary of the foundation of the municipal free public library system, this publication is a fitting tribute to the contribution which the public library system has made, and continues to make to the intellectual life of Dublin and its citizens.

Table of Contents

Sir John T Gilbert

The streets of Dublin revisited[*]

by **Douglas Bennett**

➤➤➤➤➤➤➤ ✦ ⬅⬅⬅⬅⬅⬅⬅

My Lord Mayor as you are aware the title of this lecture is the Streets of Dublin Revisited to commemorate the historian John Thomas Gilbert whose wealth of detail in his three volume *History of the city of Dublin* has made such an impact on historians down to the present day, covering as it does political, economic and social history together with a great deal more. Tonight we commemorate the year of his death, 1898, but not the actual day which was the 23 May, rather his birthday on 23 January. No doubt the organisers in their wisdom did not wish the Douglas Bennett inaugural lecture to overshadow the commemorations planned to mark the bi-centenary of the 1798 rising which coincide with the time of his departure from the earth.

[*]Gilbert Lecture, January 1998

Gilbert was born on 23 January 1829 at 23 Jervis Street, his grandfather Henry Gilbert having come to Dublin in the 1790s to establish a shipping office importing Gilbert's cider. Henry's son John was born in 1791 and in 1821 married Marianne Costello, daughter of a prosperous Roman Catholic, Philip Costello. Our John Thomas was the fifth child of the marriage. Although the father was a Protestant he allowed his wife to bring up the children in her faith. John went to St Vincent's Seminary, precursor of Castleknock College, thence to Bective College and finally to Prior Park near Bath were he left at the age of 17 to enter the family business. A bookish child he had investigated everything he could, printed or written, and transcribed anything he found about Dublin or Dubliners. When he sought election to the Royal Irish Academy at the age of 23 he was rejected, possibly due to his age and lack of academic qualifications. He was however elected three years later as volume one of the *History of the city of Dublin* was published. Among his many achievements he held the post of librarian of the Academy for 34 years. After his death his wife decided to dispose of the library gathered by him in more than 50 years of assiduous searching. Dublin Corporation of 1900 was sufficiently enlightened to vote £2,500 to purchase it and the Gilbert library in Pearse Street is a worthy memorial. In this age of computer technology, web sites, e-mail and internet my own archive is and continues to be on card indexes contained in old shoe boxes labelled, Clarkes, Winstanley, Dubarry etc. One day my widow should be able to dispose of it not so much for its historical content rather as an oddity in these modern times.

**Fish, Fruit and
Vegetable
Markets, Arran
Street
East/Mary's Lane**
Wholesale fruit
and vegetable
market opened on
6 December 1892
by the Lord Mayor
the right
honourable Joseph
M. Meade LL.D.
The fish market
was opened in 1897.
(Douglas
Bennett: Private
Collection)

A capital city includes, almost by definition, every imaginable form of architecture and every conceivable human type. Artists, architects, landscapers and developers have managed to formulate all shape and design supposedly possible in an ever changing environment. In the phantomatic streetscape is the ghost of something that has gone for ever and if Gilbert was to revisit the streets of Dublin he would recognise some of the sheer theatre of street life that had always enthralled but he would be shocked and terrified at some of the things that we call progress and we hope also be impressed with other changes.

In 1898, the year of his death Dublin City Council was established when a local government act reformed the old Corporation and a year later the Irish Literary Theatre was founded by William Butler Yeats aided by Augusta, Lady Gregory and Edward Martyn, the first production being Yeats' *The Countess Cathleen* and Martyn's *The heather field*. In Dublin, religion and politics are never far away and the new company which was to open as the Abbey Theatre in 1904 on the site of the city morgue was denounced by Arthur Griffith and some of his followers for not being used as a propaganda platform against Britain. At the turn of the century, in 1900, Queen Victoria visited Dublin for the fourth and last time. She stayed at the Viceregal Lodge and despite nationalist protests organised by Maud Gonne and James Connolly was given a glowing address of welcome by Dublin Corporation. A loving and grateful nation decided that a statue should be erected and this was unveiled outside Leinster House in 1908 and remained there until August 1948 when the first inter-party government of the state had taken office and decided that she must go. There is an amusing cartoon in that month's edition of *Dublin Opinion* showing a block and tackle over the statue while the Queen looks down on Mr De Valera and says 'Begob Eamon there's great changes around here'. The statue was removed to Bully's Acre near the Royal Hospital where it lay until Charles Haughey decided to give it to the Australian nation for their bi-centenary in 1987. Great changes indeed.

A few paces further up the street at Kildare place stands Thornycroft's statue of William Conyngham, 4th Baron Plunket one time archbishop of Dublin who after his marriage to Anne, daughter of Benjamin Lee Guinness, was appointed to St Patrick's Cathedral, then being restored by his father in law. The statue was unveiled in 1901 and when the cover was removed before a distinguished gathering it was discovered that the previous night some medical students had decided to improve the archbishop's appearance by placing his left arm and right leg in plaster of Paris. As early as the 1930s Kildare Street was in for change starting in 1935 with the impressive art deco offices of the Department of Industry and Commerce.

Dublin has always been a city of violent contrasts: the inequalities of wealth and the social and sanitary conditions of the poor quarters of the city bore no resemblance to the redbrick squares of the late eighteenth century where socialites dined and dipped into their morning papers. By the end of the nineteenth century the area between St Patrick's Cathedral and Werburgh Street had become one of the worst slums in Dublin. Starting with Sir Arthur Guinness and continued by Sir Benjamin Lee Guinness, then finished by his son the first Earl of Iveagh, the entire area was cleared and a new park built beside the

Bull Alley
Iveagh Trust public baths and laundry, built in 1905 after an architectural competition won by F.G. Hicks. Now a leisure centre. (Douglas Bennett: Private Collection)

cathedral. The Iveagh Trust was founded in 1903. The earl cleared seven acres of slums at a cost of £250,000 plus a further £50,000 towards the construction of housing for the poor. He endowed the Iveagh Hostel for working men and Iveagh Baths recently converted to a leisure and fitness centre. The flats of five storeys are at present being refurbished and the impressive hall and recreation complex known to generations of children as the Bayno which is a derivation of Beano meaning a feast, as a bun and cocoa were given daily to the children. It opened on 15 December 1909 with fifty children but the numbers rose to almost one thousand daily.

If Gilbert could revisit his city one street that he would have difficulty in recognising would be Sackville Street now O'Connell Street. In 1916 the Easter Rising took place with the most dreadful conflagration ever seen in Dublin causing £3 million of damage to the city centre. The rebel troops occupied the General Post Office and as a result of the fighting the lower end of the street from the river to the post office was devastated causing about £2.5 million worth of damage to property. Some fine re-building work continued until 1923 but in June 1922 the civil war left the area from Cathedral Street to Parnell Street in ruins. Three quarters of the street had been demolished between 1916 and 1922. In the rebuilding an opportunity was taken to drive Gloucester Street through into O'Connell Street creating Cathal Brugha Street named after one of the leaders who died in the fighting there. St Thomas Church of Ireland church in Marlborough Street was also demolished during the fighting in 1922 and a new church was erected in 1931 at the entrance to Cathal Brugha Street. The Parnell statue which was unveiled on 1 October 1911, together with Nelson and O'Connell completed what W.B. Yeats described as the three old rascals, and in his debate in the senate on divorce in 1925 suggested that their public presence was encouraging given their adulterous behaviour and that these very salutary objects of meditation might make us a little more tolerant. What in Gilbert's day had started as a fine street, O'Connell Street has now ended up with cinemas and fast food outlets that seem to dominate, and the once harmonious relationship between shop fronts is sadly missing. Nelson disappeared in 1966 although his much defaced and unrecognisable head is lovingly preserved by Dublin Corporation. He was succeeded in 1988 by a lady, Anna Livia, made in bronze. She does not lie happily in her granite jacuzzi in the company of empty beer cans and discarded beef curry take aways while confabulations of starlings hold their evening parliaments on her head and naked shoulders.

During the civil war of 1922 the Four Courts were severely bombarded. The Public Records Office set up by John Thomas Gilbert in 1867 went up in flames and the records of the country were reduced to ashes.

The Gate Theatre was founded in 1928 by Hilton Edward and Mícheál MacLiammóir. Until 1930 the company played at the Peacock, attached to the Abbey Theatre. The concert rooms of the Rotunda were leased that year. Lord Longford became a director in 1931, and after forming Longford Productions in 1936, leased the theatre for six months every year. For a couple of years in the 1950s I painted the scenery for his productions, my only payment being a free dinner in Groome's Hotel on a Friday night, providing that I had been working for him the previous week. Money was very short in those days. Alas Groome's Hotel closed in 1975 and was replaced with a four storey office block three years later. I hope that Gilbert would be pleased with the conversion of No.18 Parnell Square into the

Writers' Museum, an eighteenth century building which still retains many of its original features including a ceiling by Michael Stapleton. Here permanent displays illustrate the history of Irish literature from its earliest times to the present day. Letters, photographs, first editions and memorabilia put the featured writers into a tangible lively context. Next door in No.19 the museum also accommodates the Irish Writers' Centre which enables our contemporary writers to continue the tradition of meeting, talking and working in a friendly and comfortable environment. The dominant central house of Palace Row or Parnell Square, No.22, was bought in 1762 by Lord Charlemont. In 1932 this became the Municipal Gallery of Modern Art and later the Hugh Lane Gallery of Modern Art.

The late 1920s and 1930s saw a substantial increase in the number of large cinemas being constructed in the city. The Capitol had a seating capacity of 2,057, the Metropole held over 1,000. The Savoy held 3,000 while the Theatre Royal boasted 3,850 seats. There was a feeling of opulence when you entered those old cinemas and that 1s.6d. was well spent. The talkie cinema was here to stay. If these buildings were full you could always walk to Camden Street where the Theatre de Luxe seated 1,395. Attached to most cinemas, including the Carlton and Corinthian, there was a café/bar where you could have your tea also for 1s.6d. or if you were trying to impress a new lady friend 2s.6d. Multi-complex high technology impersonal boxes have replaced these great old bastions of entertainment.

Dublin always seems to have had a housing problem and in the 1930s it was estimated that eighteen thousand families were living in single-room tenements. New legislation on compulsory acquisition at this time resulted in impressive four-storey flats being erected in various parts of the city with courtyards and play areas including Mercer Street, Cook Street and Lower Bridge Street. Today after more than sixty years these buildings form an impressive streetscape.

Few occasions in the history of our city have been more memorable than the 31st Eucharistic Congress held in June 1932. Dublin was chosen because 1932 was then accepted as the fifteen-hundredth anniversary of St Patrick's lighting of the paschal fire at Slane. An estimated one million people attended the pontifical high mass at the Phoenix Park. These numbers would again be repeated when Pope John Paul visited in 1979. In 1932 the Dublin Port and Docks Board built a new bridge over the River Liffey named Congress Bridge. It replaced the old Butt Bridge, a centre-pivoted swing bridge erected in 1879 and named after Isaac Butt, founder of the Home Rule League. A new bridge was a necessity to take the heavy traffic of the time. It is unfortunate that it is shadowed by the city of Dublin junction railway familiarly known as the loop line which opened in 1891, an unsightly metal box affair covered to this day in advertising slogans which obliterate the view of the now completely restored Custom House. Another structure which hardly improved the skyline was the huge gasometer or gas holder on Sir John Rogerson's Quay which had until recently occupied a prominent position since 1934.

In Gilbert's day twenty five lamp lighters lit and quenched 3,750 gas lamps every day. These were gradually phased out with the opening of the Fleet Street generating station. Mercury and sodium lamps were adopted for all road lighting schemes in 1960. Mercury in the city centre and residential areas and sodium on main roads outside the North and South circular roads. 1939 saw the outbreak of World War II and in spite of neutrality German bombs fell in 1941 in Terenure and Harold's Cross with no casualties, but in May that same year the North Strand was bombed with thirty seven dead and many injured and hundreds left homeless. After the war West Germany paid £327,000 compensation. At one time it was thought that these bombs were accidentally dropped on the city but recent archival research by historians in Germany would seem to indicate that it was in reprisal for Mr De Valera allowing the Dublin fire brigade to rush to Belfast one night that year to help in the aftermath of the bombing there. Dublin was aware of rationing and lack of petrol put motor cars off the streets. Dublin was to become a city of bicyclists for a decade or more and the trams stopped running at 9.30pm each evening. There was a shortage of building materials although the Poulaphuca reservoir was built in 1940 and now supplies 24 million gallons of water to Dublin every day. There were good times as well. That year Seán O'Faoláin founded *The Bell* magazine which was to become the leading Irish literary journal of the time. It appeared regularly during the emergency, temporarily ceasing publication between 1948 and 1950, and eventually closing in 1954/5. Dublin airport also opened in 1940 to a design of architect Desmond Fitzgerald. We now come to a post-war era which brought new technology and a new vigour of philosophy to architectural design. This awakened with the opening in 1953 of Michael Scott's Busáras, the city's first modern office block and central bus station. Architects from many countries came to view Scott's new and exciting building. It should have heralded the birth of a new provocative historical period but Gilbert would have been horrified at the evidence of urban blight if he could have revisited then. It was a time of dilapidated buildings and of day-to-day destruction and over the next decade enormous cement and glass office blocks totally out of context with the streetscape would appear everywhere and the citizens of Dublin would fast get used to the heady smells of precast concrete: new cement and mortar.

As early as 1920, R.M. Butler, editor of the *Irish Builder* was to write 'Concrete, plain and reinforced, is bound to come more and more into use, the facility with which large self supporting slabs, domicile structures and so forth can be used must exert a very marked influence'.

The city had become shabby and one of your predecessors, my Lord Mayor, was to state that the city centre had 'about as much character as a second-rate knacker's yard'. It was indeed becoming a shambolic mess and this once handsome city was quickly withering into hideous old age. Another person who did not live to witness this was Alfie Byrne who died in 1956 and was ten times Lord Mayor between 1930 and 1955. I have a vivid memory of him when I was a very young child. The national school that I attended was one of the first to introduce the penny dinners and Mr Byrne came to inspect the preparation and serving of the food. As he walked along the guard of honour he looked down at this five year old and said 'not you again Douglas'. My mother at that time had been carrying on a vigorous campaign for the compulsory education of blind children in the city and was continually knocking on the Lord Mayor's door with me in tow.

I would like to remind you of 1957. The highlight of that year for me and for many others was the arrest of Alan Simpson, the director of the Pike Theatre, for producing Tennessee Williams' *The rose tattoo* and being involved (I think that everybody was except Archbishop McQuaid), in fund raising for the high court case, headed here by Cyril Cusack and in England by Sir John Gielgud and Laurence Olivier. The garda giving evidence in the case had never been in a theatre before except to a pantomime at Christmas and one phrase of his remains in my memory, 'your honour she proceeded to remove a garment' which under cross examination proved to be her cardigan. That same year Lord Gough's statue was blown up in the Phoenix Park. It was the last remaining equestrian statue in Dublin. Seán Citizen has always loved a good bang.

On May Day 1965 Liberty Hall, a seventeen storey block rising one hundred and ninety seven feet, built for the Irish Transport and General Workers' Union, opened its doors giving a slightly vertiginous view from its top floor where the muffled hum of the city seemed a long way away. Dublin had never seen anything quite like this before, a crystal tower hiding the skyscape. The city would never be the same again. Across the river the Theatre Royal in Hawkins Street, home to the Royalettes, Mickser Reid and Jimmy O'Dea was demolished, together with the Regal cinema and Ostinelli's restaurant that served the best spaghetti bolognese in the capital. They were replaced by an ugly tower block, Hawkins House. At the College Street entrance stood the Crampton memorial unveiled in memory of Surgeon General Crampton. It was removed in 1959, the corporation maintaining that it was in a dangerous state. This was the demolition era and architectural heritage was not rated very highly. Two years earlier in 1957 the Office of Public Works had pulled down two large Georgian houses in Kildare Place behind Archbishop Plunket, already mentioned, and replaced them with an unsightly brick wall. At Lower Dominick Street the corporation razed most of the Georgian buildings which had beautiful plaster-work interiors and replaced them with modern flats.

This was all too much for Desmond and Mariga Guinness who were to found the Irish Georgian Society in 1958 in an effort at least to raise a voice (albeit unpopular at the time) of protest against our, or their, fast disappearing eighteenth-century heritage.

This society was to come into its own when the ESB decided to demolish sixteen late eighteenth-century houses at 13 to 28 Lower Fitzwilliam Street. After a lengthy bitter battle, the ESB announced a competition that was won by a young company Stephenson Gibney and Associates in 1962. The letters and editorials in *The Irish Times* make interesting reading when seen in context thirty five years later, the chairman of the ESB suggesting that the eighteenth century did not have a monopoly in talent, imagination and good taste. Charles Haughey was to express the same sentiments in 1967 when he opened City Bank's new premises in Hainault House. There then followed two unfortunate incidents. In June 1963 two elderly occupants of a house in Bolton Street were killed when the building collapsed and ten days later two little girls were killed on the footpath when two tenements in Fenian Street collapsed burying them under the rubble. By 1965 Dublin Corporation in a state of panic had demolished 1,200 large houses and condemned

hundreds of others. A new breed of property speculator and developer was born. All that was needed was an anonymous telephone call to the dangerous buildings department of the corporation and another two or more houses would come down. Five Georgian houses at 74 – 78 St Stephen's Green were demolished to make way for an office block. The adjoining two were then demolished for another block. At that time the minority who believed that eighteenth-century architecture was important to the city were not foolish enough to imagine that it was important to the lives of most people or arrogant enough to think it should be. There is a letter to *The Irish Times* dated August 1966 and signed by a great many worthies including Mícheál MacLiammóir and Kevin B. Nowlan urging that the Green should be scheduled for preservation as an important cultural legacy. The Office of Public Works had obviously not read it when they removed the gates and railings at the corner facing Merrion Row to make way for what Dubliners called Tone Henge and Delaney's massive bronze of Wolfe Tone. Demolition continued in and around St Stephen's Green and Hume Street with cement replacing mellow brick.

Everywhere there seemed to be demolition squads at work and reckless speculators were erecting some curious constructions. There followed an overall degeneration in

Merrion Square

Restored doorways and fanlights at numbers 74 and 75. The square was laid out in 1752 by John Ensor for the Fitzwilliam Estate and completed towards the end of the century.

(DOUGLAS BENNETT: PRIVATE COLLECTION)

building designs, some almost of diabolical brilliance. Harcourt Road, part of the old South Circular Road leading into Adelaide Road with twenty two elegant houses in Gilbert's time became home to three of the most tasteless office blocks in the city, one of which was recently given a face lift of white tiles and a little protuberance giving a realistic public toilet effect. A city by its very nature must change and architectural designs cannot stand still but there was a high cost to pay for these wrecking activities caused by the removal of so much habitable accommodation for office space and if Gilbert could have walked at night time the streets of Dublin in the 1960s he would have found a dead city bereft of people and could have been forgiven for thinking that it was curfew hour. This head-long rush into curtain walled office blocks was to be seen in all the city centre streets including O'Connell Street, Dame Street, Nassau Street, Westmoreland Street, D'Olier Street and South Frederick Street. A commentator at the time was to suggest that the reason that the city had remained intact for so long was that we were too poor up to this time to pull it down. Nothing has changed the face of this city more than multi-storey office blocks including Áras An Phiarsaigh built in the 1970s on the sight of the historic Queen's Theatre founded in 1829 in Pearse Street. Fortunately this building was given a face lift four years ago and won an RIAI award for skilfully camouflaging the original building and at the same time realigning the façade of Pearse Street. Perhaps one day somebody will have the courage to do the same with the Mississippi paddle boat on St Stephen's Green and replace the tissue paper frills with something more in keeping with the area.

In 1966 a small group took over the derelict Tailor's Hall in Back Lane. During the 1790s the Dublin Society of United Irishmen used it as their ordinary meeting place and representatives of a great variety of other interests had held their meetings there during the 300 years since 1706. Dublin Corporation had decided to demolish the building because of its dangerous state and to make way for the new dual carriageway at High Street. After years of headache and fund raising the hall was restored and An Taisce now use it as their headquarters. It always gives me some satisfaction as I walk along the High Street and note the bend in the road at Thomas Street, the route of the new dual carriageway having been redesigned to allow for the restored building. It too is surrounded now by large office blocks but modernity and tradition are not totally incompatible. It is possible to enjoy the benefits of one while not jettisoning the other. This is a time that would include the demolition of part of Baggot Street for the £4.6 million Bank of Ireland headquarters and the Central Bank's premises in Dame Street that resulted in the removal of Commercial Buildings, a preserved complex built in 1798 which ranged round a court yard and was a convenient short cut to the quays.

Life goes on and Dublin has always cherished its personalities and the city is small enough for individuals to be known as individuals. Moore Street traders seem to thrive on words and an enormous out pouring of expression. Throughout all that previous controversial time and long before one vocal sound will be remembered coming from the person of Tommy Dudley known lovingly as Bang Bang. He lived in Bridgefoot Street and with great agility would spring grinning and glitter eyed on and off moving buses holding the central bar at the rear and shooting the enemy all around him with his large iron key. His roars of bang bang could be heard several streets away. He died on 12 January 1981. His latter years were happily spent in Clonturk House for the adult blind having long since handed up his weapon. Different forms of cultural eclecticism were found in Patrick Kavanagh and Brendan Behan with their impressive oratorical gifts while 'the pope' Eoin O'Mahony resplendent in his robes of a knight of St Columbanus and swirling his theatrical cloak managed to issue a complexity of speech even when directing American visitors to the Shelbourne Hotel. The electric kettle was invented in 1923 and the same year the first electric fridge was sold in America. Two years later the first television was on sale in the USA but it was not until New Year's Eve 1961 that television transmissions began in Ireland with the inauguration of Radio Teilifís Éireann. Big crowds turned out to celebrate this event outside the Gresham Hotel in O'Connell Street. In 1975 the saga of Wood Quay and the vain attempts to save Viking Dublin commenced. Eventually in 1983 Dublin Corporation would build their bunker offices on the site and the substantial remains of tenth-century houses, streets and quay walls would be seen for the last time. The newspapers of 1976 describe undignified scenes with violent altercations and exchanges of insults at the forty foot bathing place when women occupied what had been for generations that great bastion of 'gentlemen only'.

One of the most noticeable things in the city compared with one hundred years ago is our obsession with road widening in order to fill the areas with more commuter cars. A good example being the New Street, Lower Clanbrassil Street dual carriageway which after much controversy and protest got the go-ahead in the late 1980s and is used mostly by drivers who do not live in the area and whose vehicles emit noxious fumes from their rear ends around locals whose community has been split in two by all this concrete. The first motor cars were introduced onto Dublin streets in 1896 and by 1904 there were fifty as compared with three thousand in London. A little aside, on 52 Upper Clanbrassil Street, there hangs a commemorative plaque to the memory of Leopold Bloom who in Joyce's imagination was born there in May 1866. This was not the case. The plaque should have been erected on 52 Lower Clanbrassil Street and the startled owner of 52 Upper informed the reception committee that no Jew by the name of Bloom had ever lived there in her family's lifetime. She was quite right but the plaque remains. In 1984 the dining hall of Trinity College was burnt and was completely restored in 1986 the year that excavations commenced at Dublin Castle resulting in the restoration of the greater part of the castle complex including the Old Ship Street military barracks and the extension of the clock tower building to house the Chester Beatty library and museum. This collection was left by him in trust to the Irish nation in 1953. It contained 13,000 volumes and the collection includes Babylonian clay tablets from 2500BC and Egyptian and Greek papyri.

1986 was not without its disasters, six Loreto nuns died in a fire at their convent in St Stephen's Green and on 25 August, Hurricane Charlie caused havoc when 3.1 inches of water fell in Dublin in twenty four hours causing widespread flooding and damage to property.

Natural gas that was to replace the old coal gas was new to the city in 1987 with many

Gray Street off Pimlico
Cast iron centre-piece built as a fresh water fountain in 1898. The dome was surmounted by an eagle until the Black and Tans shot it off. The fountain was relocated with a statue of Christ in commemoration of the centenary of Catholic Emancipation in 1929. (DOUGLAS BENNETT: PRIVATE COLLECTION)

teething problems including an explosion in Ballsbridge that wrecked a new block of flats killing three people. The city celebrated its millennium in 1988, the fact that it should have been 1989 is neither here or there, after all what is one year in 1000. It made the citizens aware of their valuable heritage and an effort was made to tidy up the streets and try to come to terms with the litter problems. During that year a lot of street sculpture was commissioned, a great many of the works being very good but some of it could only be described as kitsch while others are garish and oozing with stage Irish sentimentality that was once reserved for souvenir tea towels. When writing the *Encyclopaedia of Dublin*, my photographer, Brendan Doyle, and myself set a day aside to photograph in the Coombe area. A large metal sculpture, *Parable Island* by Peter Fink, stood on waste ground at Pimlico. Local children had attached ropes with old car tyres to the various metal angles and Brendan having slowly assumed a querulous expression it was left to me to climb up and untie the knots. As we walked around it trying to get a shot that would not include too much background, dereliction, empty crisp packets and thriving clumps of purple Buddleia, three women who were standing by told us that was what they did for the poor during the millennium. Caught on film they look as if they had been standing there forever, one with a fag end with a drooping inch of ash attached to her lower lip.

The previous ten years had seen a recession in the building trade when the property market collapsed in 1974 with huge cutbacks in all aspects of construction affecting architects to labourers but this was arrested and rejuvenated with section 23 apartments encouraging people through tax incentives to live in the inner city. As to whether these tiny box flats will stand the test of time remains to be seen. Public housing policy has shown an enlightened shift in the past ten years and Dublin Corporation are to be commended on a great many streetscapes that have come to fruition recently with single family housing replacing ugly tower apartment blocks. The corporation are extending this thinking into the refurbishment of older flat complexes. From 1989 onwards the Custom House Dock development has changed the face of Docklands forever.

Shopping as a leisure pastime has come to Dublin. The Stephen's Green Centre with its Americanised malls opening on Sundays as well as during the week, encouraging shops in and around Grafton Street, now pedestrianised, to do likewise. The city centre is again alive and well in the evenings with restaurants and pubs doing a lively trade and the fog seems to have lifted. Fragmented sounds are heard from street musicians with one opus after another taking us to new peaks of enthusiasm. At times the polyphonic chorus is endless and those of you who burn the midnight oil and dance the night away will be aware of the amount of rick-shaws available to transport you home being sponsored by a foreign beer manufacturer. Streets change and are widened but rarely do they physically disappear, but on 2 November 1992 a new link road between Camden Street and Harcourt Street was opened and Charlotte Street disappeared. Back in the 1770s it was named after the seventeen-year-old bride of George III. Most of the street was absorbed into the Harcourt Centre and adjoining office blocks. Fortunately the Bleeding Horse Inn built in 1710 remains. One of the largest projects in recent years was the refurbishment of the area between Eustace Street and Fleet Street known as Temple Bar, one of the last fragments of the central area which gives a picture of Dublin city before the Wide Street Commissioners replaced its medieval street pattern with the spacious formality of Georgian streets and squares. The transformation of these previously underused and

Clanbrasssil Street Lower

Some of the last remaining houses on the west side of the street. Named after James Hamilton, second earl of Clanbrassil KP (1739–98). A dual carriage-way 88 feet wide replaced the small dairies, public houses and butcher's shops that had been operating for generations. (Douglas Bennett: Private Collection)

neglected streets focused attention on their character and distinctive potential that was greatly aided by European money. New building designs like the Ark, the Art House and the Gallery of Photography seem to fit happily into the old streetscapes but a lot of strategic buildings were lost and this is unfortunate. The area leans heavily on pub/restaurant culture and perhaps the project managers should pause for thought to get a better balance in what was and is an exciting concept.

Dublin is evolving at an extraordinarily fast rate, much of it due to the tax incentives of the Designated Areas Scheme formalised in the Finance Act of 1986, but, and here we must be careful, a lot is due to a new phrase that has come into common usage, the 'Celtic Tiger economy'. Our main street shops are fast losing any individuality that they might once have had. Vast sums of money without adequate protection for our heritage are quickly turning the inner city into an impersonal walk about, however many exciting things are also happening. A major restoration work was carried out by the Office of Public Works between 1980 – 84 on the Royal Hospital Kilmainham built for the reception and entertainment of ancient, maimed and uniform officers and soldiers, the first being admitted in 1684. The building is now used as a centre for culture and the arts and houses the Irish Museum of Modern Art. Last year the National Museum of Ireland moved its fine art collection to the newly restored and splendidly refurbished Collins Barracks and for the first time the furniture, silver, costume and other artifacts are elegantly displayed in magnificent galleries. Large numbers of hotels have opened recently including the Merrion Hotel located in an eighteenth-century house in Merrion Street with beautiful plasterwork ceilings. Open top buses now enjoy an all year round season taking visitors

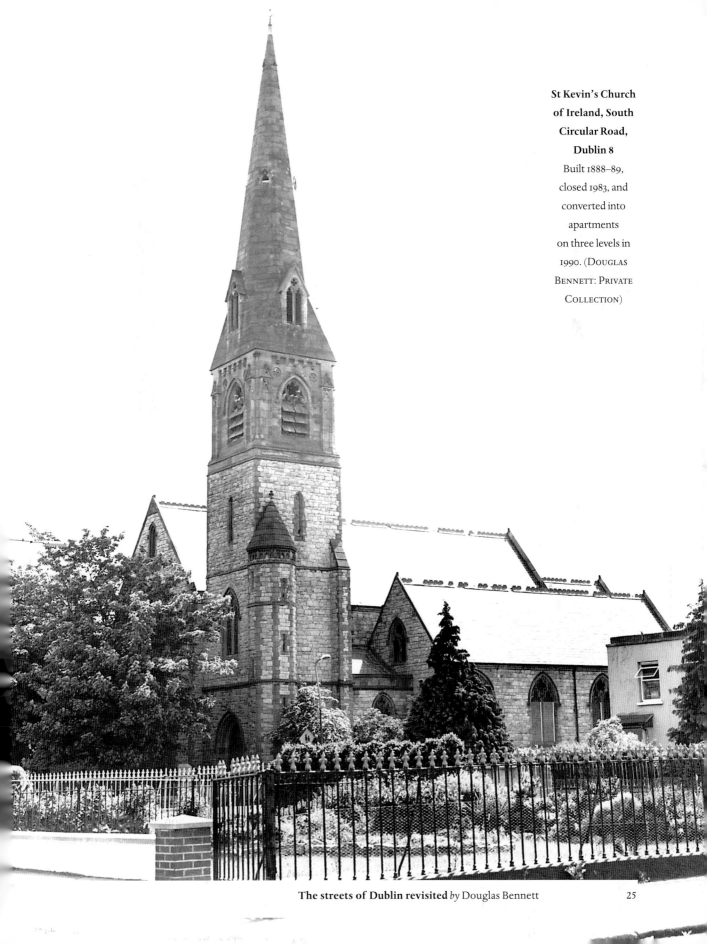

St Kevin's Church of Ireland, South Circular Road, Dublin 8
Built 1888–89, closed 1983, and converted into apartments on three levels in 1990. (DOUGLAS BENNETT: PRIVATE COLLECTION)

The streets of Dublin revisited *by* Douglas Bennett

around the sights of Dublin. To commemorate the millennium what the manufactures described as the most beautiful and astonishing clock in the world was lowered into the river Liffey at O'Connell Bridge. Such beauty could not cope with the oozy and slimy mixture to which it was subjected and was soon removed in need of a lot more than artificial respiration.

In a city that celebrated its millennium in 1988 and was designated European City of Culture in 1991, all of us have an important role to play in the creation of an attractive enjoyable environment where we feel at ease and where we may walk freely without being attacked. A city which gladdens our senses without which there is no real quality of life. There is an ever increasing awareness of the importance of the care and conservation of our heritage. Time will tell if there is a Gilbert bi-centenery lecture in the year 2098. Let us hope that the lecturer will describe the next 100 years as the age of enlightenment, that it heralded a new renaissance, that respect was paid to planning laws and that unlike the past these were rigorously enforced.

In spite of all that I may have said to the contrary, my Lord Mayor, Dublin has always been and still is a wonderful city and a great place to live in.

What a performance!*

Street entertainment in Medieval and Renaissance Dublin

by **Alan J. Fletcher**

✦

I was honoured and delighted to have been asked by Deirdre Ellis-King, Dublin City Librarian and her committee to give this second Gilbert Lecture marking the close of the centenary commemoration of Sir John T. Gilbert, distinguished historian of the city of Dublin. Tonight, I want to open up for you a neglected chapter in Dublin's history, and it is a chapter that I like to think Sir John would have enjoyed dipping into, since it was he whose diligence helped conserve many of the documents on which my research has been based.[1]

*Gilbert Lecture, January 1999

Having fun is a serious business, so it is a little strange that serious-minded historians have not paid the business of fun more attention. To be sure, their neglect is in part perfectly understandable, and is the direct result of a lack of documentary sources. It is well known that the doings of the mighty come festooned with bureaucracy, and their paper trails afford so many more opportunities for historians to pursue. At this higher social level, there is so much more produced to chew over. Consequently, kings and councils, magnates and power brokers, get the lion's share of attention in much traditional historiography. It is fair to say, then, that historians willy nilly have tended to be respecters of persons, though this has sometimes led in the direction St Paul disapproved of: the élite society of the past is the company in which the polite academic present seems to feel most comfortable in spending its time. Yet sources do exist for accessing the more lowly cultural activists that we will be thinking about tonight, even though those sources, being fewer and further between, tend to be less conspicuous. Tonight's subject, principally, will be the purveyors of fun who walked the streets of medieval and Renaissance Dublin, and the aim to bring into focus not only what these people did, but also what their wider social role and impact were.

So, given the topic, a good place to start would seem to be in an early Dublin streetscape. The earliest pictorial depiction of one that I am aware of appears in one of the woodcuts featured in John Derricke's *Image of Irelande*, published in 1581 (see Fig. 1). The woodcut betrays an interesting coincidence, and shows that the prejudices of traditional modern historiography that I began by speaking about have an ancient lineage. In the woodcut, Sir Henry Sidney, thrice appointed Lord Deputy of Ireland in the second half of the sixteenth century rides out of Dublin Castle over the bridge that crosses the castle

These trunckles heddes do playnly showe , eache rebeles fatall end,
And what a haynous crime it is , the Queene for to offend.

Although the theeues are plagued thus,by Princes trusty frendes,
And brought for their innormyties,to sondry wretched endes:
Yet may not that a warning be , to those they leaue behinde,
But needes their treasons must appeare,long kept in festred mynde.
Whereby the matter groweth at length,vnto a bloudy fielde,
Euen to the rebells ouerthrow , except the traptours yelde.

6

For he that gouernes Irishe soyle , presenting there her grace,
Whose fame made rebelles often flye , the presence of his face:
Be he I say,he goeth forth , with Marsis noble trayne,
To iustifie his Princes cause , but their demerures vayne:
Thus Queene he will haue honored,in middest of all her foes,
And knowne to be a royall Prince , euen in despight of those.

Fig. 1

Sir Henry Sidney, Lord Deputy of Ireland, and cavalcade leaving Dublin Castle (From John Derricke, *The image of Irelande* London, 1581)

moat. His cavalcade is turning left and on up into Castle Street. You can make out what I take to be Christ Church Cathedral rising above the forest of the soldiers' lances in the top right-hand corner. But apart from the viceregal bustle of this cavalcade, notice how otherwise strangely quiet this arterial city thoroughfare seems to be. If, as Shakespeare once put it, 'the people are the city', this is a loaded and partial view, for only a token populace is to be seen. Token, yes, but for all that, a carefully edited token. A man lugging a sack on his back seems visible, along with one or two other people, in the far background just to the left of the head of the lead horse of the cavalcade. A perfunctory presence, this may well seem. But consider what also may be going on here. A political detergent appears to have been applied to this streetscape, for the most part scouring out the great unwashed, and so leaving Sir Henry and his entourage spic and span at the centre of the viewer's interest. And as I mentioned, the editing is scrupulous: what populace is allowed to remain is well behaved and productive. In company with the man lugging his sack, they appear to be working.

But there is more to life than work. I want us to start imagining this squeaky-clean street in a less sanitised way, but in a way which may have been nearer to historical truth, picturing another group of folk who trod it, who came into their own mainly on high days and feast days, though doubtless at other times of the year too. Let's start thinking about fun in the raw as peddled by three lots of early Dublin street professionals: the city's gamblers, musicians, and juggling acrobats.

Gamblers first. To judge by the frequency of references to them, you might fairly guess that Ireland in general, leave alone Dublin in particular, was overrun with itinerant gamblers from the late-medieval period on. The Hiberno-English word most commonly used of them was *carrowe*, an anglicised version, now lost from Modern English usage, of the Irish word *cearrbhach* ('gambler', 'card-player'). In 1561, Thomas Smyth, a Dublin doctor, wrote a tract called 'Information for Ireland', the prime concern of which was to itemise in detail the sorts of folk we are presently interested in. (Smyth had become mayor of Dublin by the time Trinity College had been founded in 1592.) Of the *carrowe* he said, 'comenlye he goithe nakid and carise disses ['dice'] and cardes with him and he will playe the heare of his head and his eares ['and he will play away the hair of his head and his ears].'[2] It is not quite clear whether the *carrowes*' nudity noticed by Smyth was literal, or the result of his taste for hyperbole, but it seems likely that he wished to indicate that they had literally played the shirts from off their backs. Indeed, so widespread were *carrowes* that Sir Henry Sidney whom Derricke's woodcut invited us to admire felt obliged to legislate against them in 1576,[3] and when we consider the historian Edmund Campion's startling description of them, written in 1571, we can see further reason why Sir Henry, upholder of New English propriety, felt moved to do so:

'There is ... a brother-hood of Carrowes [*cearrbhaigh* = 'gamblers'] that professe to play at Cards all the yeare long, and make it their onely occupation. They play away Mantle and all to the bare skinne, and then trusse themselves in strawe or in leaves, they they [*sic*] waite for passengers in the high way, invite them to a game upon the greene, and aske no more but companions to hold them sport, for default of other stuffe they pawne portions of their glibbe [the glib was a forelock of hair characteristic of native Gaelic coiffure], the nailes of their fingers and toes, their privie members; which they lose or redeeme at the curtesie of the winner.'[4]

Richard Stanihurst, the famous Dublin historian, recycled Campion's observations a few years later in a publication of 1577, and attempted in his treatment of this passage to be somewhat more delicate, covering up the 'privie members' of Campion's account behind his own coy euphemism, 'dimissaries'.[5] This linguistic figleaf proved temporary, however, for it was partially plucked away later when Fynes Moryson, early in the seventeenth century, described the *carrowes* of his acquaintance in the following terms:

'Agayne the Irish in generall more specially the meere Irish, being sloathfull and giuen to nothing more then base Idlenes, they nourished a third generation of vipers vulgarly called Carowes, professing (forsooth) the noble science of playing at Cards and dice, which ... infected the publique meetings of the people, and the priuate houses of lordes ... And indeed the wilde Irish doe madly affect them, so as they will not only play and leese ['lose'] their mony and mouable goods, but also ingage their lands, yea their owne persons to be ledd as Prisoners by the winner, till he be paid the mony, for which they are ingaged. It is a shame to speake but I heard by credible relation, that some were found so impudent, as they had suffered themselues to be ledd as Captiues tyed by the parts of their body which I will not name, till they had mony to redeeme themselues.'[6]

It goes without saying that men dressed outlandishly in straw or leaves, tethered and led about by the genitals, would do nothing to promote the antiseptic picture that the wood-cut in John Derricke's *Image* had contrived. And had not Sir Henry tried to tidy *carrowes* out of the way in 1576? A vain hope, that, judging by the sheer frequency of reports of them. But in Derricke's optimistic *Image*, civil policies and decorous citizens are shown collabo-rating nicely. Depicting anything that would have run contrary to that would have been unthinkable.

Next, musicians. A capital on the north side of Christ Church Cathedral, carved *c.* 1200, shows a group of minstrel-musicians which may serve as template in stone of a former state of affairs in Dublin city, even if here it is in the more rarefied context of the house of God that the carving appears.[7] Beyond the precincts of the cathedral, out in the street, there was also plenty of music making to be found, with harpers and pipers especially to the fore as its purveyors. For example, at about the same date as the Christ Church capital was erected, and this time in a wholly secular context, one Thomas le Harpur was marked out in the roll of the Dublin Guild Merchant with a thumb-nail sketch of a harp placed next to his name in the left-hand margin of the roll (see Fig. 2).[8] Harpers thrived in Dublin, and most that are known about did so, it appears, in fairly tranquil circumstances. Inevitably there surfaces the odd exception: late in the thirteenth century, one Roger le Harper sued one Robert le Feure for having maliciously damaged his harp by aiming a stone at

Fig. 2
Admission of
Thomas le
Harpur to the
Dublin guild
merchant,
c. 1200; with
drawing of harp
(DUBLIN CITY
COUNCIL / CITY
ARCHIVES)

it.[9] Perhaps Robert hated the tune; history does not relate. And one sixteenth-century upset was even more fraught, when a Dublin harper, Donald O'Lalor, was pardoned for having murdered another.[10] Whatever about the tune, evidently on this occasion, Donald hated the colleague. Like the *carrowes*, many musicians were itinerant, coming and going, but some were settled, like a certain William the Piper who, in a Christ Church deed of *c.* 1260, received a grant of some land located within St Werburgh's parish.[11] The settled musicians were doubtless more fully integrated into civic life than their itinerant counter-parts. There would always be a powerful civic justification and institutional place, for example, for pipers who could sound the watch or raise the alarm, and we need look no further than the thirteenth-century seal matrix of the Dublin Civic Assembly, which shows two watchmen sounding horns on the walls of the embattled city (see Fig. 3), for evidence of their civic esteem. When horn players manage to find their way onto the city's seal, they have necessarily also already found their niche in civic culture.

In addition to instrumental music, vocal music was also available that might both raise, and lower, the tone. About seventy miles from Dublin, down in the south east in Kilkenny, Bishop Richard Ledrede, antagonist in the mid-fourteenth century of the powerful Dame Alice Kyteler, an alleged sorceress,[12] had complained that his clerics were going about polluting their throats with theatrical love ditties. As a remedy he composed a set of Latin *contrafacta*, pious poems which, in having the same metrical forms as the offending profanities that they sought to replace, could be sung to the same profane melody, thus robbing the devil of his best tunes. What happened in Kilkenny was doubtless repeated in Dublin. We would not be wrong in adding to our notional Dublin streetscape an aural dimension that was constituted not only from the sounds of musical instruments, but also from risqué lyrical songs, compositions, as I said, that both raised and lowered the tone. We have something approaching one such in a chance survival, a two-part lyric jotted into a manuscript preserved in Trinity College, Dublin.[13] The manuscript contains in the main a collection of medieval university texts, all sober enough. But inserted by someone around the year 1330 into a spare space is a short song, 'Lou, lou, lou, wer he goth', the double-entendre of whose words turning out to be anything but edifying. Translating the original Middle English into Modern English, the song would run something like this: 'Lo, lo, lo, where she goes. Lo, lo, lo, where she goes. Because of her I spill my holy water, lo.'[14] So the song is quite out of kilter with its sedate academic context. I would not wish to claim, of course, that this melody was certainly heard in a Dublin street, even though there is a whiff of the gutter about it. But it certainly wasn't heard in a church. And I imagine it would have been a little too smutty, even if we choose to entertain the idea that tastes were generally robuster in those days, to put in an appearance in polite secular society.

Now on to juggling acrobats. Tumblers, contortionists and tightrope walkers – early Irish society knew all of these skills. In fact, far beyond the Pale, in purely Gaelic areas where the colonial writ did not run, or at least did so only with difficulty, tumblers and contortionists were part of an ancient entertainment tradition that went back at least to the seventh century. Whether the people of Gaelic Ireland also experienced the thrills of tightrope walking I do not know, but by the Renaissance, the people of Dublin almost certainly did, whether the tightrope walkers were native or imported. In 1589, probably during the summer, Dublin was visited by two touring Elizabethan theatrical troupes, the Queen's Majesty's Players, and the Earl of Essex's Players. The mayor and aldermen voted them a handsome payment of £3 sterling for 'showing there Sporte in this Cittie.'[15] What was the 'Sporte'? It is safe to bet that tightrope stunts were one of the star turns in the troupe repertoire. The Queen's Majesty's Players and the Earl of Essex's Players are known to have been touring the English provinces together during this period, and had

Fig. 3
Matrix for Dublin City Seal, early 13th century, featuring watchmen with horns
(DUBLIN CITY COUNCIL/ CITY ARCHIVES)

made a detour to sandwich Dublin while touring in Lancashire.[16] We also know from other sources that 'going on the ropes' was a house speciality of the Queen's Majesty's Players, so it would be perverse to imagine that they would have gone tightrope-shy when they visited Dublin. This is what one witness says they did on a visit to Shrewsbury, Shropshire, just one year later: double somersaults; somersaults while tied up inside a bag; a 'Hungarian' tightrope walker doing the splits, dancing, pretending to fall off (gratifying that delicious frisson of danger that all audiences hanker after in such performances), then at the last moment defying expectation by hanging on by his feet. The man who reported the show was deeply impressed, noting that 'the licke was neuer seene of the inhabitantes there [i.e., in Shrewsbury] before that tyme.'[17] It is highly likely that the good citizens of Dublin had been treated to something along these lines when the Queen's Majesty's Players came calling in 1589.

In any event, tightrope walking certainly seems to have caught on in Dublin, arguably reaching its zenith by the early-eighteenth century in the person of Signora Violante Lorini, whose 'Booth' first in Dame Street, then later in South Great George's Street, pulled in the crowds. An early historian of the Irish theatre, W. R. Chetwood, observed that the 'Strength of the limbs' of performers such as the Signora was, by occupational hazard, 'shockingly indecent, but hers were masculinely indelicate and ... of a piece with the features of her face.'[18] In fact, rumour circulated that the Signora was a transvestite. But, like the Queen's Majesty's Players before her, Signora Lorini had also performed before the cognoscenti in that provincial English venue of travelling entertainers, Shrewsbury, where 'Ladies of distinction ... entertained her at their assemblies ... and soon found [the cross-dressing rumour] to be groundless.'[19] Naturally, Signora Lorini's party piece, which was to flap down a tightrope set at an incline with the rope running between her breasts, would doubtless have taken its toll on the sturdiest of physiques if repeated with any regularity. Hence the traces of gender alarm in Chetwood's description, and the mischievous rumour. No such alarm needed sounding in sixteenth-century Dublin, however, for at that date, the performers were all safely male.

Sixteenth-century Irish juggling acrobats, in the best dare-devil tradition, were also fond of manipulating knives and swords in their act. This sort of performance was ancient in Ireland too: one eighth-century Gaelic law tract specifies the compensation that you might expect if you were injured (presumably through perforation, to be precise) while watching a sword-and-spear-tossing juggler:

> **bla clesamnaig cles** .i. Slan donti eam nas na go clis in nairdi no na hubla clis
> in nairdi Masa clesa neamaicbeile iat is fiach fiancluichi indtu i laithrind 7 fiach
> cola cluiche indtu a .uii.arlaithrind Masa clesa aicbeile iat is fiach cola cluichi
> indtu cid | a | laithrind cid a .uii.arlaithrind. IS ed is clesa aicbeili ann cach cles
> arnabia rind no faebur. IS ed is clesa nemaicbeile ann cach clesarna bia rind na
> faebur. IS ed is laithrind and a tuitim ime ima cuaird i baile i mbi. IS ed is
> .uii.arlaithrind and andul uad imach i ciana.[20]
>
> 'The exemption as regards juggling/acrobatics of a juggler/acrobat, that is,

the person is exempt who multiplies the juggling spears up above, or the juggling balls up above. If they are not dangerous feats, there is a fine of fair-play for [any injuries from] them within the place [of performance], and a fine of foul-play for [any injuries from them] outside the place [of performance]. "Dangerous feats" are all the feats using [spear-]point or [sword-]edge; feats which are "not dangerous" are all those which do not use [spear-]point or [sword-]edge. "Within the place" means that they [that is, the juggling instruments] fall round about him in the place where he is. "Outside the place" means that they pass to a distance away from him.'

One of the best descriptions we have of this Irish performance art with blades dates from 1556, however. In this year, the scientist Jerome Cardan published a substantial book containing, amongst many other matters of scientific interest, a description related in forensically loving detail of the routine of an eighteen-year-old Irish juggler that he had witnessed on the continent. The lad's routine bristled with knives and swords. For example, he took two knives and inserted one into each nostril, so that the knives 'stood out perpendicular to his face'.[21] In order to do this, it was necessary to pass the knife points through the apertures by which the nose communicates with the throat. The young juggler also balanced a sword by its point on his forehead, and chopped up a number of straws sticking out of his belly with the same sword, yet without drawing a single drop of blood. In addition to this, he planted several swords and daggers in the ground by their pommels, their points sticking upwards, and resting on these points by the tips of his fingers and toes, he somehow contrived to whirl himself about from point to point. When Cardan asked whether there were any others like him in Ireland, he answered yes, dozens, and if Cardan thought that the things he had seen him doing were amazing, he should just wait until he had seen what the boys back home could do.

Gamblers, musicians, juggling acrobats – these were only three of the more prominent species of street entertainer roaming at large in medieval and Renaissance Dublin. There were many others. Various legislations enacted against them self-evidently prove two things: first, that there were those who could not tolerate them (the legislators), and second, that there were plenty of others who could, without a qualm, and more than that, who actually harboured and encouraged them, hence creating the need for the curbing legislation in the first place. Opponents of street entertainers were generally less worried about entertainment per se, as we will see, than about the antisocial fallout that their performances caused if delivered in an unlicensed package. But control of fly-by-night performers proved simply impossible. What is more, precisely because they came and went, it was feared that they took away with them strategic information about the layout and defences of the city and peddled it to Irish enemies outside the Pale, thus becoming security risks and number-one public enemies. Less ominously, but no less insidiously, they were said to have the knack of plucking out the moral backbone from the most upright of their punters, and they should therefore definitely not be encouraged. Yet as noted earlier, the very fact of the existence of reactionary legislation proves that several of their Dublin customers had managed to feel no pain at slipping an ethical disk or two. Street entertainers could thus do a great deal to upset the stable and productive world of work portrayed as the calm backdrop to Sir Henry Sidney's egress from Dublin Castle in John Derricke's woodcut.

Of course, the urge towards entertainment is irrepressible, and people will make their own entertainment if its professional purveyors are not on tap. One has only to consider the tale told by many a bone pipe and Jew's harp excavated in and around Dublin, all of them humble evidences of spontaneous music-making by the early civic community.[22] Low-key activity of this sort was not likely to rock the social boat; it was innocent enough. But other kinds, often egged on by itinerant professionals, could certainly manage to do so. And it was frequently the young men of Dublin who were involved and who got into trouble. In 1574, for example, it was announced that the apprentices and servants of Dublin's Trinity Guild, the Guild Merchant, were wasting their masters' goods by playing unlawful games. In standard Renaissance fashion, since punishment would be of little use unless exemplary, theirs was to take the form of a stripping and whipping, smartingly executed with green birch rods applied by four disguised guild members. *Pour encourager les autres*, a dozen apprentices ruefully looked on, chastened by proxy into the desired sobriety that may have come rather more naturally to their elders.[23]

Yet if such painful ritual humiliations may have put a damper on things, that is about the extent of it. It was a temporary damper. In 1612, the apprentices were at it again, playing football, coits, tennis, cudgels, and 'other unlawful games' in the streets. This time the punishment was for them to cool for twenty-four hours in the Newgate prison, no bail. Presumably the Newgate was as suitably unpleasant, in its way, as the birch twigs had been, but it is unlikely that this sanction worked entirely, either. Boys will be boys, and when in 1615 another tranche of legislation was enacted, the reforming cause of the authorities begins to look rather bedraggled, a lost cause, perhaps. This time it was illegal maypoles that were causing the problem.

Maypoles often got a bad press, both in Ireland and abroad. There survives a chilling account in the State Papers of a 1598 Dublin one to which a man was tied and his eyes put out.[24] Thus maypoles and mayhem traditionally kept company. Abroad in England, some of these festive seasonal props acquired refinements. One such at Broomfield, Somerset, had the added sophistication of a bell surmounting the top of it. The date is 1633, and we know of this elaborate maypole's existence from the key role it played in the downfall of one Thomas Cornish, a local cited for misdemeanours committed with one Joan Cole: 'on the said ffeast daie [i.e., at the annual Broomfield fair, held on the feast of All Souls] at night [Thomas Cornish] had the carnall knowledge of [Joan Cole's] bodie against the Sommer pole.'[25] In view of the maypole's aforementioned sophistication, this was not wise. The passionate frenzy below agitated the bell above, whose alarms brought the villagers running, thus making what had been intended for a clandestine tryst into a public spectacle. 'Not the maypole's fault', one might think, but that would be to miss the point. They were too often associated with riotous assembly of one sort or another for their own good.

In confirmation of their doubtful reputations, and to forestall any such incidents, Dublin's illicit, private maypoles of 1615 were to be seized, their owners fined a hefty ten shillings, and the confiscated maypoles converted to the exclusive use of Dublin Corporation.

Then there was bull and bear baiting. Young Dubliners might get into trouble at baitings all too easily. After all, youngsters elsewhere often did, so young Dubliners would be bucking the youthful trend if they did not. Dangerous live animals with wills of their own and averse to the fate hanging over their heads were a recipe for awkward situations. Another English case illustrating some of the potential dangers comes from Skilgate, Somerset, in 1592, when a bear that was being baited escaped, ran into a house and startled the pregnant woman within into labour. Pandemonium broke out as the woman dodged the bear while trying to deliver herself of a child that, the bear's presence notwithstanding, had no intention of delaying its entry into the world.[26] Unsurprisingly on investigation, it was a band of youths letting things get out of hand in the first place that had given rise to the problem. Dublin has nothing on record that is quite so graphic, but in 1620, the Act passed 'to restrain the common passage of bears and bulls through the city or any part thereof' shows that the authorities were alive to the potential dangers and that they wished to lessen the chances of any such happening.[27] The Act, we are hardly surprised to hear, noted explicitly that baitings caused *apprentices and servants*, those familiar addicts of street entertainment, to 'fall into vice and idleness'.

So, aside from reactionary legislation, whose repeated enactment suggests it was not being entirely successful, what else was to be done to let the city fathers sleep soundly in their beds, secure in their hope of *Obedientia civium urbis felicitas*? Street entertainers knew that they had eager audiences in Dublin, like the young men of the city, for example, who were always prone to the lure of their diversions. We might imagine some of these young men making up the audience for another species of street entertainment, the earliest Dublin puppet play on record that I am aware of. In 1612, that volatile puritan spirit Barnaby Rich, scourge of tobacco smokers and of the frivolous in general, published a dialogue between the upright Protestant 'Patrick Plaine', a student of Trinity College, and the unreformed priest Tady Mac Mareall, of Waterford. Rich concocted the following exchange between them (in the excerpt, Pa. stands for Patrick and Ta. for Tady):

Pa. I will neuer deny it Syr Tady, I confesse I haue seene a Masse.

Ta. Then you haue not liued altogether so irreligiously, but that you haue once seene a Masse, but tell mee truely, howe did you like it?

Pa. O passing well, I neuer sawe a thing that better pleased me, but once:

Ta. And what was that one thing, that you say pleased you better?

Pa. It was a Puppet play, that was playd at Dubline, but nowe this last summer.[28]

Although the dialogue is manifest fiction, it may still be reliable evidence of actual puppet-play performances having taken place in Dublin at around this date. If even Patrick Plaine can confess to having enjoyed a puppet show, who knows what young men without the advantages of a moral fibre such as his might have relished? Once again, Barnaby Rich knew the answer. In another of his works, he wrote:

> 'As I was dipping my pen to haue taken vp inke, I heard a muttering of mens voices, as they were passing through the streets: and looking out at a window, I saw foure young Roaring Boyes, that (I thinke) were new come from some Ordinary, … & they were consulting as they went along, how they might spend the afternoone: The one gaue his verdict to goe see a Play:'[29]

Theatre, from the vantage point that Rich chose to look at it, was, of course, the gateway to hell.

Since the young men of Dublin were liable to take entertainment into their own hands if none was professionally available, the result often being antisocial fallout, the reactive solutions that the corporation had devised were enhanced by the taking of proactive steps to channel youthful energies constructively. It is possible to regard the evolution of certain of Dublin's civic institutions as direct, proactive responses to the sheer demand for fun. Let's consider an important example. During the medieval period the office of the Mayor of the Bullring had come into existence. We might pause to note the name, the Mayor of the Bullring, which essentially refers to the presidency of the bullring set in Dublin's Cornmarket, where bulls were seasonally tethered and baited. Bullbaiting, which like bearbaiting, as we saw, was one of those potential flashpoints of street entertainment, is here through this civic office urbanised and brought within a cordon of civic control. In this way it is made respectable. We might notice, too, that the Mayor of the Bullring primarily functioned to supervise and patrol the city's ebullient young men, not just in terms of containing the potential social disturbances that might spill from their recreations, but also in terms of fortifying the morality of their recreational choices; one of the Mayor of the Bullring's duties was to watch out for young men whose entertainment choices led them to frequent the city's brothels. The office of the Mayor of the Bullring was thus central to the Dublin City Assembly's proactive plan for a constructive containment of civic fun. His office was a festive double-take on the office of the mayor itself, and like the mayoral office, it involved election for an annual term. Most of the various events over which the Mayor of the Bullring presided passed off in a spirit of entertainment. He came into his own very notably on May Day, and also during the festive ceremonies that attended weddings. As well as striving to keep the young men of Dublin out of brothels and fining whorehouse keepers (from whom, incidentally, his office derived the strangely contradictory benefit of much of its income, a fact that might give rise to speculation on how earnest his striving may have been), he organised the young men for more morally bracing pastimes, like military musters, at which they could drill their fighting skills, and for pageants, which were such crucial ceremonial aspects of civic life in many of the larger towns and cities of the British Isles in the medieval and Renaissance periods.[30]

Apart from making these institutional provisions for civic performances that could be corporately assented to as wholesome and constructive, the Dublin City Assembly also put authorised musicians on the streets in the persons of the Dublin Waits. Waits were another institution whose roots went back well into the medieval period. They may have begun life originally as sentinels or watchmen, equipped with horns for setting the watch or raising the alarm. Indeed, this is as the thirteenth-century city seal matrix of Dublin depicts them (see Fig. 3).[31] But it seems that as time went by the waits also developed other, more ceremonial and festive roles. They played to mark civic occasions, such as mayoral banquets in the Tholsel, and were under instruction to go about the streets of Dublin playing three or four mornings a week, providing the citizens, in effect, with something approaching an early-morning wake-up call.[32] At their height there were about six of them in the band. It is also clear that in their later incarnations they were not solely instrumentalists, since they were required 'to keepe always a good singinge boy from time to time'.[33] So just as on occasion there was civically authorised street fun, authorised street music was also on offer at the corporation's expense.

Alongside the various provisions made by the Dublin City Assembly, the church too played its part in providing respectable alternatives to the at best doubtful, at worst illegal, pastimes that were on offer. Recall the

Fig. 4

Motet *Angelus ad Virginem* (Courtesy Faber and Faber)

contrafacta of Bishop Ledrede of Ossory, which were pious words dubbed onto popular tunes. It is possible that a similar spirit, a baptising of the secular in the service of the sacred, is at work in this three-part motet from the Dublin Troper, a mid-fourteenth century liturgical manuscript formerly belonging to St Patrick's Cathedral and now preserved in Cambridge University Library.[34] The subject of the motet *Angelus ad Virginem*, a transcription of whose three-part version is given in Fig. 4 above, is the Archangel Gabriel's salutation of Mary, a topic impeccably religious. However, had early listeners heard the same melody sung to purely secular words, they would probably not have been surprised, for like many musical church products of this period, *Angelus ad Virginem* is a holy song with street credibility.

The late-medieval church, of course, was well prepared to enter the festive fray should it need to. The church ran a colourful and theatricalised liturgy, and thus was profession-

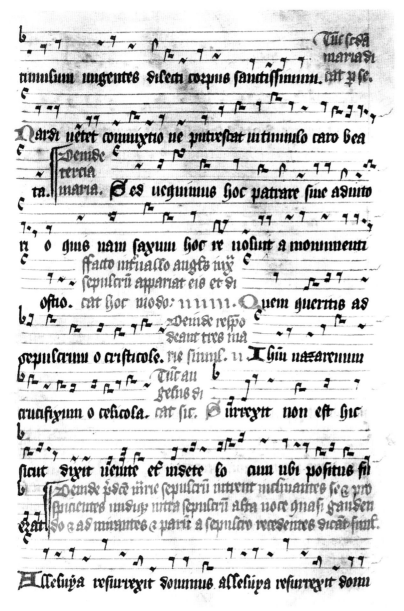

ally acquainted with several performing arts, prominent amongst which was music. If the church was moved to make its sacred riposte to secular street performance, it therefore had copious performance expertise on which to draw. In Dublin it seems especially likely that available church resources in performance would have been rich, since the city enjoyed the unusual distinction of possessing not one but two cathedrals. And if we pass on now from the street-friendly melody at St Patrick's to consider what was going on in Christ Church Cathedral up the hill, we find that the city's senior cathedral showed no sign of letting itself be outflanked. The Augustinian canons of Christ Church had invited theatrical performance into the solemnest and most prestigious moments of their liturgy.[35] The earliest play from Ireland whose text fully survives, which dramatises a visit of the three Marys to Christ's sepulchre on Easter Sunday morning in order to anoint his body with spices, may originally have had a Christ Church connection, for the two manuscripts containing it, though formerly owned by the church of St John the Evangelist that, until its demolition in the nineteenth century, stood near Christ Church, may have come to St John's as Christ Church hand-me-downs.[36] Fig. 5 shows the Marsh's Library copy of the play open at the play's central and most ancient section, the dialogue between the Marys and the angel at the sepulchre. The last melodic phrase of their exchange, the unison 'Eya, pergamus propere mandatum hoc perficere' ('Eia! Let us go quickly to fulfil this command'), could musically almost be mensural, and reminiscent, indeed, of a dance rhythm. But if this play could arguably be regarded as legitimised festivity, though surely of a kind dignified and stately in performance, one would only need to blink to miss it. It lasts for little more than fifteen minutes, and would have come around but once a year, in the early dawn hours of Easter matins. Fig. 6 shows a modern reconstruction of the costumes and accoutrements of two of the play's characters, the Apostles Peter (foreground) and John (background).

A more forceful answer from the church to banned secular pastimes is to be found in another play in which the canons of Christ Church once more had a hand, and this time it was a play not in the élite Latin of the Easter drama, but in English. Furthermore, since it was acted out in the street, it moved in the same terrain that the street entertainers themselves had made their own. This play was also performable at any time of year, not limited to single annual outings. It is the play that modern editors know as *The pride of life*, and it pivots around a vigorous battle waged between two allegorical figures, the King of Life and the King of Death. Sadly, the original copy of the play was lost in 1922 in the explosion and fire at Dublin's Four Courts, but we know what it was about, because late in the nineteenth century, the antiquarian James Mills had edited it in the course of his work on the account roll of the Priory of Holy Trinity, Dublin. The play had been squeezed onto a spare space in the account roll early in the fifteenth century.[37]

The comparative forcefulness of this early piece of Dublin street theatre is soon apparent in its plot, which went as follows. The King of Life boasts that he can live forever. His Queen, a female voice of reason, tells him not to be silly, that he is mortal, and in order to make her point stick, she invites the bishop round to put her husband right on the matter. This she does, the bishop arrives, then preaches to the King of Life on the gloomy theme that he least wishes to hear:

Fig. 6

SS. Peter and John from modern performance of *Visitatio Sepulchri* (PHOTOGRAPH COURTESY OF ALAN J. FLETCHER)

> 'Schir Kyng, thing oppon thin end   *Sir King, think on your ending*
> And hou that thou schalt dey.'[38]   *and how you shall die*

So the King of Life sends the bishop packing, and with a colloquial vigour that was doubtless matched somehow on stage, perhaps even by boisterous episcopal manhandling:

'Wat! bissop, byssop babler,	*What! Bishop, Bishop Babbler,*
Schold Y of Det hau dred??	*should I dread Death?*
Thou art bot a chagler –	*You're nothing but a windbag.*
Go hom thy wey, I red.	*Get off home, I advise you.*
…	
Troust piou I uold be dead	*Do you think I'd wish to be dead*
In mi yyng lif?	*in my young life?*
Thou lisst, screu, bolhed;	*You're lying, villain, bull-head.*
Euil mot thou thriwe!'[39]	*May you come badly unstuck.*

To this the bishop replies mildly, but sticks stolidly to his theme:

'Qwhen thou art grauen on grene,	*When you're buried in the ground,*
Ther metis fleys and molde,	*where flesh and earth meet together,*
Then helpith litil, I wene,	*then I think your handsome*
Thy gay croun of golde.	*crown of gold will be of little help.*
Sire Kyng, haue goday,	*Sir King, good day to you,*
Crist I you beteche.'[40]	*I entrust you to Christ.*

At which point the King has had enough:

'Fare wel, bisschop, thi way,,	*Farewell on your way, Bishop,*
And lerne bet to preche.'[41]	*and learn how to preach better.*

This section of dialogue gives a flavour of what theatrical energy this early piece of Dublin street theatre was capable of. What subsequently happened was that the King of Life issued a challenge to the King of Death. The King of Death responded, they fought, and naturally, the King of Life was defeated. But just as it seemed that the King of Life's soul was destined to be whisked off to hell by devils, a kind of *dea ex machina* was introduced in the form of the Blessed Virgin Mary. She interceded for the King of Life, and in standard medieval fashion her son, who always found such maternal pleas irresistible, saved the soul of the King of Life, and everything ended happily. An impression of what its staging may have looked like is given in Fig. 7.

While this makes for a spectacle based squarely on orthodox medieval theology, it goes further than that, for the canons of Christ Church Cathedral, under whose auspices this very different breed of play would have been performed, are shown here taking the popular performers head on, meeting them with canonically sanctified fun at their own level in the street and doing something dramatically that was a little similar to what Bishop Ledrede had been doing lyrically. For what this play also represents is a baptised version of a popular and originally thoroughly pagan storyline. Consider the play's ingredients and their sequence: a boasting hero (or anti-hero, the King of Life); a challenge; a fight; the death of the hero; the intervention of a miracle-worker; and the resuscitation of the hero. These ingredients match those that make up the traditional storyline behind the

Fig. 7

Reconstruction of staging of *The pride of life* play (COURTESY ALAN J. FLETCHER)

mummers' plays of immemorial tradition, the cyclical, hero-combat narrative of death and rebirth.[42] Thus *The pride of life* is another manifestation in dramatic terms of medieval Christianity's appropriative way of thinking: the canons of Christ Church were preparing for hygienic general consumption of a traditional storyline that had once been essentially popular and secular. To put this in more stringently sociological terms, we could say that in this play we observe an organism of official culture containing any threat that unofficial culture might pose by absorbing the unofficial into itself. But inevitably, such processes cannot pass off without the official being changed in some important respects.

Another similar instance of cultural hybridity, as I noted earlier, is to be seen in the evolution of the office of Mayor of the Bullring. Here, the energy of the young men of Dublin was less suppressed than absorbed and reoriented in socially useful directions. The institution of the office of the Mayor of the Bullring, an officially sanctioned, proactive response to the inevitability of boys being boys, caused the sum total of the civic structure to alter. Thus high-level, official culture in fact needed low-level, unofficial culture, then as still now, for a host of reasons, not least amongst which was self-definition. For in order to define what you consider yourself to be, it is often convenient to assert what you think you are not: that is something that John Derricke's streetscape was also doing, as Sir Henry rode out against his orderly, productive, and teflon-clean civic backdrop.

But this survey, though very short, has shown us how the reality was actually far broader than that which John Derricke wanted us to believe. Dublin's streetscape, especially on high days and feast days, was clamourously alive with inescapably necessary alternatives. So we cannot afford to be snobbish about 'high' at the expense of 'low' when both are in fact locked in interdependence. Much less should the serious-minded historian that I began by evoking dismiss the performing arts as ephemeral pastimes before passing on to the hard stuff that really matters. Not often, granted, but sometimes, it transpired that the performing arts, undoubtedly ephemeral, were nevertheless matters of life and death, and what harder stuff could there be than that? For example in 1535 simply the performance of a song seems to have stood between life and death for two men, singers from the chapel in Maynooth Castle. In March of that year Sir William Skeffington had sortied out of Dublin with troops to lay siege to the castle, the stronghold of the earls of Kildare, in a decisive retaliation for James Fitzgerald's attempt to take Dublin by siege in 1534. Skeffington prevailed and the castle garrison in Maynooth was all slaughtered, but a certain James Delahyde and one Haywood, doubtless thinking that their end was in sight, sang *Dulcis amica*, a song asking the Blessed Virgin to be present when the hour of death came. They sang so beautifully, said the chronicler, that their lives were spared.[43]

Lord Mayor, ladies and gentlemen, friends and colleagues, the next time you walk down Grafton Street, spare a thought for the musicians and the jugglers, for the solo street theatres like the 'Dice Man' of happy memory. These people are the unknowing heirs of an old civic tradition. And spare a thought too for their ancient predecessors who animated the early cultural life of the capital in ways that the powers that be may not always have found appropriate, but which were nevertheless unstoppably productive of the city's sense of selfhood. And I hope that the presiding spirit of Sir John Gilbert will not have been too appalled by this walk on the wild side of streets that he, with far greater decorum than I am capable of, also loved to celebrate.

Notes

1 Many of the documentary sources referred to in this paper are published in Alan J. Fletcher, ed. *Drama and the performing arts in pre-Cromwellian Ireland: a repertoy of sources and documents from the earliest times until c. 1642* (Cambridge, 2001); hereafter cited as *DPA*. For a fuller narrative history of drama and performance in medieval and early modern Ireland, see Alan J. Fletcher, *Drama, performance, and polity in pre-Cromwellian Ireland* (Toronto, 2000; Cork, 2000); hereafter cited as *DPP*

2 *DPA*, p. 173, lines 37–9.

3 *DPA*, pp 175–6.

4 *DPA*, p. 175, lines 6–13.

5 L. Miller and E. Power, ed. *Holinshed's Irish chronicle* (Dublin and New York, 1979), p. 114.

6 *DPA*, p. 190, lines 27–39.

7 R. Stalley, 'The medieval sculpture of Christ Church Cathedral, Dublin', *Archaeologia* 106 (1979), pp 107–22.

8 *DPA*, p. 221, line 2.

9 *DPA*, p. 222, lines 2–5.

10 *DPA*, p. 245, lines 2–3.

11 *DPA*, p. 222.

12 On Alice Kyteler, see L. S. Davidson and J. O. Ward, ed. *The sorcery trial of Alice Kyteler: a contemporary account (1324), together with related documents*, Medieval and Renaissance texts and studies (1993).

13 Dublin, Trinity College, MS 270, fol. 37v.

14 The spilling of the 'holy water' is a double-entendre for male orgasm.

15 *DPA*, p. 276, lines 16–17.

16 See *DPP*, p. 252, for discussion and references.

17 J. Alan B. Somerset, ed. *Shropshire: records of early English drama*, 2 vols (Toronto, 1994), i, 247, lines 11–38.

18 W.R. Chetwood, *A general history of the stage* (Dublin, 1749), p. 60.

19 Carson's Dublin Intelligence, 22 November 1729 (cited in John C. Greene and Gladys L.H. Clark, *The Dublin stage 1720–1745: A calendar of plays, entertainments and afterpieces* (Bethlehem, London and Toronto, 1993), p. 25.

20 *DPA*, p. 147, lines 2–8 of *Bretha Étgid*.

21 'ut ad perpendiculum faciei superstarent'; *DPA*, p. 482, lines 3–4.

22 Ann Buckley, "Muscial Instruments in Ireland from the Ninth to the Fourteenth Centuries" in Gerard Gillen and Harry White, eds. *Irish musical studies* 1: *musicology in Ireland* (Dublin, 1990), pp 13–57

23 *DPA*, pp 260–1, lines 2–16.

24 *DPA*, p. 290, lines 2–12.

25 J. Stokes and R. J. Alexander, ed. *Somerset including Bath: records of early English drama*, 2 vols (Toronto, 1996), i, 63, lines 28–9.

26 Stokes and Alexander, *Somerset including Bath*, i, 212–19

27 *DPA*, p. 320, lines 2–14.

28 Barnaby Rich, *A Catholicke conference betvveene Syr Tady Mac. Mareall a popish priest of VVaterforde, and Patricke Plaine, a young student in Trinity Colledge by Dublin in Ireland* (London, 1612; *STC* 20981), f. 21v, sig. [F 3v].

29 Barnaby Rich, *The Irish Hvbbvb, or, The English hve and crie* (London, 1622; *STC* 20991), p. 37.

30 The pageant especially associated with the Mayor of the Bullring was that of the Nine Worthies of Christendom. For further explanation of this pageant and the way it was organised, see *DPP*, pp 145–8.

31 The horn blowers on the seal matrix appear to be raising the alarm, for the city, it will be noticed, is shown embattled.

32 For a study of the Dublin waits, see *DPP*, pp 148–53.

33 *DPA*, p. 330, lines 7–8 of the 1636 Dublin Assembly Rolls entry.

34 Cambridge, University Library, MS Additional 710. The version of *Angelus ad Virginem* given in Fig. 4 below is present on fol. 130v of this manuscript.

35 There is likely to have been liturgical drama in St Patrick's Cathedral too, but the extant evidence for it is not extensive; see *DPP*, pp 78–80.

36 One manuscript, an opening of which is shown in facsimile in Fig. 5, is preserved in Dublin, Marsh's Library, MS Z.4.2.20; the other is preserved, in Oxford, Bodleian Library, MS Rawlinson liturg. D. 4. For a full discussion of both, see *DPP*, pp 281–5.

37 James Mills, ed. *Account roll of the Priory of Holy Trinity, Dublin, 1337–1346*, with an introduction by James Lydon and Alan J. Fletcher (Dublin, 1996).

38 Norman Davis, ed. *Non-cycle plays and fragments*, Early English Text Society, ss 1 (London, New York and Toronto, 1970), p. 102, lines 391–2.

39 Davis, *Non-cycle plays*, p. 102–3, lines 407–10 and 419–22.

40 Davis, *Non-cycle plays*, p. 104, lines 443–8.

41 Davis, *Non-cycle plays*, p. 104, lines 449–50.

42 For a more detailed account, see *DPP*, pp 121–3.

43 Miller and Power, *Hollinshed's Irish chronicle*, p. 279.

Dublin in the year 1000[*]

by John Bradley

[*]Gilbert Lecture, January 2000

In 1996 I had the pleasure of visiting Oberlin College in the American Midwest, one of that country's great liberal arts colleges and renowned for its School of Music. It was graduation day and the campus was thronged with proud parents, many of whom were lost in the sprawling complex of university buildings. Americans are naturally friendly people and one parent, noticing that I was wandering around somewhat haphazardly, asked me if I was there for the graduation ceremony.

'No', I said, 'I am just visiting'.

'Where are you from?' she asked.

'Dublin', I replied.

'Oh, I'm from Dublin also. Whereabouts do you live?', she asked.

'Rathgar', I said.

She looked puzzled. 'Towards the Terenure end', I added.

More puzzlement. To rescue the situation, I thought I had better ask her where in Dublin she lived.

'Clifton Heights', she replied.

I did not recognise the name and thought that it must be one of those new housing developments that are edging their way up the Dublin Mountains. 'Is that on the south side?' I asked.

'No, the east side', she replied.

'The east', I said, 'close to the sea, then?'

Her brow furled and she looked at me as if I was an axe-murderer. 'What Dublin are you from?' she said.

'Dublin, Ireland', I replied.

'Well', she said with a touch of triumph, 'I am from Dublin, Ohio'.

In the year 2000 there is not just one Dublin. Dublin, Ohio, has a population of 150,000 people and there are at least eight other Dublins in the United States, one in Canada and one in Australia, countries (and continents, indeed) which were unknown to Dubliners in the year 1000. Dublin has not merely come a long way in a thousand years, it has literally gone a long way as well.

Sir John Gilbert, whose colossal achievements in rescuing Dublin's history are commemorated by this lecture series, had little to say about the Viking Age town. This was not because he was uninterested. It was simply because, when he wrote his *History of Dublin* between 1854 and 1859, the data was not available. The great editions of the Irish annals had not appeared and the source from which most of our knowledge of Viking Age Dublin was to ultimately derive had, in the 1850s, only begun to register with individuals like Gilbert, George Petrie and William Wilde. This was the earth on which Dublin was built. Gilbert recorded the 'boggy' nature of the soil over much of the old city and assumed, like many others of his time, that the city had been built upon a marsh.[1] What he did not realise was that this 'boggy' earth was the peaty soil that had accumulated as archaeological deposits century by century until, in places, it was almost 9 metres (thirty feet) deep. Gilbert noted some of the discoveries made during building and drainage works —swords, burials and the occasional object[2]—but the intellectual framework in which to interpret these objects and use them to reconstruct the past, simply did not exist. Those developments have only occurred within our own lifetimes. Archaeological excavation commenced at Dublin Castle in 1961 and was subsequently carried out by the National Museum of Ireland at High Street, Christ Church Place, Fishamble Street and Wood Quay between 1963 and 1981.[3] Increasing redevelopment in the late 1980s and 90s has occasioned an enormous expansion in the number and variety of excavated sites and our newspapers are regularly brightened up with the news of one new discovery after another. Among Irish cities, indeed among European cities, Dublin is special to the archaeologist because its archaeological deposits are so well preserved. This is due to the fact that they are water-logged and, as a consequence, organic materials such as wood and leather, plants, insects, even the moss that was used as toilet tissue, all survive because the bacteria that cause decay cannot live under water. Indeed, much of the most exciting new information has been derived from studies of the animal bones, plants and flora. Dr Pat Wallace has spoken of how the archive of archaeological information on Viking Age Dublin is now so extensive that, potentially we can know more about life in the Viking Age town than we can about any succeeding period of Dublin's history until the Age of Swift. Sir John Gilbert, I think, would have been impressed.

On the 30 December 999, Brian Bóruma defeated the army of Máel Mórda, king of Leinster and his Dublin allies under their king Sitric Silkenbeard at the Battle of Glenn Máma, fought in the foothills of the Dublin Mountains near Saggart. Brian Bóruma's victory was complete and on the following day, 1 January 1000 he marched on Dublin and laid siege to it.

If we had a time machine and could travel back to Dublin in the year 1000 what would we find? What would it be like if we were to march (say) with Brian Bóruma's soldiers from Saggart to Dublin? Well, if we position our time machine like an Aer Lingus jet, at an elevation of (say) 1000 feet, we would discover that the landscape was very different from that of today—not just in terms of an absence of buildings but in terms of an absence of land as well. Dublin Bay was much larger than it is today and it began just east of where Capel Street Bridge is now. Huge swathes of the modern city were under water. On the north side, everything east of Jervis Street, including O'Connell Street, and as far north as the foot of Parnell Square, were tidal flats, much the same as we find stretching from Sandymount to Blackrock today. On the south side, almost everything east of College

Green, including Trinity College, Merrion Square, much of Ballsbridge and Sandymount would also have been under water. Outside the door of the Mansion House, we could have walked down the green slope on which Dawson Street was later built, to find the seawaters lapping against the beach at the foot of Nassau Street and enjoy an uninterrupted view across the Dublin Bay to the hill of Howth.[4]

Grafton Street, Dawson Street, Stephen's Green and the environs for miles around were countryside, worked mainly as farmland but with patches of woodland and scrub, and smoke coming from the occasional settlement dotted thinly across this vista. The fields were separated from one another by fences and hedges. There was more grassland than tillage.[5] A closer look at the hedges enables us to identify hawthorn, sloe and blackberry bushes as well as crab-apple trees, while herds of cattle, sheep, pigs and horses were kept in the fields.[6]

'Ireland', wrote the Venerable Bede, 'is far more favoured than Britain by latitude and by its mild and healthy climate. Snow rarely lies longer than three days, so that there is no need to store hay in summer for winter use, or to build stables for beasts'.[7] Haymaking was not practised until after the coming of the Normans, but even in the year 1000, some grass was harvested and dried for use as floor covering and bedding.[8]

Bede, incidentally, also tells us that Ireland was warm enough to grow its own vines and the climate is thought to have been between 1 and 3 degrees warmer on average than today.[9]

The arable land in the vicinity of the town was considerable. Bread and porridge were staple parts of the diet, eaten for breakfast, dinner and supper.[10] It has been calculated that an average person consumed 2lbs (almost 1 kg) of bread or porridge per day and in order to feed the population of Dublin in the year 1000, a minimum area of about 6000 acres would need to have been under grain.[11] When one allows for the well-known liking of Dubliners for beer and ale, as well as allowing for what would have been destroyed by weather, disease, mismanagement or warfare, the minimum estimate of land under cereals would need to be about 20,000 acres.[12] The principal crops grown included wheat, barley, oats, and beans.[13] There is no evidence for rye even though this was a staple of diets in Scandinavia.

Woodland was confined almost entirely to the river valleys—the curving sweep of the Liffey itself, but also the valleys of the Camac, Coombe, Poddle and Steine.[14] Enormous quantities of hazel were required by the townspeople, particularly for making the post and wattle screens that were such a feature of their houses, that functioned as fences dividing properties and that acted as pathways when placed flat on the ground. Indeed, with an average of fifty new houses being built each year and with so many others requiring repairs, the cutting of hazel had to be managed by means of coppicing.[15] Other trees in the river valleys included alder, birch, willow, ash and holly.[16] There were some oak trees but for large oaks, which might be required in ship-building, one had to go even then to the woodlands of Shillelagh.[17] A substantial amount of timber was required for firewood and this too was brought downriver to Dublin. The woods themselves were inhabited by herds of deer and, in wintertime, they were frequented by wolves.

From our time machine, at a height of 1000 feet we would notice the smoke coming from individual settlements scattered across the landscape and in the distance, clusters of houses nestling around old church sites and forming little hamlets or villages around Swords, Lusk, Finglas, Clondalkin, Tallaght, Dalkey. Here and there are abandoned settlements—the ringforts (or raths) that gave their name to Rathfarnham, Rathmines and Rathgar. But there were new settlements also, often indicated by a large mound or several smaller ones where the pagan Scandinavian ancestors of the Dubliners had buried their dead. The high ground along the Parnell Square ridge where the Municipal Gallery is today was dotted with such mounds, which looked directly down onto Dublin Bay.[18] In what is today College Green and along the Andrews Street ridge there was another collection of mounds looking back towards Dublin across the open meadow that is now Dame Street.[19] Indeed there were so many burial mounds in the College Green area that up until the foundation of Trinity College and for some time afterwards it was known as Haugen Green, from the Scandinavian word *Haugr*, meaning a burial mound. Close to the College Green area, on a spit of land extending out towards Pearse Street Garda Station there was the *stein*, a large pillar-stone erected to commemorate the landing place of the first Scandinavians.[20]

A mile or so to the west of Dublin was the largest concentration of low mounds, an extensive cemetery of burials focusing around the old church site at Kilmainham, another closer to the Liffey at what we call Islandbridge, and a third in what is today the Phoenix Park.[21] The burial mounds were sacred land and some, indeed, may well have been within or close to sacred forests. We know the name of one such, Thor's Wood, because it is recorded that in the year 1000 Brian Bóruma had Thor's Wood (*Caill Tomair*) cut down to indicate his supremacy over the Dubliners.[22]

There were few roads but such as there were homed in like elongated fingers on to one crossing point of the Liffey, Áth Cliath, the ford of the hurdles, situated a little to the west of where the Four Courts is located today. The River Liffey at this point was shallow and broad, some twenty times its present width, inundating what are now the quays on the south side, up as far as the tower block portion of Civic Offices at Wood Quay, while on the north side, the Four Courts and the first fifty metres or so of Capel Street were under water.

Overlooking the ford on the south side of the river was the principal settlement of the region, Dublin. In the year 1000 the enclosed area of Dublin stretched from what is now Dublin Castle on the east to Christ Church Cathedral on the west, from the tower block portion of the Civic Offices at Wood Quay on the north to the rear of Jury's Christ Church Hotel on the south.[23] Dublin in the year 1000 occupied an area that would fit comfortably within a supermarket car park. Not only that but one may note that Dublin of the year 1000 would fit twice over into the area occupied by the Liffey Valley Shopping Mall. To our eyes Dublin in the year 1000 was incredibly small, but to the Dubliners who lived in it, the settlement, with a population of perhaps 2000 people, was the largest and richest in the country.

Technically, Dublin was 159 years old in the year 1000 since it had been established as a *longphort* (or ship fortress) in 841. I say technically because there is a hitch with this calculation. The *longphort*, established in 841, was abandoned in 902 and Dublin had to wait another fifteen years before it was re-founded in 917.[24] So, in reality in the year 1000, the settlement of Dublin was 83 years old and, if none of the actual initial founders were still alive, their sons and daughters were probably present to bring in the millennial year.

There is some dispute as to the location of the initial settlement of 841. Some scholars maintain that it was in the vicinity of Kilmainham-Islandbridge, where a great cemetery was discovered about one hundred and fifty years ago during the construction of the railway line at Heuston Station.[25] Others maintain that the *longphort* of 841 was in the vicinity of Dublin Castle, perhaps in the Aungier Street area or on Usher's Island.[26] In 902, however, the *longphort* was captured by an alliance of the Meathmen and Leinstermen and the destruction of the settlement was so thorough that Dublin was abandoned.

When the dispossessed Scandinavians returned in 917, however, there is no doubt about where they settled. Successive archaeological excavations, conducted by Dr Pat Wallace and others, have shown beyond any doubt that the settlement of 917 was located on a spur of high ground overlooking the confluence of the Rivers Liffey and Poddle in the vicinity of the present Christ Church Cathedral. Several years ago now, Dr Howard Clarke of University College Dublin, suggested that this new foundation was not built on open ground.[27] There may have been a settlement overlooking the ford of *Áth Cliath* and an ecclesiastical community at *Dubhlinn*, just above the 'dark pool' from which Dublin derives its name. The likely location of this pool is just south of Dublin Castle in the recently restored Castle Gardens. If there were settlements at *Áth Cliath* and *Dubhlinn*, however, they were almost certainly of rural character. Dublin's beginnings as a town with streets, houses and market-places originates with the returning Scandinavians of 917.

In the year 1000 Dublin was protected by a roughly circular earthen bank, 5 m broad and 3 m high, which was crowned by a fence of thickly-woven, post and wattle. The post and wattle probably formed a breastwork, which would give added protection to the defenders.[28] Virtually all settlement concentrated within this enclosure but just to the west, a row of suburban houses was beginning to appear along the line of what later became known as High Street, linking the settlement on the ridge with the ford across the Liffey, the *Áth Cliath* or ford of the hurdles.[29] A bridge did not exist at this time but in 1001 Máel Sechnaill, king of Mide, built a causeway from the north bank that extended across the mud flats to the mid point of the river.[30] It was an act of patronage that presumably also reflected the extent of his power.

Inside the defences, all settlement focused around a cross-roads, the junction of Castle Street, Fishamble Street, Werburgh Street and Christ Church Place (known as Skinner's Alley until the nineteenth century—and much narrower then than now). Within the town virtually all of the buildings were of wood. Post-and-wattle construction was the most common and ash was the most popular wood. In these buildings the walls were composed of upright, hammer-driven circular posts with layers of wattles or rods woven between them in basketry fashion. In many houses a double row of post and wattle was present and the space in between was filled with ferns or straw to provide insulation.

In the year 1000, the settlement consisted of about 400 houses. The houses tended to be located on the front end of long narrow plots, which originally seem to have stretched from the street frontage to the town defences. These plots were privately owned and fenced off from one another. About two-thirds of Dublin's houses were identical in size, shape and location.[31] The buildings were rectangular with rounded corners; they measured 7.5 by 5.5 m on average; the walls were 1.25 m high and were almost always of post and wattle construction. The roofs were thatched; they were hipped rather than gabled, and they were supported on four main posts arranged in a rectangle within the floor area. It was normal to find two opposed doors, located in the end walls, one giving access to the street, the other to buildings at the rear of the plot. Internally, the floor space was divided into three, with the central strip, sometimes paved or gravelled being the broadest. A rectangular stone-lined fireplace was located in the centre. Along the side walls, two low benches were used both for sitting and sleeping. Sometimes corner areas near the doors were partitioned off to form a private space. Smaller versions of this building type, but lacking hearths, were frequently located behind the larger house. They may have functioned as granny flats although they could hardly be used in wintertime. In addition there were sheds and animal pens. Cats and dogs, goats, pigs and domestic fowl were all kept within the town and enclosures and pens were built for at least some of them. At Christ Church Place there was an open-air wooden platform which may have functioned as an altar or had some other related ceremonial purpose.

In the year 1000 the population of Dublin is estimated to have been around 2,000 but in the course of the following century there is clear evidence for a doubling of the population. The eleventh century was a period of great expansion and the intensity of occupation was such that by about the year 1050, the build-up of debris seems to have caused problems of structural stability. There was no refuse collection and, with earthen floors and no such thing as electric light, it was difficult to keep interiors clear of debris. It has been calculated that ground level grew at a rate of about one centimetre per annum. Over a hundred year period, this amounts to one metre, and by the later eleventh century, the soft ground was almost two metres deep, making it difficult to obtain good foundations. This is the 'boggy' earth that Gilbert and his colleagues noticed a century ago. Rafts of wattle and timber were used to cover the demolished ruins of the previous building, larger wattle posts were needed in the walls, and roof-posts were given the added support of padstones. The eleventh century also witnessed a growth in the skill of the carpenter and the quality of the houses improved. Perhaps the most outstanding example of this improvement is the stave-built house of oak from Christ Church Place, dated by dendrochronology to 1059.[32] It measured 9.5 by 4.5 m and had a single entrance slightly off-centre in the south wall. The sides of the building were straight and the corners right-angled. The floor consisted of a damp layer of fermenting vegetation with a texture akin to mouldy hay and analysis indicated that flies, fleas and mites were present in abundance. Indeed George Coope, the scientist who analysed the hay, has suggested that 'this fermenting carpet was deliberately contrived to maintain warmth within the building'.[33] Sawdust and wood-chips were also laid on the floors and, like compost heaps, the breakdown of nutrients raised the temperature. There is little doubt but that this material was deliberately brought in as a primitive form of central heating. The high numbers of two beetles, one that attacks wickerwork, the other, the common furniture beetle, indicates that the house was badly infected with woodworm. Indeed, it has been estimated that, given the activity of woodworm, the average life-span of a house was no more than twenty to twenty-five years.

Although such an environment might sound quaint or rustic, Siobhán Geraghty points out that 'there was a tolerance of circumstances that would nowadays be regarded as unacceptable'.[34] The town was in effect, a vast dung-heap, composed of an ever-increasing mass of fermenting wood-chips and mouldy grass, augmented with the usual detritus of human life and punctuated with cess pits. Indeed, to our hygiene-conscious age the most striking anomaly was the location of cess pits beside wells, with the detritus of one oozing into the drinking water of the other. In wet weather the town was liable to become impassable [Gridlock 1000 AD style] and elaborate systems of drains and gullies were constructed so as to remove surface water, while paths were usually paved or boarded.

Well, so much for the physical environment, what of the people themselves? Bones from excavated graves of this period indicate that the Dubliners of the year 1000 were as tall as we are today. The popular misconception that people were smaller in the past largely arises from the fact that the inhabitants of nineteenth-century towns tended to be smaller than today because they lived in overcrowded and under-nourished conditions, resulting in a poor physique. The life span of the early Dubliners, however, was shorter than that of today. Infant mortality was high. 50% of women were dead by the age of 35, worn out primarily by child-bearing; 10% of the population lived past the age of 60, and nine out of ten of these were men—a complete reversal of modern life-span expectations.[35] The average diet of Dubliners was one that modern nutritionists would regard as well balanced: substantial quantities of wholemeal bread and porridge, supplemented by fruit [apples and pears], nuts [particularly hazelnuts], berries and beans; some meat and fish, including ling, ray and herrings.[36] In terms of meat, beef was most common but mutton and pork were also eaten and there is evidence that pigs were raised within the town. Goats were also kept, probably as a source of milk. Among shellfish, mussels and winkles were the most commonly eaten. Eggs and dairy produce would have supplemented the diet. A sweet and sour relish (a combination of honey and fermented sloe juice) was popular and herbs such as mint were used as flavourings. All was washed down with beer, which was certainly safer to drink than the water.

Viking Age Dublin was a town of merchants and craftsmen. It was as ocean-going travellers that the Vikings had made their name. Their ships were the finest in Europe and with their shallow draft (you could float one virtually in a bath), they were also able to trade deep into the interior of Ireland. Balance scales, gold and silver ingots and a large number of imported coins indicate the importance of merchants who traded with England, particularly the Chester area, and with the northwest of France.[37] The presence of walrus ivory, soapstone vessels and amber indicates that trade was maintained with Scandinavia, while the discovery of silks shows that Dublin was part of a trading network which stretched as far as the Silk Road to China. Silver coins from Samarkand, Tashkent and Baghdad have all turned up in the Dublin excavations. Dublin's major exports were wool, hides and slaves. It was the slave trade, indeed, which generated the town's wealth. It has been pointed out that the Vikings were interested in luxury commodities, obtained cheaply in distant places and sold for high prices to consumers. The classic items are gold and silver, wine, slaves and furs. One of the furs that the Vikings traded was vair, which is the soft, underbelly fur of a Siberian squirrel. Highly prized in the early middle ages, it became almost impossible to obtain in Western Europe after the year 1300. So when, in the seventeenth century, the French children's stories of Perrault were being translated into English, the translator discovered that Cinderella's slippers were made of *vaire*. The only English word he knew for *vaire* was 'glass', and hence the absurdity of a glass slipper. Cinderella's slippers were made from that luxurious fur, vair, which the Vikings so-liked to trade. Ireland was limited as a source of fur but in Dublin the furs of red squirrels, pine martens and domestic cats were used. Indeed there are indications that cats were bred and kept for their fur. But the quality of this fur was not good enough for export. Silver was probably exported through Dublin but the source of the town's wealth (as it was to be the source of Bristol and Liverpool's wealth in a later age) was the slave trade.[38] Slaves were obtained not just in raids. Individuals whose debts were too great sometimes had to sell themselves into slavery. But the most common way of obtaining slaves was by trade. The lives of captives taken in battle were forfeit to the victors. If the captives were not aristocratic and capable of paying a ransom, it was more profitable to sell the captives as slaves than to kill them. The majority of individuals in the Dublin slavemarkets then were purchased from one victorious Irish king or another. Ireland was not the only source of slaves. England, Scotland and Wales supplied their share. Indeed even in the 1100s the merchants of Dublin were condemned for selling English Christians into slavery in Ireland. Slaves were brought from further afield as well. The first reference to blackmen, *gentib gorma*, in Ireland occurs in the Viking Age when it is assumed that these were Moors captured from Spain or Morocco.[39] Perhaps the most graphic testimony to Dublin's overseas trade, however, was the discovery some years ago of a Dublin ship in the harbour of Roskilde, the ancient capital of Denmark. Here excavations in the 1960s uncovered the remains of five ocean-going vessels.[40] It was only in 1991, with advances in dendrochronology, that it was recognised that the largest of these ships, which required 50 oarsmen to propel it, was built from oak felled in the east of Ireland in *c*.1060–70.[41]

The range of artisans and tradesmen in the town included carpenters, coopers, turners, shipwrights, carvers, blacksmiths, silversmiths, goldsmiths, bronze-smiths, copper-smiths, and lead-smiths.[42] Antler, naturally shed, was recovered for making pins, combs and gaming-pieces. Some individual workshops have been identified: a bronze pin manufacturer at High Street, comb-makers at High Street and Christ Church Place, amber jewellers at High Street and Fishamble Street. Wool and linen were prepared, spun and woven while tanning and leather-working were also practised.

By the year 1000 it is probably fair to say that many (if not most) Dubliners were Christians. Olaf Cuarán, king of Dublin from 945 to 980 had abdicated so that he might go and die in the habit of a monk at Iona. His son was the famous Sitric Silkenbeard, who was king in the year 1000. We know that Dublin received its first bishop and cathedral during his reign and, since he abdicated in 1036, the date conservatively given for the foundation of Christ Church Cathedral is 1035. It is more likely to have been about 1028, however, the year in which Sitric Silkenbeard made the hazardous pilgrimage to Rome, almost certainly coming back with papal approval for his new diocese.

The hinterland of Dublin, the area under the rule of Sitric Silkenbeard, comprised roughly the area of the modern county, stretching westwards as far as Leixlip, north to Skerries and south into the barony of Rathdown.[43] Bilberries, rowan berries, heather and *sphagnum* moss (all acidic plants) are known to have been brought into the town from the Dublin mountains.[44] Further afield the fishing villages and settlements at Arklow, Wicklow and the towns of Wexford and Waterford kept in close touch with Dublin and for much of our period were governed by the Dublin ruling family.

Let us return now to Brian Bóruma and his army, laying siege to Dublin at the beginning of January in the year 1000. From the refoundation in 917 until 980, the Dubliners had endeavoured to go their own way and set up an independent kingdom within Ireland. Their hopes came to grief in 980 at the battle of Tara, however, when they were defeated by Máel Sechnaill, king of Mide, who followed up his victory by quickly capturing Dublin itself. Huge numbers of hostages were released into Irish hands and the treasures of Dublin were brought back to Meath. The Dubliners had lost battles before and the settlement had been captured before, but this time was different. Dublin had fallen to an ambitious, energetic and able king at the height of his powers. When the Dubliners tried to break away from his control in 989 he besieged the town, cut off their sources of fresh water, so that the annalist tells us 'they were reduced to drinking sea-water' and after three weeks, Dublin surrendered. It was on this occasion that Máel Sechnaill levied an annual tax of one ounce of gold on every plot in Dublin—a minimum of 400 ounces of gold, not bad even at today's prices but a fortune at this period when the only gold was ancient gold, and the gold of Africa still lay undiscovered. It was this capture of Dublin in 989 that afforded the occasion for celebrating the Dublin Millennium in 1988. In 995 Máel Sechnaill captured Dublin again. Ostensibly this was to punish the Dubliners for a raid on Donaghpatrick (near Kells), and this time Máel Sechnaill humiliated the townspeople by removing their most valued possessions, the sword of Carlus (a weapon which was believed to belong to Charlemagne himself) and the ring of Thor, presumably a great silver arm-ring of the form used for solemn oath-takings in Scandinavian societies. It was probably the insignia of the urban community much as the mace and seal would be to a later age.

It is not clear how much of a role Máel Sechnaill played at Glenn Máma in 999 but he did not attempt to prevent Brian Bóruma from besieging Dublin on 1 January 1000.[45] Five days later, on Little Christmas, Dublin fell to the forces of Brian Bóruma. He and his conquering army remained in Dublin until 1 February.[46] The town was burnt and plundered, its population and that of its hinterland decimated; its women and young people carried into slavery, with only those wealthy enough to purchase their freedom left behind. A supporter of Brian Bóruma, writing somewhat later leaves us in no doubt about what happened:

> 'Oh', he writes, 'the piercing and hacking of bodies,
> The cleaving of fair and handsome heads,
> Feet kicking and arms flailing in all directions
>
> …
>
> The Dál Cais put to death on that day
> Four thousand people,
> From others they removed their cows
> In return for sparing their lives
>
> …
>
> On that occasion, we carried off silks from Dublin
> We carried off beds and soft furnishings,
> We brought horses, strong and swift,
> And white-skinned women in the bloom of youth[47]

In Dublin, he says, 'were found the greatest quantities of gold and silver, of gilt-metal and precious stones, gigantic drinking horns and beautiful goblets. Garments of all colours were gathered likewise. Many women, and boys and girls also, were ruined ['sexually abused', we would say today] before being carried off into slavery.'[48]

At this point the chronicler was evidently touched by compassion because in the next sentence he felt he had to give an explanation of the Munstermen's behaviour. 'The Dubliners', he explains, 'deserved this because they were foreigners …'[49]

And he continues: 'It was bad luck for the Dubliners when Brian Bóruma was born, for it was by him that they were killed, destroyed, exterminated, enslaved and bondaged. So that there was not a house from Howth to Dursey Island that did not have a foreigner in bondage in it, nor was there a grinding stone without a foreign woman to work it. So that no son of Erin deigned to put his hand to a flail or any other manual labour. Nor did any Irish woman have to put her hands to the grinding of a quern, or to knead a cake, or to wash her clothes, but that she had a servile Dublin man or a Dublin woman to do the work for them.'[50]

One would like to think that such scenes as the capture and pillage of towns were confined to the Middle Ages, yet it is one that we have seen all too frequently on our television screens throughout the 1990s.

Despite its destruction in the year 1000, Dublin recovered. For the remaining fourteen years of his life Dublin remained loyal to Brian Bóruma. It did not dare to do otherwise. Occasionally there were grumblings and Sitric Silkenbeard was instrumental in bringing the forces of Sigurd, Jarl of Orkney, to Clontarf in 1014, but when it came to the battle,

Dublin remained neutral. Few tears would have been shed in Dublin when news was brought of Brian Bóruma's death and the victorious Ua Briain army found that the gates of Dublin were closed to them as they marched home from Clontarf.

A thousand years ago then, in January of 1000, Dublin would have been an awkward place to be (unless of course you were a Clare man). Once the warriors had left, however, the townspeople were able to get on as best they could and rebuild their lives. It is a tribute to their persistence and determination that they rebuilt not only their lives but also the town. The tiny area occupied by Dublin in the year 1000, no bigger than a supermarket car park, was the nucleus around which a millennium of development created the city we know today. Yet even in its infancy, many of the features that characterise the later city were present almost like the genetic coding of a simple cell. The roads that led out from this nucleus were to become the streets of the later city; the individual property plots (known to a later period as burgages) were to remain the standard building blocks of the city into the twentieth century; and the nucleus itself was to remain the hub of economic, social and religious activity. When the second millennium was rung out last New Year's Eve, it was from Christ Church Cathedral. People gathered in Christ Church Place, Winetavern Street and Fishamble Street, just as they would like to have done a thousand years ago, although I suspect that they were too preoccupied with the aftermath of the battle of Glenn Máma to have had much time to notice the arrival of the year 1000. Without us even being aware of it, the decisions of a thousand years ago continue to influence our lives.

In the year 2000 it is, perhaps, salutary to remember that no matter how great our problems are: traffic, housing, drugs, crime or refugees, they pale in contrast to the life and death struggle for existence that Dublin faced in the year 1000. It is only fitting then, that on the eve of the third millennium, we should remember and salute the Dubliners of a thousand years ago, just as a thousand years hence we may hope to merit a nod from the new Dubliners who will be living not in Dublin, Ohio, but in the several Dublins on the moons of Jupiter and the most distant planets.

Notes

1 J. T. Gilbert, *A history of the city of Dublin* (3 vols, Dublin, 1854–9), reprinted with an introduction by F. E. Dixon (Dublin, 1978), i, pp 130, 208.

2 For example, ibid, pp 45, 101, 144.

3 Reports on the National Museum of Ireland's excavations in medieval Dublin have appeared as follows: H. A. Murray, *Viking and early medieval buildings in Dublin* (Oxford, 1983); G. F. Mitchell, *Archaeology and environment in early Dublin* (Dublin, 1987); J. T. Lang, *Viking Age decorated wood* (Dublin, 1988); P. F. Wallace (ed.), *Miscellanea 1* (Dublin, 1988); P. F. Wallace, *The Viking Age buildings of Dublin* (2 vols, Dublin, 1992); Seán McGrail, *Medieval boat and ship timbers from Dublin* (Dublin, 1993); Thomas Fanning, *Viking Age ringed-pins from Dublin* (Dublin, 1994); Siobhán Geraghty, *Viking Dublin: botanical evidence from Fishamble Street* (Dublin, 1996); M. P. Barnes, J. P. Haglond and R. I. Page, *The runic inscriptions of Viking Age Dublin* (Dublin, 1997).

4 H. B. Clarke, *Dublin c.840 to c.1540, the medieval town in the modern city* (Dublin, 1978).

5 Geraghty, *Viking Dublin: botanical evidence*, pp 64–6.

6 Ibid., pp 63, 68.

7 Bede, *Historia ecclesiastica gentis Anglorum*, I.i, translated by Leo Shirley Price and R. E. Latham as *A history of the English church and people* (Harmondsworth, 1968), p. 39.

8 Geraghty, *Viking Dublin: botanical evidence*, p. 64.

9 Bede, op. cit.

10 Geraghty, *Viking Dublin: botanical evidence*, p. 67.

11 Ibid., p. 65.

12 Ibid., pp 48–9.

13 Ibid.

14 Ibid.

15 Ibid., pp 63, 66.

16 Ibid., p. 63.

17 Ibid., p. 61; Aidan O'Sullivan, 'Woodmanship and the supply of timber to Anglo-Norman Dublin' in Conleth Manning (ed.) *Dublin and beyond the Pale: studies in honour of Patrick Healy* (Bray, 1998), pp 63–73.

18 Raghnall Ó Floinn, 'The archaeology of the early Viking age in Ireland' in H. B. Clarke, Máire Ní Mhaonaigh and Raghnall Ó Floinn (eds), *Ireland and Scandinavia in the early Viking age* (Dublin, 1998), p. 134.

19 Ibid., pp 135–7.

20 Charles Halliday, *The Scandinavian kingdom of Dublin* (2nd ed., Dublin, 1884; reprinted Shannon, 1969), pp 151–2.

21 Elizabeth O'Brien, 'The location and context of Viking burials at Kilmainham and Islandbridge, Dublin' in Clarke, Ní Mhaonaigh and Ó Floinn (eds), *Ireland and Scandinavia in the early Viking age*, pp 203–21.

22 Seán Mac Airt (ed.), *The annals of Inisfallen* (Dublin, 1951), sub anno.

23 John Bradley, 'The topographical development of Scandinavian Dublin' in F. H. A. Aalen and Kevin Whelan (eds), *Dublin city and county: from prehistory to the present, studies in honour of J. H. Andrews* (Dublin, 1992), pp 43–6.

24 Ibid., p. 44; H. B. Clarke, 'The bloodied eagle: the Vikings and the development of Dublin, 841–1014' in *Ir. Sword* xviii (1990–2), pp 91–119.

25 Bradley, 'Topographical development of Scandinavian Dublin', pp 43–4.

26 H. B. Clarke, 'The topographical development of early medieval Dublin' in *R.S.A.I. Jn.*, cvii (1977), pp 42–5; idem, 'Proto-towns and towns in Ireland and Britain in the ninth and tenth centuries' in Clarke, Ní Mhaonaigh and Ó Floinn (eds), *Ireland and Scandinavia in the early Viking age*, pp 346–52; Anngret Simms, 'Medieval Dublin: a topographical analysis' in *Ir. Geog.*, xii (1979), pp 32–3. Cf. Linzi Simpson, 'Forty years a-digging: a preliminary synthesis of archaeological investigations in medieval Dublin' in Seán Duffy (ed.), *Medieval Dublin I, proceedings of the Friends of Medieval Dublin symposium 1999* (Dublin, 2000), pp 20–1.

27 Clarke, 'The topographical development of early medieval Dublin, pp 29–51; Cf. Simpson, 'Forty years a-digging', pp 11–19.

28 P. F. Wallace, 'Dublin's waterfront at Wood Quay, 900–1317' in Gustav Milne and Brian Hobley (eds) *Waterfront archaeology in Britain and northern Europe* (London, 1981), pp 110–13.

29 Murray, *Viking and early medieval buildings in Dublin*, pp 43, 203.

30 W. M. Hennessy (ed.), *Chronicum Scotorum, a chronicle of Irish affairs … to A.D. 1135* (London, 1866), sub anno 999. The editor maintained, incorrectly in my view, that this was a duplicate account of an entry relating to Athlone. See now H. B. Clarke, *Dublin, part I* (Irish historic towns atlas no. 11, Dublin, 2002).

31 Wallace, *Viking age buildings*.

32 Murray, *Viking and early medieval buildings*, pp 95–7; A. B. Ó Ríordáin, 'The High Street excavations', in Bo Almqvist and David Greene (eds), *Proceedings of the seventh Viking congress, Dublin 15-21 August 1973* (Dublin, 1976), pp 139–40.

33 G. R. Coope, 'Report on the coleoptera from an eleventh-century house at Christ Church Place, Dublin', in H. Bekker-Nielsen et al (eds), *Proceedings of the eighth Viking congress, Århus 24–31 August 1977* (Odense, 1981), p. 56.

34 Geraghty, *Viking Dublin: botanical evidence*, p. 69.

35 Barra Ó Donnabháin and Benedikt Hallgrímson, 'Dublin: the biological identity of the Hiberno-Norse town' in Seán Duffy (ed.), *Medieval Dublin II, proceedings of the Friends of Medieval Dublin symposium 2000* (Dublin, 2001), pp 65–87. The mortality figures cited here are from J. D. Dawes and J. R. Magilton, *The cemetery of St Helen-on-the-walls, Aldwark* (The archaeology of York 12/1, York, 1980).

36 The following paragraph is based on Geraghty, *Viking Dublin: botanical evidence*, pp 67–8.

37 P. F. Wallace, 'The economy and commerce of Viking Age Dublin' in Klaus Düwel, Herbert Jankuhn, Harald Siems and Dieter Timpe (eds), *Untersuchungen zu Handel und Verkehr der vor- und frügeschichtlichen Zeit in Mittel- und Nordeurope* (4 vols, Göttingen, 1987), iv, pp 200–45.

38 Paul Holm, 'The slave trade in Dublin, ninth to twelfth centuries', *Peritia*, v (1986), pp 317–45.

39 J. H. Todd (ed.) *Cogadh Gaedhel re Gallaibh, the war of the Gaedhil with the Gaill* (London, 1867), p. 68

40 Olaf Olsen and Ole Crumlin-Pedersen, *Five Viking ships from Roskilde Fjord* (Copenhagen, 1978).

41 Niels Bunde, 'Found in Denmark, but where do they come from?' in *Archaeology Ire.*, xii, no. 3 (1998), pp 24–9.

42 P. F. Wallace, 'A reappraisal of the archaeological signifi-cance of Wood Quay' in John Bradley (ed.), *Viking Dublin exposed, the Wood Quay saga* (Dublin, 1984), pp 112–33.

43 John Bradley, 'The interpretation of Scandinavian settlement in Ireland' in John Bradley (ed.), *Settlement and society in medieval Ireland, studies presented to F. X. Martin, o.s.a.* (Kilkenny, 1988), pp 49–78; Mary Valente, 'Dublin's economic relations with hinterland and periphery in the later Viking age' in *Medieval Dublin I*, pp 69–83.

44 Geraghty, *Viking Dublin: botanical evidence*, p. 61.

45 Ailbhe Mac Shamhráin, 'The battle of Glenn Máma, Dublin and the high-kingship of Ireland: a millennial commemora-tion' in *Medieval Dublin II*, pp 53–64.

46 *Cogadh Gaedhel*, pp 116–17.

47 Ibid., pp 112–13.

48 Ibid., pp 114–15.

49 Ibid., pp 116–17.

50 Ibid.

The four parts of the city[*]

High life and low life in the suburbs of medieval Dublin

by **Howard B. Clarke**

‐►‐►‐►‐►‐► ✦ *‐◄‐◄‐◄‐◄‐◄‐◄*

*Gilbert Lecture, January 2001

Commemorative lectures in honour of those who have gone before us tend to be unique events. Nevertheless a common feature shared by all such occasions is that the passage of time opens up a void between speaker and subject. The former, addressing a contemporary audience, will necessarily bring a measure of contemporary colouring to what is said and how that is expressed. It is a commonplace, yet valid, observation that each generation interprets the past in the light of the present. Over a century separates this point in time from Sir John T. Gilbert's death in 1898. As a contemporary of Queen Victoria, living in an Ireland that was fully part of the British state, his background and outlook were fundamentally different from our own, just as ours will be from those of our successors at such a remove. A commemoration of this kind can produce only a faint echo of the man and his times, whose resonances will be inescapably modern.[1] That being so, I have retained much of the jocular spirit of the lecture as delivered, in order both to preserve something of the atmosphere of the occasion and to remind readers that Gilbert himself had a strong sense of humour. The evening in question was dignified by the presence of the Lord Mayor of Dublin, Alderman Maurice Ahern, who graciously accepted his previously unannounced role as a 'character' in the action. It was my own particular honour in the first year of the new millennium to involve him as the first citizen of Dublin in this avowedly contemporary celebration of the achievements of a most remarkable nineteenth-century scholar.

Until a short while ago, Lord Mayor, you and I shared a delectable secret. You yourself may not have been so consciously aware of it as I was, but as a practised observer of the civic scene something of what was passing before us is likely to have registered with you, if only subconsciously. The secret to which I refer is that only you and I, from our particular directional vantage-point, could observe why these good burghers of your fair city have come here this evening. Along with burghers, of course, I include 'burgheresses' or, as may be more politically correct these days, 'burgher-persons'. You and I, Lord Mayor, could observe this in some people by the light of anticipation in their eyes; in others by the somewhat surreptitious manner in which they took their seats, accompanied by furtive glances to one side and the other, as if entering a certain lingerie establishment opposite the G.P.O. without being seen by their friends, and still worse their neighbours, from the upper deck of a passing bus; in yet others by the bold-as-brass, devil-may-care nonchalance with which they strode to their chosen places. You and I could see plainly that these people have not come here to learn about high life in the suburbs of medieval Dublin — about what Thomas Carlyle in a totally different context called 'heroic toil and silence and endurance, such as leads to the high places of the Universe and the golden mountain-tops where dwell the spirits of the dawn'.[2] No, sir, they have come here this evening to learn about low life in the suburbs of medieval Dublin.

After all, what are suburbs if not low-down places? Consider, if you will, classical Latin *sub*, 'below', 'beneath', 'under' and *urbs*, genitive singular *urbis*, 'walled town', 'city'. In classical times, the adjective *suburbanus* denoted generally 'suburban' and more specifically 'situated near Rome'. By *suburbani* Cicero and other writers meant 'the inhabitants of the towns near Rome'. Accordingly there was something inherently *infra dignitatem urbis*, 'beneath the dignity of the city' to be living *in suburbio*, 'in a suburb', or more commonly in small towns in the agglomeration below the elevated citadel that sheltered craftsmen, traders and other inferior types. In medieval Europe the suburb (often used in the singular) signified commercial and residential areas belonging to a town or city lying immediately outside and adjacent to its walls or boundaries. In late seventeenth-century England, as in classical Italy, the adjective 'suburban' was applied with particular reference to the chief city, London, where the word took on a pejorative colouring associated with inferior, debased and especially licentious habits of life. And with what do we associate present-day Irish suburbs? My own personal list would include the following: Grotesque assemblages of fairies, gnomes, leprechauns and other assorted folkloric figures disporting themselves in minuscule front gardens; Unbelievable amounts of litter, household waste and miscellaneous detritus in linkways between housing estates and other public spaces; Bizarre sexual and kindred practices that find themselves on a regular basis in the Sunday newspapers; and, most Unprecedented of all, at least in darkest Dundrum, representatives of that strange, exotic hybrid — wife-swapping sodomites![3]

At the outset of this consideration of the suburbs of medieval Dublin, we need to establish two things. One is the existence of suburbs and the other is their location and nature. When you received your invitation, many of you may have been surprised to learn that there were indeed suburbs in the middle ages. The popular image of a medieval town or city is that of a

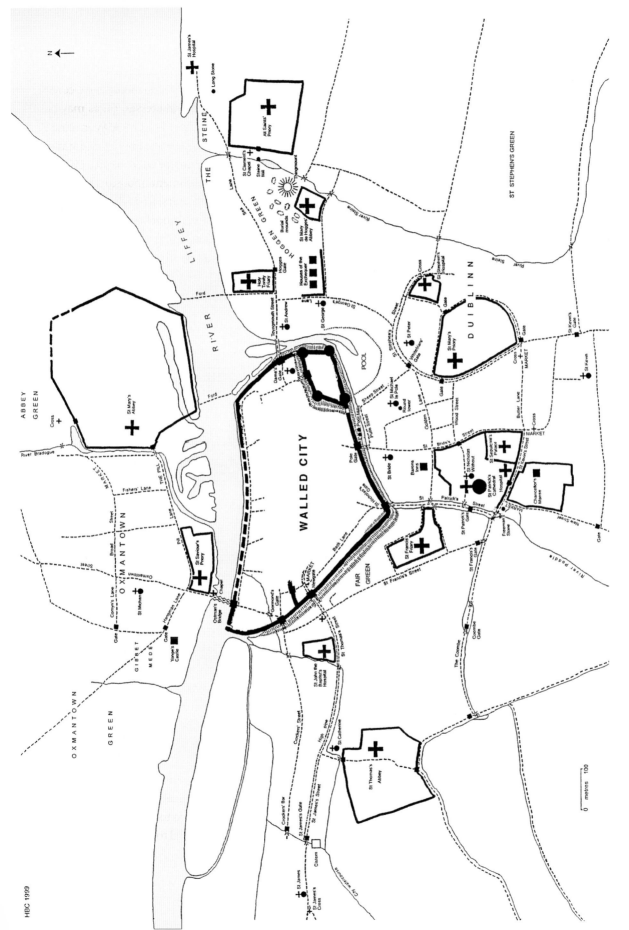

Fig. 1 The medieval suburbs in relation to the walled city

HBC 1999

densely built-up, walled and gated enclosure, outside which extended the surrounding countryside full of peasants. Inside the walls there was wealth and sophistication; outside them poverty and ignorance. To some extent, medieval townspeople themselves fostered such images.[4] The obverse of Dublin's common seal of the thirteenth century, for example, portrays a powerful gateway with two flanking towers and a third watchtower above. Heralds with trumpets and archers with crossbows deter unseen attackers, while three impaled human heads over the gate serve as a warning to external malefactors. When the course of Dublin's medieval walls was worked out more or less accurately by the late Paddy Healy *c.* 1969, he produced a plan that for many people remains the standard concept.[5] The walled city of the thirteenth century and later contained a network of streets, focused on the east-west alignment running parallel to the River Liffey. To one side of this central spine stood Christ Church Cathedral in an appropriately central position, while to the other, tucked away in a defensive angle, there was Dublin Castle. Six principal gates gave access to and egress from the walled city: Dam Gate, Pool Gate, St Nicholas's Gate, Newgate (containing, like London's, a prison), Gormond's Gate and Bridge Gate. Merchant's Quay and Wood Quay appear not to have been walled completely at any stage (which would have obstructed access to and from ships), but the 'old', inner north wall is referred to quite often from the mid-thirteenth century onwards.[6]

The walled enclosure, extending down to the quays, contained only 18 hectares (44 acres), less than inside the defences of some other, ostensibly smaller towns in medieval Ireland such as Drogheda-in-Uriel and New Ross. Clearly there must have been more to high medieval and late medieval Dublin than this, as a reverse image demonstrates with dramatic effect (Fig. 1). Relative to the suburban areas, the walled city was quite small — a fundamental reason why historians should never attempt to estimate population size from that of the defensive enclosure, or enclosures in some cases. Dublin is a classic demonstration of the fact that we might misconceive totally the true character of a medieval town or city by confining our attention to the space delimited by walls, banks, ditches and other defensive arrangements. There was a further dimension to the real size of the medieval city from the late twelfth century onwards — its municipal boundary (Fig. 2). This appears to have been laid down at that time, soon after the arrival of the Anglo-French (or Anglo-Normans) and very possibly during King Henry II's sojourn in the cold winter of 1171–2 outside the town walls near St Andrew's Church. The area so defined would become the 'liberty' of the city of Dublin, that is, the territory within which, in principle, the rights and privileges of fully enfranchised citizens obtained and over which the city authorities, from 1229 under their mayor (Latin *maior*), exercised jurisdiction. The size of this liberty was a measure of the king's determination to build up his city of Dublin into the main focus of loyalty to the English crown in the new colony in Ireland. There was ample scope, therefore, for the development of suburbs in all directions inside the city's own liberty. Even at its greatest extent, however, the built-up area did not occupy more than a fraction of the available space. Nevertheless Dublin did develop into by far the most populous settlement in thirteenth-century Ireland, attaining an estimated 11,000 inhabitants by *c.* 1300.[7]

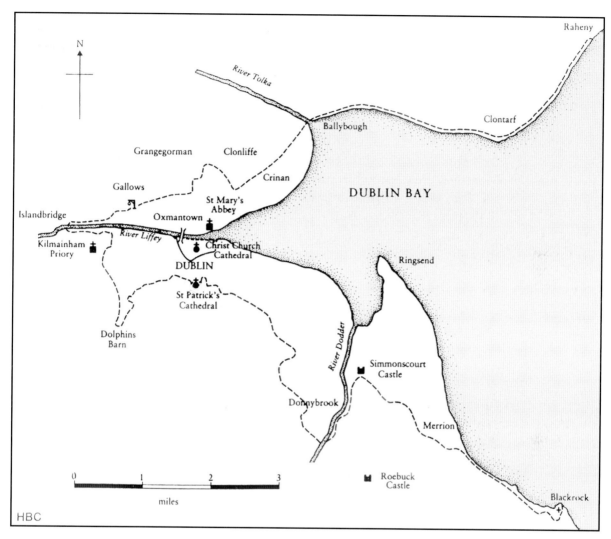

Fig. 2

The territorial liberty

A significant proportion of these people must have been living and working outside the city walls. I have been able to discover only one documentary clue as to what that proportion might have been.[8] It dates from the year 1319 and therefore relates to a time when the medieval population is likely to have reached its peak, about thirty years before the first outbreak of plague in Dublin in 1348. The background to this document is dramatic. Two years earlier the mayor of Dublin, Robert de Nottingham, had issued an order that the city's suburbs should be demolished and burnt to the ground. He was not mad. A Scottish army led by the king, Robert Bruce and his brother Edward, was encamped at Castleknock and was threatening to besiege and capture Dublin. To deprive the enemy of cover in front of the walls and the approaches to them, it was necessary to remove all structures. In a later siege of the city, that conducted by Silken Thomas in 1534, the rebels cut through the side walls of the wooden houses along Thomas Street so as to attack Newgate.[9] In the event, this attack by an Anglo-Irish lord failed, but the western suburb was a particular source of danger. Accordingly, in February 1317, much of it was razed to the ground, including St John the Baptist's Hospital outside the main gate.[10] The fires may have got out of control; there may have been a prevailing westerly wind; at any rate it seems that most of suburban Dublin was either totally destroyed or suffered serious damage. Across the bridge, St Saviour's Priory, home to the city's Dominican friars, was demolished and its stone used to strengthen the defences on the south side; one contemporary source refers to its broken walls, trees felled in the friars' garden, and general devastation.[11] These desperate measures had the desired effect in that the Scots, who had spent a whole year in capturing Carrickfergus Castle, decided against a prolonged siege and went away. Two years later, in their negotiations with the English king, Edward II, seeking compensation for the damage caused in the name of the crown, the city authorities claimed that three-quarters of the fee-farm (that is, the city rent payable annually to the Irish exchequer) came 'from the suburb [from which] they previously received the greater part of the crown rent, but, by the execution of the ordinance above referred to throughout *the four parts of the city*, they are unable to pay the entire amount'.[12]

It may already have occurred to you, Lord Mayor, that herein lies a possible solution to Dublin's current traffic problems. This solution is at once elegant in its simplicity, infallible in its nature and instantaneous in its result: issue an order to burn the lot and start again! Indeed, if you were to be suitably devious about the whole business, as I am sure you would be as a seasoned politician on Dublin City Council, you could even emulate your medieval predecessor by seeking compensation from the British government, for having created such rotten suburbs in the first place. Back in the middle ages, therefore, 'the four parts of the city' were home to large numbers of people. Some of these may have been unenfranchised occupants of mere cabins and were Irish or of Irish extraction. After 1348 the relative proportion of the population of the walled city to that of its suburbs probably changed, even dramatically. The Black Death struck hard, the victims in 1349 including both the mayor, Kenewrek Scherman, and the archbishop, Alexander Bicknor. The former, incidentally, is credited with funding the reconstruction of the east window and the bell tower of the church of the Dominican friary after the destruction of 1317.[13] As those who enjoyed the protection of the walls died off, survivors from the four suburbs may have been tempted to abandon their by then reconstructed homes and to move inside. The four suburbs could have lost a significant proportion of their inhabitants quite quickly. Another possibility is that better-quality housing became available to cabin-dwellers. There is good evidence from many parts of Europe for rising standards of living in the post-Black Death period or, to put it more pithily, there was more high life for low lifers than before.

Dublin's suburbs certainly continued to exist and, from around the middle of the fifteenth century, we hear about a large number of extramural gates, some of them located at a considerable distance from the walled enclosure. These extramural gates were probably intended to control access to the suburbs, especially at night-time. They may have had the usual fiscal functions as well, for there were a number of suburban market-places in late medieval Dublin. The positions of these gates suggest that at least the main approach roads

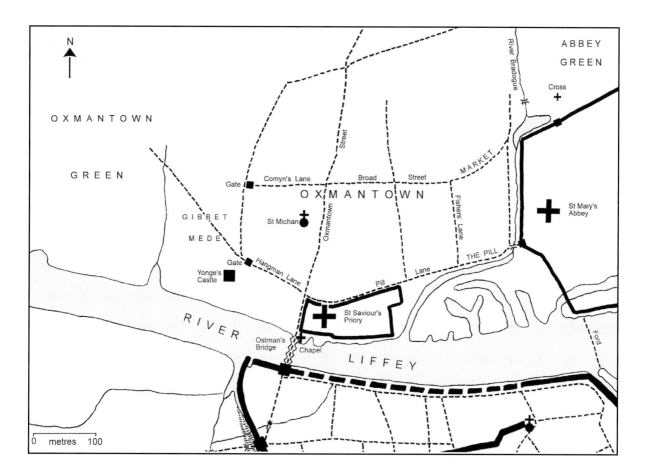

Fig. 3

**The northern
suburb**

to the city were largely built up and occupied, despite the initial and probably continuing outbreaks of plague that may have caused the total population to fall to between 5,000 and 6,000 inhabitants by the early fifteenth century. Their number may have stabilised at around that level for quite some time. In broad terms, therefore, Dublin's medieval suburbs expanded rapidly between the late twelfth and the early fourteenth centuries, contracted in the second half of the latter century, and then stagnated for the rest of the middle ages.

I propose now to conduct you on a brief tour of the four parts of the city, before turning to the question of lifestyles therein.[14] We shall proceed in a clockwise direction, starting in the north across the River Liffey (Fig. 3). Oxmantown took its name from the Hiberno-Norse exodus from the walled town on the south side after the Anglo-French takeover in 1170–2. Even as late as 1483 the main north-south thoroughfare, known to us as Church Street, was being referred to as the 'street of the Ostmen'.[15] Oxmantown was a classic transpontine suburb, situated across the single bridge spanning the Liffey. A medieval bridgehead, potentially at least, was a prime commercial site, though at Dublin one side was monopolised entirely by the mendicant friars of St Saviour's. By the mid-thirteenth century Church Street, named after the parish church of St Michan, is denoted as the 'high street'.[16] The northside suburb came to occupy the ground between the private, enclosed space of St Mary's Abbey to the east and the public, open space of Oxmantown Green to the west. Its street pattern has the appearance of a grid or chequer plan, representing an example of medieval town planning dating presumably to the last decades of the twelfth century. The main east-west alignment comprised Broad Street (now Mary's Lane) towards the abbey and Comynes Lane (now May Lane) towards the green. Nearer to the river another east-west alignment comprised Pill Lane leading towards The Pill — the Cistercians' fishing harbour on the Bradogue estuary — and Hangman Lane (now Hammond Lane) leading towards a typically medieval combination of deterrence and entertainment — the hanging of criminals on what was eventually known as Gibbet Mede.[17] In the thirteenth century the eastern end of Broad Street may have served as a market-place (not far from the present markets), disposing of surplus produce from the vast estates of St Mary's Abbey. Oxmantown, in fact, possessed many of the attributes of a typical country town in the middle ages: an urban street pattern, a market-place, a harbour, a single parish church serving what is described as a large parish,[18] and two religious houses. It had no defensive wall, but two street gates were built in the years 1466–70.[19] By the following century the inhabitants of Oxmantown even had one of those symbols of ordered town life: to improve their time-keeping a bell was added to the public clock over Bridge Gate in 1571.[20]

The morphology of the eastern suburb was quite different, being disposed around two open spaces, both of which had Viking associations (Fig. 4). Hoggen Green took its name from the *haugar* or burial-mounds of Scandinavian kings and war-leaders, one of which survived until its removal in the middle of the seventeenth century.[22] Nearby was the ancient Viking place of assembly, the Thingmount or Thingmote, a motte-like, earthen structure with steep sides and a flat top. Seán Duffy has suggested, rightly I think, that Thingmote became a district name in the thirteenth century.[22] The ancestor of Dame Street was called the (high)way to the Hogges, then Te(y)ngmouth Street,[23] reflecting a consciousness, however corrupt verbally and remote in time, of the predecessors of the Anglo-French or English inhabitants. Like the little river that separated Hoggen Green from its companion, the open space farther east was named The Steine after the Long Stone (Old Norse *steinn*, 'stone'), a tall megalith that is believed to have commemorated the first Viking landfall at Dublin back in the mid-ninth century.[24] These open spaces, once upon a time redolent with pagan Scandinavian ritual, were progressively christianised, initially by none other than Diarmait Mac Murchada, the king of Leinster who founded both the nunnery of St Mary de Hogges (*c.* 1146) and the Augustinian monastery of All Saints (*c.* 1162). Over a century later another Augustinian house, this time a friary, was established near the river bank as well as a ford across the Liffey that was blocked off in 1466 because it was considered dangerous to horseriders attempting to take a short cut.[25] Also near the shoreline stood St James's Hospital, a hospice where pilgrims heading for the

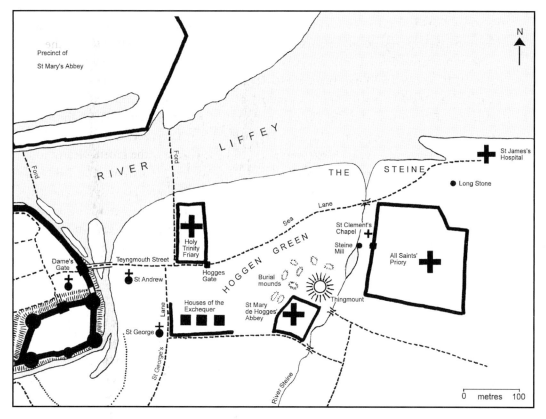

Fig. 4
The eastern suburb

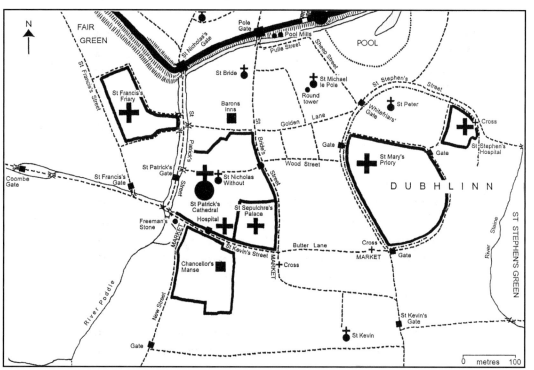

Fig. 5
The southern suburb

The four parts of the city by Howard B. Clarke

famous shrine at Compostela in north-western Spain waited for ships and for suitable weather, as well as rested on their safe return to Dublin.[26]

The southern suburb evinced extraordinary historical and morphological complexity (Fig. 5). Here coexisted a cathedral (St Patrick's), an archbishop's palace, five parish churches, two friaries and a leper-house in the religious sphere, along with a large number of extramural gates, three market-places and, in the far south-east, the southside citizens' common pasture, St Stephen's Green. An aboriginal feature, from which the city derives its international name, was a tidal pool in the River Poddle. After the construction of a dam across the river outside Dam Gate, this pool went out of use as a waterway, though it seems to have been surrounded by numerous gardens and orchards for the water was no longer salty. Nevertheless its former presence lived on in local nomenclature: the Pool Gate, Pulle Street, the Pool Mill and the parish church of St Michael le Pole. As late as 1494 St Bridget's Church is designated as St Brigid of the Polle.[27] St Michael's possessed an unusual attribute that hints at earlier times, a round tower that survived down to the late eighteenth century. This striking feature of Irish monasticism, however, was probably later in date than the nearby monastery,[28] whose characteristic outline was preserved by medieval streets that went around rather than across the site. This monastery may well have been occupied by the first Dublin-based Vikings in the years 841 and 842, before they moved on elsewhere.[29] Most of the ancient enclosure remained an ecclesiastical preserve throughout the middle ages. Even more conspicuous is the cathedral complex, including the archiepiscopal palace and chapel of St Sepulchre. Both came to be surrounded by stone walls, as was the mansion of one of the great cathedral officers, the chancellor, on the south side of St Kevin's Street. This street was so called because it led to the southernmost parish church in the medieval city, whose dedication reflected an earlier link with Glendalough in the mountains. The extramural gate with the same name is the earliest on record on the south side, being mentioned c. 1213,[30] a few years after the disaster of Black Monday, when a large number of citizens taking their Easter Monday walk were massacred by the local Irish at the archbishop's manor of Cullenswood — what we call Ranelagh. New Street Gate may have been erected at about the same time, but it is not documented before 1326.[31] Earlier still, perhaps in the 1190s, the River Poddle had been rerouted away from its old tidal channel along both sides of St Patrick's Street and in front of the realigned south wall of the main defensive barrier.[32]

We arrive finally at the western suburb, the principal approach to the city from the interior that was the chief concern of the mayor in the military emergency of 1317 (Fig. 6). Alone of all the suburbs, this one lay at a higher level than the walled city, which permitted the construction of an ingenious piece of medieval engineering. This was a gravity-flow system of fresh water, reaching the main cistern or holding tank via the city watercourse and then continuing as the high pipe along the side of St James's Street and St Thomas's Street before entering the defensive enclosure at Newgate.[33] These streets were named respectively after medieval Dublin's westernmost parish church and the great royal foundation of St Thomas's Abbey towards the south. As a suburban thoroughfare St Thomas's Street was a creation of

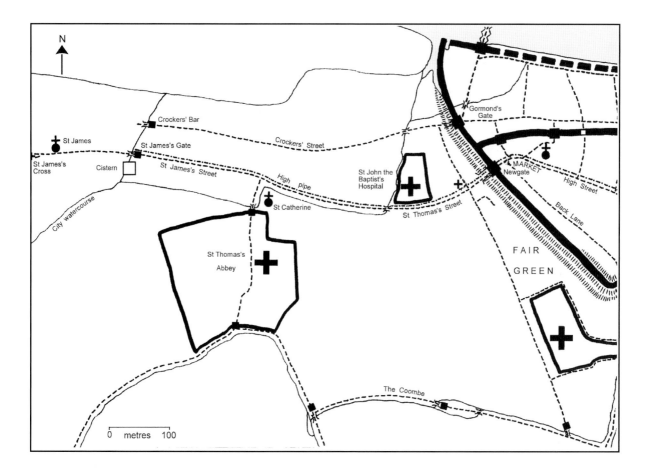

the late twelfth century, when it is called the 'great street' and the 'great new street'.[34] Its commercial potential lay in its length on the side facing the western hinterland and in the fact that it led directly to Newgate and to the heart of the city. Not surprisingly, therefore, we learn that, in the middle of this great artery for food and other necessities entering the city, an eight-day annual fair was authorised by King John in 1204 'at the bridge of St John the Baptist'.[35] The institution referred to here was a charitable one run on monastic lines and catering for the sick poor in particular, its monastic component sheltering both men and women. At a later stage the fifteen-day fair was transferred to a more spacious venue known as the Fair Green in front of the city ditch, which protected the only part of the walls to lack the water-based defences provided by the Liffey and the Poddle.[36] The original fair site seems to have become a horse market, which is described as 'old' in the middle of the sixteenth century.[37] Parallel to this great thoroughfare there was a back lane called Crockers' Lane or Street, the presumed pottery-making quarter where local wares were produced. This area was protected by Crockers' Bars, an extramural barrier whose defensive capability was increased in the 1460s around the same time as the western limits of Oxmantown.[38]

Fig. 6

The western suburb

We come now to the question of high life and low life in these medieval suburbs. One of their most striking features is the large number of monasteries they contained; indeed, all but one of Dublin's religious houses were situated outside the city walls, the exception being the Augustinian priory of the Holy Trinity attached to the south side of Christ Church Cathedral. In this respect, Dublin differed from medieval London, for example, which had six friaries or priories, two hospitals, a hermitage and the college of St Martin le Grand inside its much bigger walled enclosure.[39] We do not know a great deal about the observance of the contemplative life in these monasteries, but it may reasonably be assumed that they were typical of their day in colonial Ireland and that the basic rules were followed. The cartularies and registers that have survived tell us mainly about the ownership of property and its administration; one of the striking features here is the gross disparities of wealth between the various religious houses and hospitals. The only comprehensive and systematic measure that we now have is the surveys made at the time of dissolution *c.* 1540 — the monastic extents. On this basis we can divide Dublin's suburban establishments into three groups. First come the big three: St Mary's Abbey (Cistercian), St Thomas's Abbey (Augustinian) and Kilmainham Priory (Knights Hospitaller). According to the extent of St Mary's Abbey, the enormous precinct contained the church (then being used to store artillery and munitions), the abbot's house, guest-house, garden and stable, the monks' garden, a large orchard, an enclosed pasture, another enclosure, a bakehouse, a brewhouse, a stable and a granary over the outer gate, a water-mill and watercourse, a horse mill and a messuage with a garden, along with shops, houses, gardens and plots of land spread through eleven city parishes, especially that of St Michan in Oxmantown.[40] All of this takes no account of the monks' estates in the country-side.[41] Secondly there were two institutions of a middling sort in terms of wealth: All Saints' Priory and St John the Baptist's Hospital (both Augustinian). When the latter was surveyed in 1540 it was found to contain a hospital building with fifty beds, the prior's quarters, various rooms and a separate house called The Revestre, along with houses, gardens and plots mainly in the western suburb.[42] Finally there were four surviving mendicant houses and the nunnery of St Mary de Hogges.

Thus we may assume that life in Dublin's suburban monasteries varied from very high to pretty low. In terms of material comfort, our best direct evidence comes from an account roll dating from the years 1336–43 and relating to the city's only intramural monastery, Holy Trinity Priory.[43] The community was headed by a prior who was a mitred abbot next in rank to the archbishop and had a seat in parliament. He had a separate suite of rooms in the priory, equipped with close-fitting doors, window glass and a chimney. His table-ware was made of pewter and his table sat twelve people. A washer-woman was employed in the prior's chamber to wash his linen and was paid the princely sum of 12*d.* a year. Breakfast for the prior and his guests included bread, capons, pasties, oysters, salmon, wine and ale; dinner and supper focused more on various meats (beef, mutton, lamb, pork, goose, fowl, rabbit, pigeon, lark and plover). On Fridays and during Lent fish predomi-nated: salmon, herrings, salt-fish, trout, turbot, plaice and gurnard, together with oysters and eels. Condiments and luxury items included almonds, figs, ginger, mustard, olive oil, pepper, rice, saffron, salt, walnuts, and the inevitable 'spices'.[44] It is manifest beyond any doubt that these Augustinian canons regular were living extremely well. Their much poorer confrères may have been more than a little envious, which may explain why the Dominican prior from St Saviour's felt constrained to proclaim in public in 1369 that he would not be responsible for debts run up by members of his order for victuals and other items, unless he had taken personal responsibility.[45] Uniquely, it seems, the monks of St Thomas's Abbey enjoyed a special source of income — a tax charged on ale and mead being produced for the city's taverns. This custom, called tolboll, amounted to one and a half gallons of the best and the second-best batches of every brewing operation.[46] Here the principle seems to have been that the drunker the citizens got, the richer the monks got. In English monasteries, by the way, the monks themselves were commonly allocated a gallon of ale or cider a day; as every modern pop-artiste knows, chanting and singing make for thirsty work.

As for the laity, much of what we know about standards of living comes from late medieval wills and inventories of personal goods, of which about a hundred survive for Dublin.[47] To take an example preserved in the White Book, John Hamound was a shoe-maker and part-time farmer who probably lived in the southern suburb. When he died in 1388 he left in his shop 232 shoes and other materials, a yard or store containing wheat, barley, oats and hay, and six horses. He had at least three male servants, who were all owed money at the time of his death.[48] The inventory of the goods of John Cor, who wished to be buried in St Michan's Church and probably lived in Oxmantown, is more modest and amounted to some metal objects, five cows, five sheep and three pigs.[49] A more substantial parishioner was Nicholas Barret, who appears to have been a bell-maker, farmer and moneylender. To his unmarried daughter, Joan, he bequeathed two brass bells weighing 230 and 18 pounds, together with the practical necessities whereby a young woman from a respectable social background might set up home.[50] Wives sometimes made wills independently of their husbands, as did Ellen Kymore, also of St Michan's parish, in 1478. Her husband, John Bulbeke, seems to have been essentially a farmer, although the couple had a number of male and female servants and may have been engaged in other business in addition.[51] Other women acted alone: for example, Margaret Obern, whose recorded assets were those of a small farmer, directed that she be buried in St Kevin's Church, to whose upkeep she contributed the modest sum of 12d.[52] By its nature, of course, this kind of evidence tells us about the upper and middling social levels in the city and its suburbs.

One explanation for high living in the wealthiest monasteries is that these institutions were endowed with jurisdictional liberties. The territorial liberty of the city was in principle subject to the jurisdiction of the city court, known as the 'hundred' and meeting once a week. This court dealt with civil and criminal matters of many different kinds. Most punishments took the form of a fine, but there were also city prisons and a city gallows. The first city prison on record was situated just inside the walls, at the east end of the lane known to later generations as Hoey's Court.[53] There was another in the Tholsel, the late medieval 'city hall' on the site of the present Peace Garden; this was apparently situated on two levels of the building.[54] The south tower of Newgate also housed a prison by the end of the fifteenth century. There, prisoners were chained by the neck and by the legs, smaller equipment being used for children.[55] In 1525–6 there were seven prisoners in Newgate: four for indebtedness, two for felony and one for trespass. Thus the city's judicial role was taken seriously.

In practice, however, landownership by great ecclesiastics inside the city's liberty caused complications, resulting in the establishment in the early thirteenth century of a number of private liberties. The greatest beneficiary, as one might expect, was the archbishop with three liberties attached to Christ Church Cathedral, St Patrick's Cathedral (after c. 1220) and St Sepulchre's Palace. The abbots of St Thomas's had two liberties — St Thomas's (later Thomascourt) and Donore.[56] The precise status of the liberty of St Mary's Abbey was a source of confusion and conflict. In c. 1282 the abbot, who had arrested a felon and put him in the abbey's prison, argued successfully that St Mary's was not in the civic jurisdiction; the mayor was fined and the city's liberties revoked temporarily.[57] Yet in 1328, after a search of charters, the justiciar's court determined that the abbey did lie within the boundaries of the city.[58] Much later, in 1488 during the course of riding the franchises, the mayor Thomas Meyler and his party were twice accosted by the abbot of St Mary's and his monks, who complained about the route that had been taken. The mayor rebuked the monks with these words: 'Nay, for by our boke when we did retorne bakward fromm the Tolkan' we shold haue rid to Our Lady Churche of Ostmanneby'.[59] Evidently medieval mayors had no fear of a belt of the crozier! Immediately beyond the western suburb lay the liberty of the prior of Kilmainham. Even though his liberty lay completely outside that of the city, there were still occasions for dispute. In 1220, for example, part of the city's fishery in the Liffey above Kilmainham had been destroyed, apparently because of a watermill erected by the Knights; half a century later the enraged citizens marched out and demolished the offending mill.[60] One consequence of the existence of all these jurisdictions, whose rights included that to hang common thieves, was that the city's approaches were adorned with gallows and their gruesome occupants.[61] Another consequence was attempts by litigants to secure a better deal in a different court. In 1308 a resident of St Patrick's Street, William le Deyer, bought some woad and other materials from a merchant from Wales on the quayside at Dublin. When brought before the king's court for indebtedness, William did not deny that he owed the money, but argued that the actual contract was drawn up in St Patrick's Street, in the archbishop's liberty, and that the case should be heard in the latter's court.[62]

Outside the formal records of courts of law, examples of low life are harder to pick up. Poverty was probably widespread, as it usually seems to have been in all historical periods. Some poverty may have been self-induced: in c. 1319 the new archbishop of Dublin, Alexander Bicknor, delivered a fierce sermon in Christ Church Cathedral denouncing sloth and idleness, citing in particular the large numbers of vagrants and beggars infesting the streets of the city and its suburbs; even mendicant friars were not excused.[63] In the mid-sixteenth century we are told that the poor tended to congregate at the city's gates and a bellman provided with a special livery was appointed to expel strange beggars.[64] Medieval churchmen had their own view of the foibles of the laity. A general inquisition concerning public sins was conducted through the city and its suburbs once or twice a year and in 1267 Archbishop Fulk de Ferings made an agreement with the city authorities about public penance. Those found guilty of a particular offence for the first time were fined a sum of money; second offenders were beaten with rods round their parish church; third offenders were similarly chastised on a holy day in front of the procession outside one of the cathedrals; thereafter the mayor and one of his assistants were to be informed so that the persistent offender could be expelled from the city or at least scourged through its streets.[65] Misdemeanours that did not offend against public morality are listed in the city's by-laws and were normally punished by fines. Citizens, whether from the walled enclosure or from the much more extensive suburbs, who insulted the mayor were fined 40s.; those who did likewise as he presided over the hundred court were fined £10. Striking the mayor would cost you four times that amount and, if blood were shed, £100 or the loss of your right hand or perpetual imprisonment. Insulting a mere neighbour was more affordable at 2s. and for not cleaning the pavement in front of your house even more so at 12d. Women brewers, found guilty of making inferior ale, were fined 15d. for a first offence, as were bakers for producing faulty bread, whilst a baker who failed to stamp his loaves with his own name was fined 6s. 8d.[66] Relatively minor infractions of law and morality might result in a spell in the pillory, which stood at the important road junction south-east of Christ Church Cathedral. Judging by a late sixteenth-century reference, the citizenry would enter into the spirit of things with gusto, for the nearby fresh-water aqueduct was being polluted by missiles thrown at the unfortunate occupants.[67]

In a period before the advent of newspapers, we tend to hear most about more serious crimes, many of these involving violence. Robbery was probably common enough. In 1310 Adam, son of Robert de Cauntetoun, together with accomplices broke into the church of the Friars of the Sack, a shortlived mendicant house on the southern fringes of the city, and stole 40s.[68] In the following year one John Kellagh was found guilty by jurors from the north side of the city of breaking into the house of Hugh and Isabelle de Sauntref (Santry) and of stealing clothing; he was sentenced to be hanged for he had no land or chattels.[69] Some violence occurred aboard ships in the harbour, as in 1311 when Adam de Cokerford came at Richard del Shoppe with a big stick called by sailors a 'spek'. Richard used the ship's mast as a shield and then struck Adam with his cutlass and killed him. The jurors said that this was justifiable homicide and Richard was pardoned.[70] That same year some mariners, including men from the English ports of Liverpool, Sandwich and Whitehaven, assisted in the killing of Robert Thurstayn. Five of them were found guilty and sentenced to be hanged. Afterwards two of them, having been taken down from the gallows presumed dead, were taken by cart to Kilmainham for burial. However, they were still alive and took refuge in the church there, whereupon they were pardoned.[71] A surprising amount of violence was perpetrated by clerics and monks. Again in the same year, Robert of Corbaly, a canon of St Thomas's Abbey, cast aside his monastic habit, shaved his head completely and put on lay garments. He then broke the locks of the abbey's coffers, mutilated charters and other muniments, and stole 60 pounds of silver and other plate.[72] In 1379 eight members of the Augustinian friary of the Holy Trinity, situated in the eastern suburb, were accused of murdering another friar, Richard Dermot, an Englishman. After midnight, i.e. during the curfew, they carried the body to Adam Bron's garden and dumped it down his well. Subsequently they retrieved it and buried it in the friars' churchyard.[73] In the following year there was an affray in the Dominicans' cemetery, in the course of which at least one friar was wearing a coat of mail under his habit and, upon the ringing of the church bell, none other than the mayor of Dublin and a party of men came to the assistance of the friars.[74] Both of these outbreaks of suburban violence have the same background which offers an insight into these otherwise bizarre events.[75]

Medieval towns and cities have a reputation for being unhealthy places to live in and it is probably true that their death-rates were higher than those in the countryside. Nevertheless many regulations for waste disposal were drawn up; the big problem was to ensure compliance. Unlike nowadays, most medieval waste was organic and could be disposed of safely provided that elementary precautions were observed. Human waste was commonly disposed of in cess-pits dug in the back gardens of houses, though no doubt some of it found its way into street drains where these existed. Cess-pits in Dublin could not be sited within 2 feet 6 inches (0.8 metre) of a neighbour's property. We know of at least one public latrine in medieval Dublin; this was situated next to Isolde's Tower and would have discharged directly into the River Liffey.[76] Animal waste, on the other hand, was a valuable commodity as one of the main sources of fertiliser. There were recognised public dung-heaps beyond Hangman Lane in Oxmantown, on Hoggen Green and near the Franciscan friary, and one of the tasks of the city constables was to see that the streets were kept free of dung.[77] As well as dogs, pigs roamed the streets and would have played their part by consuming anything that was edible. Medieval pigs were smaller and more agile than their modern descendants and from time to time a swine-catcher was appointed by the city authorities to impound or kill stray pigs. In 1460 the driving of swine being kept in the suburbs through the walled city was banned.[78] This regulation is but one of several that suggest that what was tolerated in the suburbs of medieval Dublin was not permitted inside the walls. There, butchers were prohibited from slaughtering beasts 'to prevent the excessive and noxious stenches hitherto caused by slaughter of cattle';[79] the inference must be that butchers practised their craft in the suburbs. Carters who brought dung inside the city walls for use in gardens were fined 12d. unless the offending material was put to use by the owner on the same day.[80] At least during the nervous 1450s and 1460s, when efforts were being made to defend the outer suburban area in particular, the walled city became a prohibited zone for the lodgement of Irish men, men with 'beards above the mouth' (which seems to have amounted to the same thing), their horses and their horse boys, on pain of a fine of 6s. 8d.[81] The same period witnessed another special provision: any woman crying out within the walls in time of war was to be fined half that amount 'and also to les

[lose] hyr clothys that ys abowt hyr'.[82] Suburban women, we are left to conclude, could go on shouting as much as they liked!

This brings us to high and low aspects of relations between the sexes in the suburbs of medieval Dublin. What has been termed 'the ineradicable nature of the heterosexual condition' meant that female prostitution was as much a feature of this city as of any other. Indeed there was talk of a special prison for fornicatiors to be built in a house called Tune *c.* 1378; two centuries later Richard Stanihurst, that proud Dubliner of the Elizabethan age, refers to the city's brothel-houses, though he does not say where they were.[83] Because the gates were closed at night-time, a red-light district in the city centre would have been no good at all to the dwellers of the suburbs. In the case of medieval London we happen to know that there was a concentration of brothels along the river frontage at Southwark, on the south side of the Thames opposite the main city. By a typically medieval confusion of values, many of these establishments were owned by none other than the bishop of Winchester. Here the principle seems to have been that the more pleasure bad men got, the more money the good bishop got. These facilities came to be known as the stews of Southwark, which leads me to remind you that, when you say 'I was in a stew' about something or other, you are not referring directly to something you ate. A familiar sight in medieval London, apparently, was that of men in little boats rowing city-wards across the Thames in the early hours of the morning.[84] Any London wife, spying her husband at this time and looking more exhausted than he should have done from the mere act of rowing his boat, would have been in no doubt as to what he had been up to the night before. Whether the River Liffey was pullulating with men in little boats coming over from Oxmantown in the early hours, history does not record. The late Leo Swan, however, made the archaeological discovery of a handy little harbour near Bridge Gate that would have been ideal for the purpose of making a discreet landfall.[85] Before they got married, unwedded bachelors (as they are called) were spied upon by a curious official, the mayor of the bullring. The bullring itself was in Cornmarket, just inside Newgate, but the 'mayor' was chosen by custom in the churchyard of St Andrew's Church, in the eastern suburb. One of his functions was to prosecute the keepers of houses of ill repute; another was ceremoniously to assist about-to-be-wed bachelors to celebrate their last hours of 'freedom'.[86]

During the course of this lecture, I hope that I have convinced you of two things: first that suburbs did exist in the middle ages, and extensive ones at that; secondly that the neglected question of life in them is a subject worthy of consideration in its own right. There would have been a good deal of interaction between the four parts of the city. Alan Fletcher has suggested, very plausibly, that late medieval Corpus Christi pageants assembled near St John's Hospital in the western suburb and then proceeded along the internal spine of the walled city, past the High Cross and the Tholsel, before exiting at Dam Gate and finishing at St George's Church in the eastern suburb.[87] Public spectacles would have drawn people

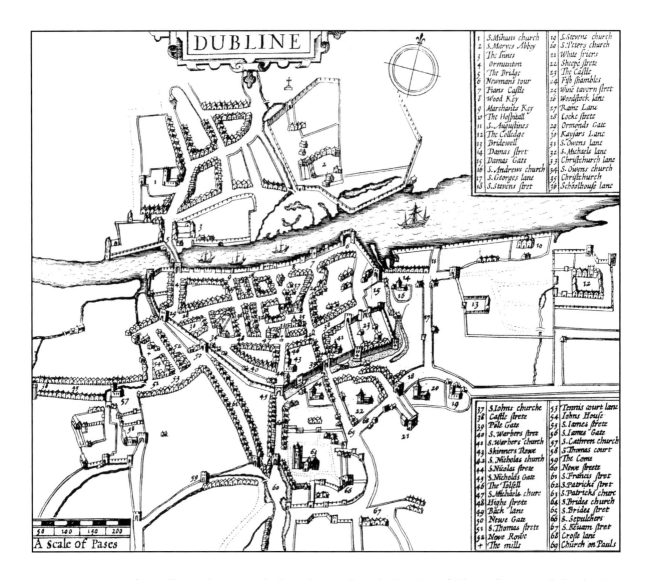

Fig. 7

John Speed's map of Dublin in 1610

from all over the city, including plays such as the Passion of Christ, first recorded as having been performed on Hoggen Green in 1506.[88] Such plays would have been presented in front of a standing audience, using a playing space at ground level and a number of scaffolded platforms.[89] Another example of interaction is the annual procession of the newly elected mayor and his fellow officers from the city centre, across the bridge to St Saviour's Priory in Oxmantown. There the prior would deliver a sermon on civic duty and civic rights.[90] What a good idea, Lord Mayor! What was said on these occasions is not recorded, but we can at least fondly hope that, as paper became a less expensive and more familiar commodity in the course of the fifteenth century and on into the sixteenth, those high-minded Dominicans gave careful instruction to the mayor and his colleagues as to proper and improper uses of brown envelopes.

A city of many parts is precisely what is depicted on the earliest surviving map of

Dublin, that engraved on behalf of John Speed in 1610 (Fig. 7). Despite the changes that had taken place since the dissolution of the monasteries, Speed's map is essentially a portrait in bird's-eye-view style of the late medieval city. The author of this work decided, correctly, to include the four suburbs as well as the main walled enclosure. The resulting contraction in scale placed severe limits on what could be shown in a map of a city of this size and degree of diffusion.[91] Intramural Christ Church Cathedral, for example, is reduced by pressure of space to the dimensions of a small parish church, whereas suburban St Patrick's stands out proportionately in its large enclosure surrounded by stone walls and interval towers. The two biggest monastic sites inside the map frame suggest that some of their buildings and much of their system of boundary walls (some of them apparently crenellated), towers and gates had survived. On the other hand, no trace is indicated of the Augustinian and Franciscan convents apart from the name of the former. The number of houses is under-represented to a considerable extent, with the result that the map cannot be used as a basis for estimating the number of inhabitants either inside or outside the walls. Oxmantown is shown to have been still seriously depopulated and the same may have been true of the other suburbs. Even so, Speed's map does succeed in giving due recognition to 'the four parts of the city' that had been inherited from the middle ages.

We have gathered here this evening to celebrate the work of a great scholar, who did fundamental work not only on medieval Dublin but also on many other aspects of Irish history. John T. Gilbert was a pioneer in the field and we have always to remind ourselves that his three-volume history of the city was published by the time that he had reached the age of thirty. This topographically-arranged work shows that Gilbert was generally aware of the coexistence of a walled area and suburbs. Volume 1 (1854) covers most of 'the ancient city within the walls'.[92] The two other volumes deal with the eastern suburb (roughly Temple Bar) and beyond as far as Kildare Street and South William Street, where the city council had been holding its regular meetings between 1809 and 1852 in the Exhibition Room of the Society of Artists (now the Civic Museum).[93] There is no systematic treatment of the southern, western and northern suburbs, though at least one further volume was planned and indeed announced as being in the press.[94] In 1854 Gilbert and members of his family moved from Jervis Street to Blackrock, in the nineteenth-century suburbs. Their home in Merrion Avenue had a typically suburban name, Villa Nova, reflecting an incident in Portugal over twenty years earlier and the family's involvement in the wine trade.[95] Gilbert is known to have tended his suburban garden, watching the birds and squirrels and incorporating the latter into his armorial bearings when he was knighted in 1897.[96] In the following year, on the afternoon of 28 May, he died a quintessentially suburban death, aboard a no. 8 tram between Merrion and Haddington Road, as he was travelling inwards from Blackrock to attend a meeting of the council of the Royal Irish Academy.[97] As Nodlaig Hardiman puts it so appositely, 'Gilbert, the man noted for his impish sense of humour and fondness for puns and word play, would have appreciated the truly Gilbertian absurdity of the death of a knight errant, in a tram car on a journey from

Blackrock to Dublin, attended only by a man called Pratt'.[98] Nevertheless, just over a century later, it is still generally agreed that John T. Gilbert had earned a well-deserved place among the 'mighty men which were of old, men of renown'.[99]

Acknowledgements

I wish to thank Stephen Hannon of the Cartographic Laboratory of the Department of Geography, University College, Dublin, for his computer-drawn versions of the sketch-maps of the four suburbs (Figs 3–6), which also constitute the basis for Fig. 1; and Dublinia Ltd for permission to reproduce Fig. 2.

Notes

1 For commemorative essays focused more specifically on the man and his times, see Mary Clark, Yvonne Desmond and N.P. Hardiman (eds), *Sir John T. Gilbert 1829–1898: historian, archivist and librarian* (Dublin, 1999).

2 Thomas Carlyle, *History of Friedrich II of Prussia, called Frederick the Great*, i (London, 1858), p. 415.

3 The acronym GUBU was coined by Conor Cruise O'Brien in 1982 in response to a comment by the then taoiseach, Charles Haughey, about the discovery of an alleged (and later convicted) murderer in the home of the attorney general. 'Wife-swopping sodomites' was an accusation hurled at journalists by a lady from Dundrum at the time of the divorce referendum in 1995.

4 For a detailed discussion, based largely on the incomparable records of medieval Italy, see Chiara Frugoni, *A distant city: images of urban experience in the medieval world*, trans. William McCuaig (Princeton, 1991).

5 First published in *Current Archaeology*, ii (1969–70), p. 312; subsequently revised for Curriculum Development Unit, *Viking settlement to medieval Dublin* (Dublin, 1978), p. 30.

6 For example, in *Register of the hospital of S. John without the New Gate, Dublin*, ed. E. StJ. Brooks (Dublin, 1936), pp 58 (*c.* 1279), 75 (*c.* 1243).

7 J. C. Russell, *Medieval regions and their cities* (Newton Abbot, 1972), pp 136–8. This is a reasonable estimate by an author whose methods have been much criticised.

8 Printed from the memorandum roll in *Historic and municipal documents of Ireland, A.D. 1172–1320, from the archives of the city of Dublin, etc.*, ed. J. T. Gilbert (London, 1870), pp 409–12; calendared from the White Book in *Calendar of ancient records of Dublin in the possession of the municipal corporation*, ed. J. T. Gilbert and R. M. Gilbert (19 vols, Dublin, 1889–1944), i, 150–1, being the return by a jury of twenty-nine men sworn to investigate the losses incurred by the citizens when the suburbs were destroyed.

9 Raphael Holinshed, *The first and second volumes of chronicles … newlie augmented and continued … to 1586 by Iohn Hooker alias Vowell* (2 vols, London, 1587), ii, pt 1, p. 93.

10 *Chartularies of St Mary's Abbey, Dublin … and annals of Ireland, 1162–1370*, ed. J. T. Gilbert (2 vols, London, 1884–6), ii, 299, 353; *Rotuli parliamentorum, 1327–77*, p. 393.

11 G. O. Sayles (ed.), *Documents on the affairs of Ireland before the king's council* (Dublin, 1979), p. 87.

12 Printed from the memorandum roll in *Hist. & mun. doc. Ire.*, p. 408; calendared from the White Book in *Anc. rec. Dublin*, i, 149 (italics mine): 'per quatuor partes ejusdem civitatis'. Cf. Sayles, *Affairs of Ire.*, p. 87: 'les suburbes en quatre parties de la cite' and the list of the citizens' grievances *c.* 1317, where the context is not specifically suburban (*Anc. rec. Dublin*, i, 133, 134).

13 *Chartul. St Mary's, Dublin*, ii, 391.

14 I am grateful to Conleth Manning (editor) and to Wordwell Ltd (publisher) for permission to re-use material from 'Urbs et suburbium: beyond the walls of medieval Dublin' in Conleth Manning (ed.), *Dublin and beyond the Pale: studies in honour of Patrick Healy* (Bray, 1998), pp 45–58, and to reproduce Figs 3–6.

Broadly speaking, the historical details cited here relate to the period from the late twelfth to the early sixteenth centuries.

15 M. J. McEnery and Raymond Refaussé (eds), *Christ Church deeds* (Dublin, 2001), no. 1046.

16 *Anc. rec. Dublin*, i, 96.

17 *The Irish fiants of the Tudor sovereigns ...* (4 vols, Dublin, 1994), Hen. VIII, no. 238: Gybbetes Meade (1541). Other spellings are recorded.

18 N. B. White (ed.), 'The *Reportorium viride* of John Alen, archbishop of Dublin, 1533' in *Anal. Hib.*, x (1941), pp 180–1.

19 *Anc. rec. Dublin*, i, 322, 341.

20 Ibid., ii, 69.

21 Walter Harris (ed.), *The whole works of Sir James Ware concerning Ireland, revised and improved* (3 vols, Dublin, 1739–64), ii, 145. A 'little hill' covered this elaborate tomb, which on the balance of probabilities dated from the early Viking period. A drawing is reproduced as plate I, no. 9, facing p. 37.

22 Seán Duffy, 'Ireland's Hastings: the Anglo-Norman conquest of Dublin' in *Anglo-Norman Studies*, xx (1997), pp 83–5.

23 *Anc. rec. Dublin*, i, 83–4 (1239); *Christ Church deeds*, nos 636 (1347), 239 (1348); J. L. Robinson, 'On the ancient deeds of the parish of St John, Dublin, preserved in the library of Trinity College' in *R.I.A. Proc.*, xxxiii (1916–17), sect. C, p. 189 (1364).

24 Charles Haliday, *The Scandinavian kingdom of Dublin* (2nd ed., Dublin, 1884), pp 151–2.

25 *Anc. rec. Dublin*, i, 325.

26 Roger Stalley, 'Sailing to Santiago: medieval pilgrimage to Santiago de Compostela and its artistic influence in Ireland' in John Bradley (ed.), *Settlement and society in medieval Ireland: studies presented to F. X. Martin, o.s.a.* (Kilkenny, 1988), pp 397–420.

27 *Christ Church deeds*, no. 360.

28 H. B. Clarke, 'Conversion, church and cathedral: the diocese of Dublin to 1152' in James Kelly and Dáire Keogh (eds), *History of the Catholic diocese of Dublin* (Dublin, 2000), pp 45–6; Margaret Gowen, 'Excavations at the site of the church and tower of St Michael le Pole, Dublin' in Seán Duffy (ed.), *Medieval Dublin II: proceedings of the Friends of Medieval Dublin symposium 2000* (Dublin, 2001), pp 39–40, 49–51.

29 As suggested hypothetically in H. B. Clarke, 'Proto-towns and towns in Ireland and Britain in the ninth and tenth centuries' in H. B. Clarke, Máire Ní Mhaonaigh and Raghnall Ó Floinn (eds), *Ireland and Scandinavia in the early Viking age* (Dublin, 1998), pp 346–50.

30 *Calendar of Archbishop Alen's register, c. 1172–1534*, ed. Charles McNeill (Dublin, 1950), p. 41.

31 Ibid., p. 171.

32 Claire Walsh, *Archaeological excavations at Patrick, Nicholas and Winetavern Streets, Dublin* (Dingle, 1997), pp 26–7, 77.

33 Valentine Jackson, 'The inception of the Dodder water supply' in *Dublin Hist. Rec.*, xv (1958–9), pp 33–41; repr., with map, in H. B. Clarke (ed.), *Medieval Dublin*, i, *The making of a metropolis* (Dublin, 1990), pp 128–41.

34 *Reg. St John, Dublin*, p. 22 (c. 1190); *Register of the abbey of St Thomas, Dublin*, ed. J. T. Gilbert (London, 1889), p. 404 (c. 1195).

35 *Calendar of documents relating to Ireland, 1171–1251*, p. 35.

36 *Anc. rec. Dublin*, i, 10 (1252), 119 (1335), 120 (1359). Only the last two references are indicative of the fair's location.

37 Ibid., p. 456 (1556).

38 Ibid., pp 314 (earthen wall), 324 (additional tower).

39 M. D. Lobel (ed.), *The city of London from prehistoric times to c. 1520* (Oxford and New York, 1989), maps for c. 1270, c. 1520.

40 *Extents of Irish monastic possessions, 1540–41, from manuscripts in the Public Record Office, London*, ed. N. B. White (Dublin, 1943), pp 1–8.

41 Even a monastery as wealthy as St Mary's could get into debt. On 16 June 1308 two citizens of Dublin complained that the abbot owed them £10, which he promised to repay by the beginning of November (*Calendar of the justiciary rolls or proceedings in the court of the justiciar of Ireland, 1308–14*, p. 83). One factor here may have been loss of income from outlying estates, for in 1312 the abbot, his monks and their servants were pardoned for having disturbed the king's peace when seeking to recover their animals and other property (ibid., p. 246; *Chartul. St Mary's, Dublin*, i, 275).

42 *Extents Ir. mon. possessions*, pp 55–7.

43 *Account roll of the priory of the Holy Trinity, Dublin, 1337–1346*, ed. James Mills (Dublin, 1891; repr., Dublin, 1996).

44 Brian Mac Giolla Phádraig, 'Fourteenth-century life in a Dublin monastery' in *Dublin Hist. Rec.*, vii (1944–5), pp 69–80; repr. in H. B. Clarke (ed.), *Medieval Dublin*, ii, *The living city* (Dublin, 1990), pp 112–22, here at p. 116. Much of this food was prepared in the priory's kitchen, but ready-made food was also purchased in nearby Cook Street (*Account roll of Holy Trinity, Dublin*, p. 111).

45 *Anc. rec. Dublin*, i, 236.

46 Ibid., pp 179, 182 (1524). See also H. F. Berry, 'Proceedings in the matter of the custom called tolboll, 1308 and 1385: St Thomas's Abbey v. some early Dublin brewers, etc.' in *R.I.A. Proc.*, xxviii (1909–10), sect. C, pp 169–73; Virginia Davis, 'Relations between the abbey of St Thomas the Martyr and the municipality of Dublin, c. 1176–1527' in *Dublin Hist. Rec.*, xl (1986–7), p. 61.

47 The principal collection is *Register of wills and inventories of the diocese of Dublin, in the time of Archbishops Tregury and Walton 1457–1483 ...* , ed. and trans. H. F. Berry, (Dublin, 1898).

48 *Anc. rec. Dublin*, i, 127–30.

49 *Register of wills and inventories*, pp 56–8 (1473).

50 Ibid., pp 68–72 (1474).

51 Ibid., pp 102–3.

52 Ibid., pp 104–5 (1478).

53 *Anc. rec. Dublin*, i, 235 (1309).

54 H. F. Berry, 'History of the religious gild of S. Anne, in S. Audoen's Church, Dublin, 1430–1740, taken from its records in the Haliday Collection, R.I.A.' in *R.I.A. Proc.*, xxv (1904–5), sect. C, p. 47; J. T. Gilbert, *A history of the city of Dublin* (3 vols, Dublin, 1854–9; repr., Dublin, 1978), i, 162.

55 Lists of restraining equipment survive in the Chain Book for 1486, 1512, 1525–6 and 1526–7 (*Anc. rec. Dublin*, i, 237–8, 247–9).

56 In 1305 the court of the abbot of St Thomas's was meeting fortnightly, suggesting that judicial business was brisk (*Cal. justic. rolls Ire., 1305–7*, p. 6).

57 *Anc. rec. Dublin*, i, 164–5.

58 Ibid., p. 155.

59 Ibid., pp 495–6.

60 *Cal. doc. Ire., 1171–1251*, pp 149, 150, 171–2; *Cal. doc. Ire., 1302–7*, p 82.

61 The archbishop of Dublin, for example, had a gallows about half way along The Coombe, on the western boundary of the liberty of St Sepulchre (*Alen's reg.*, p. 302).

62 *Cal. justic. rolls Ire., 1308–14*, p. 65.

63 Aubrey Gwynn, 'The medieval university of St Patrick's, Dublin' in *Studies*, xxvii (1938), p. 441, citing Harris (ed.), *Whole works of Sir James Ware*, i, 331–2.

64 *Anc. rec. Dublin*, ii, 28–9 (1563), 53 (1568).

65 Ibid., i, 99; *Alen's reg.*, p. 130.

66 *Anc. rec. Dublin*, i, 219, 221, 222, 224–6 (early fourteenth century).

67 Ibid., ii, 220–1 (1589).

68 *Cal. justic. rolls Ire., 1308–14*, p. 150.

69 Ibid., p. 222.

70 Ibid.

71 Ibid., p. 219.

72 Ibid., p. 212.

73 F. X. Martin, 'Murder in a Dublin monastery, 1379' in Gearóid Mac Niocaill and P. F. Wallace (eds), *Keimelia: studies in medieval archaeology and history in memory of Tom Delaney* (Galway, 1988), pp 468, 470–1, 494–6.

74 Ibid., pp 478–9; Benedict O'Sullivan, 'The Dominicans in medieval Dublin' in *Dublin Hist. Rec.*, ix (1946–8), pp 41–58; repr. in Clarke (ed.), *Living city*, pp 83–99, here at pp 91–4.

75 Martin, 'Murder in a Dublin monastery', pp 479–80.

76 Linzi Simpson, *Excavations at Isolde's Tower, Dublin* (Dublin, 1994), pp 15–17, 21.

77 *Anc. rec. Dublin*, i, 292 (1456).

78 Ibid., p. 306.

79 Ibid., p. 236 (1366).

80 Ibid., p. 326 (1467).

81 Ibid., p. 298 (1458).

82 Ibid., p. 314 (1462).

83 Sayles, *Affairs of Ire.*, p. 248; *Anc. rec. Dublin*, ii, 542 (1577).

84 D. W. Robertson, *Chaucer's London* (New York, 1968), p. 58.

85 D. L. Swan, 'Archaeological excavations at Usher's Quay, 1991' in Seán Duffy (ed.), *Medieval Dublin I: proceedings of the Friends of Medieval Dublin symposium 1999* (Dublin, 2000), pp 126–58.

86 *Anc. rec. Dublin*, ii, 542 (1577).

87 A. J. Fletcher, *Drama, performance, and polity in pre-Cromwellian Ireland* (Cork, 2000), pp 101–13.

88 Ibid., p. 134.

89 Ibid., pp 87–8 and fig. 8.

90 O'Sullivan, 'Dominicans in medieval Dublin', p. 89.

91 J. H. Andrews, 'The oldest map of Dublin' in *R.I.A. Proc.*, lxxxiii (1983), sect. C, p. 211.

92 Gilbert, *History of the city of Dublin*, i, p. xiii.

93 Ibid., iii, 350.

94 Ibid., i, p. vi. Cf. C. T. M'Cready, *Dublin street names, dated and explained* (Dublin, 1892; repr., Blackrock, 1987), p. xii.

95 N. P. Hardiman, 'The entire Gilbert: the life and times of John T. Gilbert' in Clark *et al.* (eds), *Sir John T. Gilbert*, p. 11.

96 Ibid., p. 19.

97 Ibid., p. 23.

98 Ibid., pp 23–4.

99 *Genesis*, vi.4.

Managing the Dublin slums, 1850–1922[*]

by **Jacinta Prunty**

✦➤✦➤✦➤✦➤✦➤ ✦ ✦◄✦◄✦◄✦◄✦◄✦

*Gilbert Lecture, January 2002

A s a native of Dublin city and a major user of the Gilbert collection in Pearse Street Library for the purposes of this research, it gives me great pleasure, Lord Mayor, ladies and gentlemen, to present this paper tonight. As one of the many who benefited immeasurably from Dublin City Public Libraries in Drumcondra and later Ballymun and elsewhere, as school child, teenager and adult, I am particularly pleased to acknowledge in public the wonderful service which the Libraries have provided over the years, in city and suburbs. We cannot put a value on this in purely monetary terms, but I know from my own experience and that of my circle of school friends in Ballygall and Glasnevin something of what the Public Libraries have done to foster the love of reading and widen the world of opportunities. I come here tonight as one of the beneficiaries of that investment, which dates back to the later nineteenth century, and is itself part of the movement towards more enlightened city management.

But first, let us introduce Dublin at mid century. Under the Dublin Improvement Act of 1849 the powers and responsibilities of the Commissioners for making Wide and Convenient Streets were transferred to Dublin Corporation, in what can be seen as just one stage on the road towards establishing an efficient administration for the city. In 1848 the Nuisances Removal and Diseases Prevention Act was introduced, and though clumsy, marks the beginning of modern public health legislation. The municipal and legislative reforms therefore of the late 1840s marks the opening of tonight's story, a whole new chapter in the history of the city of Dublin.[1] What was the new corporation faced with? What problems had it inherited from its predecessor bodies?[2] In particular what were the public health challenges? What legislative tools did they have, and more importantly, what could they do that would work in practice?

While we are dealing with the city area proper, in the latter half of the nineteenth century, we must not ignore the development of independent townships outside the city limits which gathered pace during this period (Fig. 1). It was a constant complaint of the city's councillors and officials, depriving the city of income from property rates just at the time when the demands on the city's resources were increasing massively. Perhaps more significantly, suburban township development deprived the city of the energies and active interest of many well-to-do residents who could continue to enjoy all the privileges of city

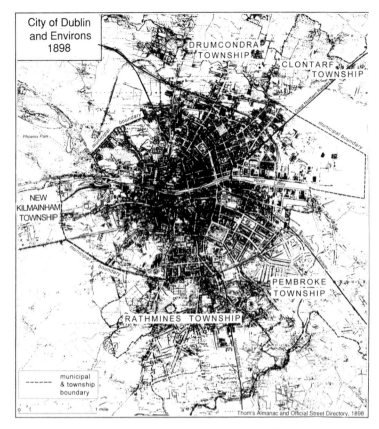

Fig. 1 **Dublin city and townships,** *Thom's almanac and official street directory,*
1898

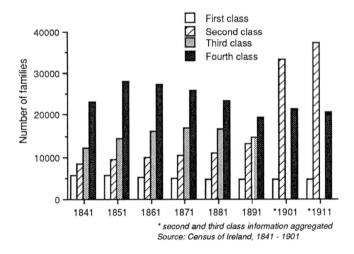

Fig. 2 **House accommodation of families, Dublin city 1841–1911**

life – the commercial opportunities and social gatherings – without having to shoulder the tax burden that the city's decaying infrastructure and massive underclass generated. They were just beyond the limits, on the far side of the canals and circular roads that marked the city's administrative boundary until 1900.[3]

In terms of knowing the city, the nineteenth-century census established universal data-collection; the Ordnance Survey brought maps. In combination therefore we have an extraordinarily useful means of judging the state of the city at mid-century. Housing was a special focus of the census, as 'there can be no more obvious indication of the advances and condition of the people than improvement in the quality of their residence'. House accommodation (Fig. 2), was a sophisticated measurement, as it depended not alone on the quality of the construction, but on how many families you shared this with! The numbers in fourth class accommodation[4] peaked in 1851, at 28,039 or 49% of the total number of families recorded for the city. Combining the census returns with the new OS town plans, it was possible as early as 1841 and again in 1851 to work out a sophisticated street classification, based on house class and occupation or status of the householder (Fig. 3). Correlating the street classification with mortality returns (admittedly not very reliable yet), revealed enormous dis-crepancies in life expectancy between occupations and thus between areas (Fig. 4); legal practitioners and librarians lived to 'extreme old age'.

More seriously, the loss of infant life in the poorest wards, such as South City, was massive, among a total baptised infant population of 1,076, 62% were dead before their 10th birthday. The comparable figure for an average first class residential street was 30%, and the figures for the poor were certainly understated as it did not include the vast numbers who died in the workhouses, hospitals and other institutions or were simply not recorded. Field work revealing the extent of Dublin poverty had been a feature of the period 1790s through to the 1840s; but the census allowed poverty to be measured as reflected in its housing stock, and brought social investigation in Ireland directly into the mainstream of European statistical science.

Of real significance was the establishment of the Registrar General's Office in 1864, now at Lombard Street. The idea that there was an acceptable 'death rate', that there was a target figure which should not be breached, transformed attitudes to public health and the management of the city environment. Weekly, quarterly and annual returns were compiled throughout the British Isles and indeed for most major European cities, making it possible to construct 'league tables', comparing city with city, and country with country, year on year. The limit of 17 deaths in a 1,000 was set by the Registrar General for England in 1854, who claimed that 'any deaths in a people exceeding 17 in 1,000 are unnatural deaths'. This figure was adopted by the Irish authors of the *Manual for public health* (Dublin, 1875). Figure 5 reveals how Dublin was faring, when set against urban centres in Ireland and Britain. No matter how the figures are reworked and what excuses are

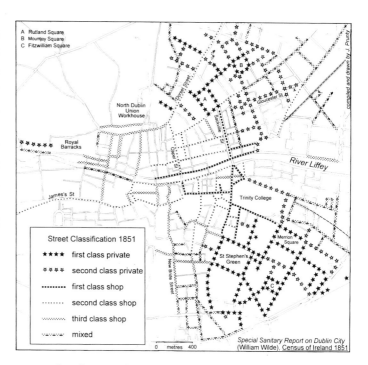

Fig. 3 **Classification of major Dublin streets, William Wilde, 1851.**

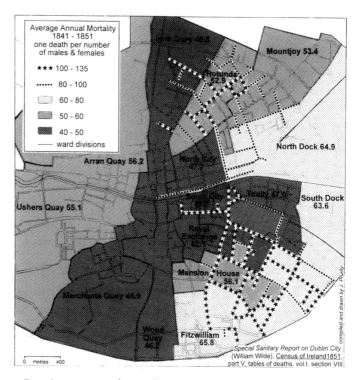

Fig. 4 **Average annual mortality according to location, Dublin 1851**

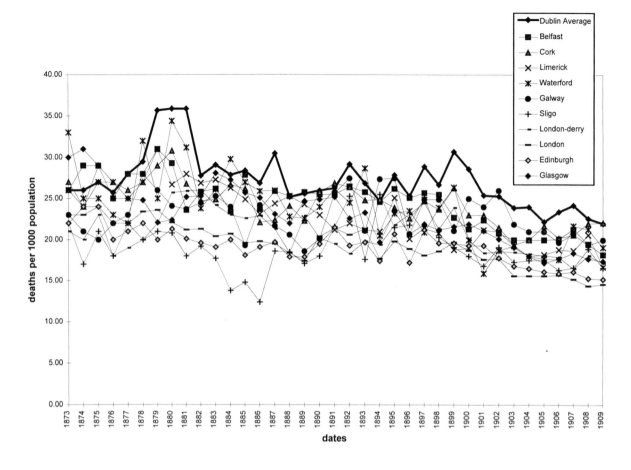

Fig. 5 **Annual mortality, Dublin and selected British and Irish urban sanitary districts, 1873–1909**

made, the conclusion is unavoidable: Dublin city had the worst health record in the British Isles for the century before independence.

Behind the scandalous mortality figures of the period 1867 onwards (which incidentally rose sharply in 1879 when cemetery returns were first correlated with registered deaths), was the lack of industrial opportunities. There were a few large-scale industries which were important to the city and held their own in the United Kingdom market such as Guinness and Jacobs, but really there were very few opportunities for the many anxious for work. As a major port city it acted as a magnet for the distressed and destitute of other counties, and a place of return for Irish people disappointed elsewhere, such as soldiers' widows and cast-off camp-followers who disembarked at Dublin rather than return to their provincial roots.

Statistically, the census records the preponderance of third and fourth class accommodation (Fig. 2). Visibly, the city was run down. The single room tenement was by mid-century dominating the housing market, with the break-up of the Gardiner estate on the north side in 1846, and its sale piecemeal to speculators fuelling this trend. These tenement rooms could be found in older seventeenth- and eighteenth-century houses in once-respectable terraces (Fig. 6), in barely-converted stable dwellings (Fig. 7), and in the countless

Fig. 6 Interior, Cornmarket, unfurnished, 1s. 9d. per week, 1913 (RSAI 75)

Fig. 7 Henrietta Buildings, Henrietta Place, 1913 (RSAI 62)

Managing the Dublin slums, 1850–1922 *by* Jacinta Prunty

Fig. 8 **Plunkett's Cottages off Sandwith Street, 1913 (RSAI 31)**

cheap dwellings that were thrown up in yards and gardens in response to market demand (Fig. 8). The long plots of much eighteenth-century development lent itself to infill in more straitened times.

The management of this slum city was in the hands of the corporation in a few important respects only. In the areas that really mattered – such as landlord-tenant relations, child welfare, nutrition, education – the corporation had little or no powers at all. With regard to the management of the private housing market (the only housing market at this point), the greatest problem was that of legal ownership. And who could be held responsible for upkeep? F.R. Falkiner QC reports on how there were often several owners of a single house, holding 'fractional undivided shares in common, some of these persons living far away, some minors, some women or otherwise under disability, some of most limited means'; where there were several owners the right of doing the work had to be offered to each owner in turn; the owner ordered to execute the works had the option of demolishing the premises, but could not prejudice the operation of existing leases in the covenant![5] In Dublin, the system of immediate lessors 'little removed socially from their lodgers, letting in tenements at the last possible shilling, and at the least possible outlay' made regulation well nigh impossible. Under the 1868 Artisans' and Labourers' Dwelling Act (Torrens Act), the local authority, on the report of their medical officer for health that a building was 'in a statue injurious to health or unfit for human habitation', could order the owner to execute the necessary structural improvements according to prepared specifications; if he did not do it, the corporation could do it and obtain a court order demanding payment.[6] On top of all the report making by the officer for public health and the city engineer, and serving these on the owner, then a sitting to hear objections, then the preparation of plans, then a second hearing to get objections to the plans, and at each stage innumerable opportunities to appeal to the Quarter Sessions and to the Queen's Bench, the guilty party might (or might not) be fined, which he might (or might not) pay.

A good example of the impossibilities of managing the city environment is the 1875 complaint by Mercer's Hospital to the Local Government Board for Ireland, against the 'nuisance and injury caused to the patients' by the presence of this dairy yard; it is among the many useful case studies in the *Reports and printed documents of the city of Dublin*, housed in the City Archive at Pearse Street (Fig. 9). The secretary of the Public Health Committee of the corporation inspected it, found 70 cows, 4 pigs, 4 horses, 'all kept in a fairly cleanly condition', the yard paved and sewered, and a heap of manure 'about 30 cart loads'. The corporation could not act once the yard was kept in a 'cleanly state', it could only move against the manure heap. Their orders ignored, legal proceedings dragged on, and the manure heap overlooked by the hospital wards

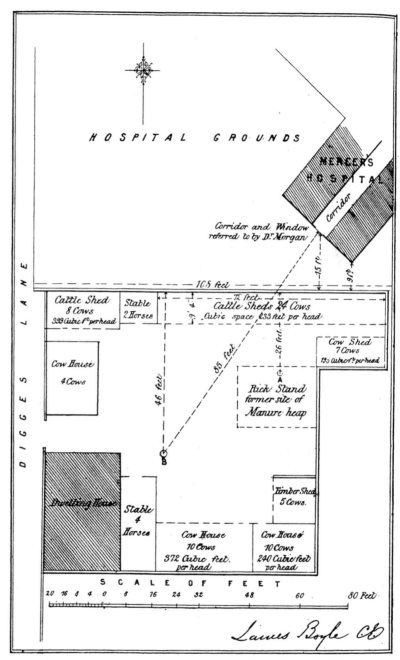

Report of Public Health Committee, *RPDCD*, I (36) 1875, p 11

Fig. 9 **Sketch plan concerning nuisance occasioned by dairy yard adjoining Mercer's Hospital, Dublin, 22 July 1875.**

increased in size and in nastiness. At the court case the corporation's officer stated he could cite innumerable examples of worse conditions about which they could do nothing, including one yard where there were 470 head of cattle held at 230 cubic feet per animal. The Mercer's cows had 470 cubic feet space per animal; the London legal minimum was 600 cubic feet. The best that could be done in this case was to order that further accumulations of manure to be kept at point B (Fig. 9), hardly a victory for the hospital and public health authorities. There was nothing that could be done without stronger legal powers, and a decided shift in public opinion in favour of 'interfering' in private matters for the sake of the common good.

The question of privies or dry toilets was also of major public interest. To what extent could, and should, the corporation intervene in the sanitary arrangements of individual private houses, even where these have been sublet to an unreasonable degree, and the toilet accommodation designed for one family is now shared by up to 100 persons? In many the original minimal facilities (a dry toilet in the yard, and cess pit), were in place for over a century. In evidence before the 1879 Royal Commission of Enquiry on the Sewerage and Drainage System of Dublin, the city engineer, Parke Neville, and the medical superintendent of health, Dr. Charles Cameron, gave facts and figures. There were an estimated 7,800 water closets in Dublin (only a tiny fraction of which could be considered plumbed and sewered satisfactorily). At least 17,200 houses relied exclusively on dry privies and many of the cess pits were in direct communication with each other. The corporation's spokesmen reported on the size, smell and nature of the problem, and cannot be accused of polite restraint. In one yard behind a crowded tenement house, the stones were 'swimming in black putrescent matter which on being disturbed gave out horrid stenches'. The cess pits were rarely if ever emptied, and the ashpits, which were supposed to hold only dry ash and cinders ready to shovel over the excrement, were too often turned into cess pits also. Where the yard surface was of clay – ubiquitous in the poorer quarters – the filth would percolate through and endanger the children, who were too often without shoes. The worst of all arrangements was where a tenement house had no yard at all, and the privy was to be found in 'some such objectionable situation, such as the area or the kitchen', that is, the small space below ground level fronting the cellar kitchen, with no possibility of removing effete matter. Individual courts and houses are named in the evidence. Maguinness Court, Townsend Street, for example, was full of 'certainly no less than a ton weight of semi-fluid filth, exhaling the most disgusting odour' so that residents of rooms overlooking this cesspit could not open their windows; the response of the Public Health Authority was to demand that 'the nuisance be considerably reduced in size, and provided with a cover'.[7]

Drastic overhaul was required, and the corporation as the health authority for the municipal area, was forced to give leadership. Under the Public Health (Ireland) Act, 1878, the local authority had, for the first time, the legislative tools to make a real difference; the 'chaotic jumble of sanitary statutes'[8] that was the 1866 Act might be passed over, noting only that this earlier legislation did create the corporation's Public Health Committee.

The 1878 Public Health Act can be regarded as a boundary stone marking a real shift in the way in which the Dublin slums were managed between 1850 and independence. The earlier period ('pre 1878') was largely concerned with sanitary legislation and trying, rather ineffectively, to force the public to comply with minimal standards; post-1878 there is a push towards more pro-active involvement, resulting in slum clearance and housing construction. Advances were piecemeal and, it could be argued, forced on a reluctant corporation, but nevertheless there is a decided shift in favour of more effective action. The corporation starts to employ significant numbers in what we might today call environmental management, and professional career structures with formal job descriptions are put in place. In 1851 there was a single 'inspector of nuisances' employed, a policeman, paid by the corporation, whose city-wide one-man public health operations included enforcing the removal of swine from dwellings, and from yards where kept offensively, and ordering the construction, repair and cleansing of out-offices and closets. By 1859 the sanitary staff numbered three officers, and the first medical officer of health was appointed in 1864. The corporation was instructed by the Local Government Board for Ireland on 21 October 1874 to create three key posts: consulting sanitary officer, medical officer for health, and executive sanitary officer, and the 'inspectors of nuisances' were now to be styled 'sanitary sub-officers'.[9] By 1873 the corporation had a sanitary staff of 24 (one medical officer, public analyst, secretary, 15 police officers acting as sanitary inspectors, a clerk, three inspectors of food, two disinfectors); by 1885 the staff numbered 36, not counting the stablemen, whitewashers and labourers. The main increase was in the employment of 12 civilian sanitary inspectors, while the services of 9 police officers were also retained. Another milestone was reached in 1899 when the first lady sanitary sub-officers were employed, as a result of competitive exams open to men and women. Dr. Cameron had campaigned for years to get women officers; he considered 'they would prove most useful, especially in persuading the women of the tenement houses to keep themselves, their dwellings, clothes, bedding, and children in a cleanly condition' and in encouraging them to 'teach their children the elementary principles of decency and cleanliness'.[10]

In 1866 legislation is passed to enable slum clearance and the construction of housing for the working classes; that this legislation was clumsy and unworkable is not the point (the 1875 Cross Act, as amended in 1883, proved much more useful). What matters is the recognition that reform of slum housing requires action on the part of the municipality well beyond issuing directives, imposing fines and engaging in a little desultory street-sweeping. The late 1870s was marked by optimism, as medical officers and other concerned persons really did feel that there was going to be significant improvement, and that Dublin would catch up on its British neighbours.

Returning to the question of the privies, by 1878 it was obvious to any observer that reform of the privy system would have to be at public expense, whatever the protestations of the rate payers and business interests. The stink from the Liffey meant that it was impossible to deny that there was a problem, and the scandalous mortality figures exposed Dublin's poor standing among the towns of the United Kingdom (Fig. 10). The miasmic

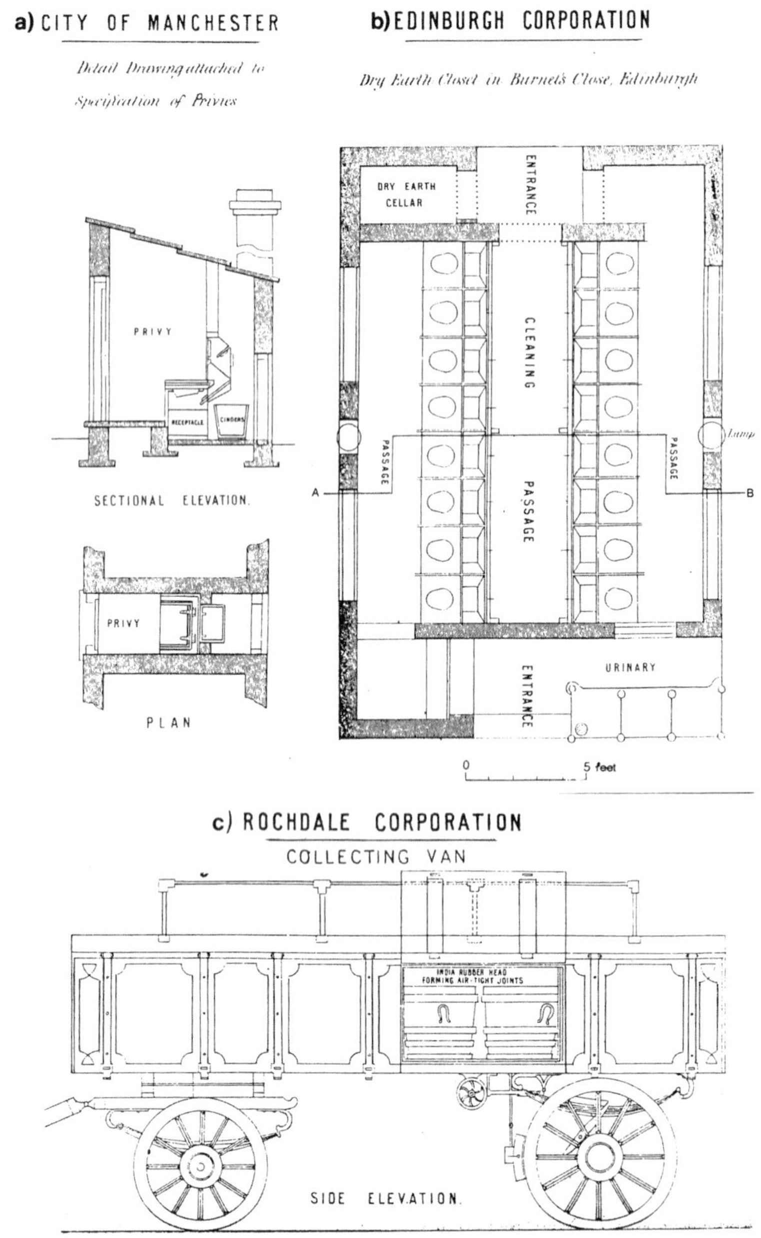

Detail Drawing attached to
Specification of Privies

b) EDINBURGH CORPORATION

Dry Earth Closet in Burnet's Close, Edinburgh

c) ROCHDALE CORPORATION
COLLECTING VAN

Report of the City Engineer, *RPDCD*, III (184) 1879, pp 164-167

Fig. 10 **Sanitary arrangements approved by British municipal authorities, report of Parke Neville to public health committee, Dublin Corporation, 1879.**

theory of disease prevailed, so that sewer gas was in itself regarded as responsible for typhoid fever, sore throats and diarrhoea. Maps held by the corporation's water department show the sewer net-work at mid-century: red lines link a few main sewers, emptying neatly and directly into the Liffey. Major work to replace the old brick-lined flat-bottomed sewers started in 1851, but the larger question of whether Dublin was to embrace water-borne sewage disposal entirely had still to be addressed. In its anxiety to keep abreast of developments in this area, and at a time when the dry privy vs. waterclost debate was at its height, the corporation dispatched its chief sanitary engineer on a fact-finding tour of British cities, where he was very kindly shown the latest advances in municipal waste management. He duly gave a full, and illustrated, account to the Public Health Committee, emphasising that the only way to restore the Liffey to an acceptable quality was to prevent the sewage going into it in the first place.[11] He was especially impressed by the systems adopted in Rochdale, Manchester and Edinburgh (Fig. 10). Edinburgh was eliminating its old cess pools by clearing them out, filling them with dry builders' rubble, and then constructing single or multiple privies on cement floor, the contents to be carried away every second day, at municipal expense. In Rochdale a superior type of collecting van had been developed, well sprung with such closely-fitting door seals that

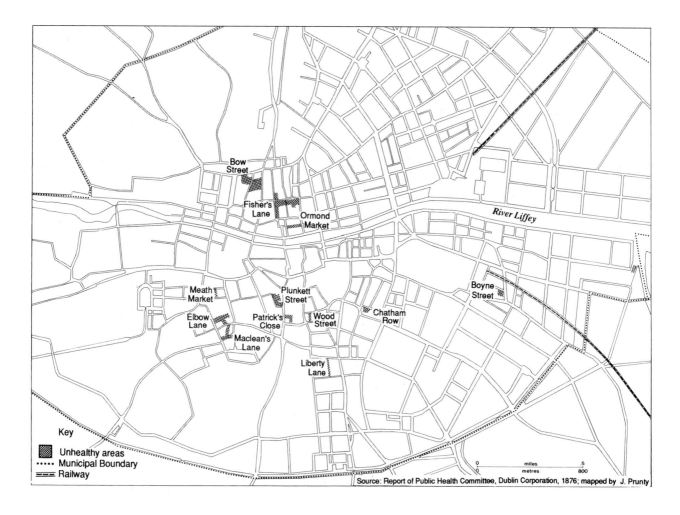

Key
■ Unhealthy areas
···· Municipal Boundary
▦ Railway

Source: Report of Public Health Committee, Dublin Corporation, 1876; mapped by J. Prunty

you could drive it though your living room (practically) without anyone catching a whiff of what it contained. The outcome of the privy vs. watercloset debate in Dublin need not be laboured; medical opposition to storing human waste for any length of time (as required by even the best-regulated dry privy system), and the preference of the public, who started installing water-closets regardless of the ability of the main sewers to cope, won out, but in 1878 the outcome was not at all certain.

From piecemeal 'fever nest' clearance schemes, to opening up 'lungs', to total clearance of a small number of sites, through to individual closures and mundane 'sanitary operations'. This in brief summarises key shifts in the corporation's management approach to the slum housing crisis from the late 1870s to the end of the century. The passing of the Artisans' Dwellings Act, 1875 (also known as the Cross Act) is behind the identification of twelve notorious 'fever nests' by Dr. Mapother (Fig. 11), the city's medical officer of health, and listed in his report for 1876. Seven of the twelve areas were in the old Liberties: Meath Market, McClean's Lane, Elbow Lane, Plunket Street, Patrick's Close,

Fig. 11 '**Unhealthy areas' in Dublin city, as identified by Dr. Mapother, 1876.**

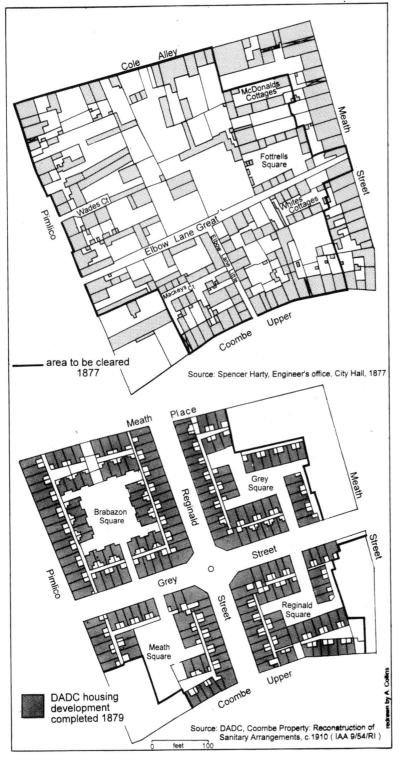

Fig. 12 **Coombe scheme, Dublin, 1877–79**

Wood Street, and Liberty Lane. There were two other south side 'unhealthy areas' pinpointed: Chatham Row, and Boyne Street near Trinity College. The north city areas were Bow Street, Fisher's Lane and Ormond Market beside the Four Courts. As Dr. Cameron himself noted, these were only a selection of some of the worst fever nests, but perhaps headway could be made on this list as a start? All of the 'unhealthy areas' selected had housing that was 'unfit for human habitation and incapable of repair' due to 'dilapidation, closeness of the passages preventing ventilation and lighting, want of decent sanitary accommodation and the difficulty of affording it owing to absence of yards and soakage of the earth with animal refuse from ashpits, slaughterhouses, etc.', resulting in high death rates especially among infants, also lung disease, rheumatism, and 'a low tone of general health, filthy habits, intemperance, and debased morals'.[12] The men leading this campaign on the city's behalf really did believe that slum housing dehumanised its occupants; managing the city slums was to take on strong moral overtones.

The immediate and practical results of the Mapother 'fever nest' study of 1876 are disappointing, but the reports, minutes of meetings and correspondence around this expose the impossibility of the task facing the corporation as the local health authority. Schemes were drawn up for two only, the Coombe (Elbow Lane) and Boyne Street; the latter was quickly shelved as the full costs of the Coombe scheme became apparent, a clearance scheme for Plunket Street was adopted in 1879 and largely completed in 1887. The 1876 report by Dr. Mapother, and its endorsement by the city engineer Parke Neville, had focused on widening thorough-ways to allow sunlight to penetrate and the free circulation of air, and 'macademised surfaces' which would not emit foul disease-carrying smells. But even the most modest plans quickly expanded in concept and cost. The proposal to widen Elbow Lane Great and Elbow Lane Little quickly became the more ambitious Dublin Improvement Scheme, area no. 1 (1877), Coombe, and deserves special attention as the first slum clearance scheme in the city under the new legislation (Fig. 12). The case for total demolition and rebuilding of the Elbow Lane area was made on sound medical grounds by Dr. Grimshaw at a public inquiry in April 1877. But the costs skyrocketed, as very poor occupiers sought, understandably, to maximise the amount of compensation to be paid by the corporation. The corporation valued the premises, an arbitrator more than doubled these valuations, and a jury made further massive increases.[13] The corporation merely bought, cleared and serviced the four-acre site, then leased it to a philanthropic housing company, the Dublin Artisans' Dwellings' Company who were contracted to erect 199 houses, to be 'well and substantially built and ventilated, and furnished with water supply, proper drainage, and sanitary appliances and apparatus, to the satisfaction of the corporation or their architect'. 120 houses were built, of four different classes, those of the best quality (and highest rents) facing the main wide (and macademised) through ways, the smallest one-storey cottages grouped around a courtyard (surfaced in concrete 'so that no foul matter can percolate into the earth'). Weekly rents for houses in the new scheme ranged from 3s.6d. to 7s., well beyond the ability of the former residents of this area, who paid rents from 1s.6d – 2s.9d.

The corporation's first major venture into slum clearance was such a fraught and costly experience (carried out under intense public scrutiny) that the adoption of an alternative, less visible and more easily managed strategy is understandable. The Plunket Street scheme (John Dillon Street) lurched along, taking eight years to complete, not counting the time lost in assembling the site; it was similar in many respects to the Coombe, but on a smaller and more irregular site, and regarded as a model of best sanitary practice by its supporters. But from September 1879 the corporation determined to 'prune out here and there throughout the city houses in narrow alleyways and courts than to clear out a whole district'. Once demolished, 'only such new houses could be erected in their stead as would have sufficient yard accommodation'. A veritable crusade followed, giving the newly-enlarged sanitary staff, under Dr. Cameron's direction, the chance to prove themselves. From 31 August 1879 to 31 December 1882, 1,325 houses were closed and detenanted as unfit for human habitation, and a further 389 cellars were shut up, not to mention the hundreds of individual rooms closed.

Figure 13 is an extract from the report of 1883, giving a summary of the pragmatic slum

RETURN OF SANITARY OPERATIONS CARRIED OUT IN THE YEAR 1883

Sewers and House Drains constructed on demand of Sanitary Authority	... ...	537
Do.	repaired and cleansed... ...	2263
Water-closets constructed	... ...	970
Privies constructed ...	... ...	42
Ashpits constructed ...	... ...	313
Ashpits rebuilt and altered according to specification supplied by Public Health Committee	... ...	15
Privies and Water-closets cleansed	... ...	637
Dwellings repaired ...	... ...	6457
Privies and Water-closets repaired	... ...	2490
Dwellings cleansed ...	... ...	8531
Dwellings condemned and closed, being unfit for human habitation	... ...	271
Rooms in other Houses closed, being unfit for human habitation	... ...	128
Dwellings reported to the City Engineer as being dangerous		56
Cellar Dwellings condemned and closed	... ...	41
Yards and External Premises cleansed ...	... ...	2225
Lanes and Alleys cleansed by private parties	... ...	396
Accumulations of Manure removed	.. ..	944
Swine removed from Dwellings	... ...	32
Other Animals removed from Dwellings	... ...	28
Swine removed from Yards where kept offensively	...	306
Miscellaneous Nuisances abated	... ...	1269
Inspections of Tenement Houses	.. ..	49976
Do.	Tenement Rooms	204743
Do.	Nightly Lodging Houses	2176
Do.	Bakeries	1588
Do.	Slaughter Houses	2640
Do.	Dairy Yards	2909
Certificates of Destitution to entitle to Gratuitous Interment		501
Water-taps supplied to Tenement Houses	... ...	265
Sanitary Defects discovered ...	... ...	33978
Do.	remedied	33748
Infected Dwellings inspected and cleansed	... ...	1073
Do.	chemically disinfected	1073
Reports received from Medical Sanitary Officers ...	...	561
Patients removed by Hospital Cabs	... ...	160
Removals for Disinfection by Vans	... ...	2062
Disinfecting Chamber used by Persons ...	... ...	1081
Number of Articles Disinfected	... ...	11153
Infected Mattresses and Beds burned, their owners compensated ...	... ...	1117
Detections of Unsound Food ...	... ...	202
Convictions for selling Adulterated Food	... ...	39
Do.	Refusing to sell Food to Inspectors... ...	4
Do.	for Breaches of Explosives Act	5
Do.	for Nuisances from Smoke	1
Do.	for Breaches of Building Laws	4
Do.	Nightly Lodging-keepers, for Breaches of By-laws	2
Do.	of Dairy Yard Owners, for Filthy Premises ...	4
* Do.	for Establishing noxious Trades Workshops without due Notice	2
Do.	for Ordinary Sanitary Offences	3135
Notices served ...	... ...	13750
Summonses served ...	... ...	3211
Total Number of Convictions...	... .	3196
Cases Dismissed	... ...	15

* **Mr. D. Toler**, Food Inspector, prosecuted two manufacturers of sausages whose premises were in a very filthy condition. They were fined £1 and 5s. respectively.

Source: Public Health Report for 1883, *DCRPD*, 1894, vol II, no. 70, pp 68-69

Fig. 13 **Return of sanitary arrangements carried out in the year 1883,**

Dublin Corporation

management approach formally adopted by the corporation from 1879, little seen but vital work that undoubtedly benefited a larger percentage of the citizenry than the model slum clearance schemes. But it did not do much for the corporation's public image, and accusations that it was not managing the crisis at all were understandable.

The slum management focus tonight is mainly on the work of the corporation, but it would be important to note that it was not only officialdom that concerned itself with the slum problem. Numbers of medical men, clergymen, bible readers and charity workers have all left accounts of the living conditions within the Dublin tenements, and how from their different perspectives they got involved in the 'management' or amelioration of conditions in the Dublin slums. Their records are most important for the word pictures they draw, the analyses they make of the problem, and the practical assistance they extended. Just one example must suffice, in this case the Ladies' Association of Charity (Fig. 14), already mentioned in the context of distributing food, fuel and clothing to the 'sick poor'. The Metropolitan or Marlborough Street branch was founded in 1851 by Margaret Aylward (who later went on to found St. Brigid's Orphanage, schools, and Sisters of the Holy Faith);[14] its published reports describe the scenes encountered by the 'lady visitors'. In one of the 'narrow lanes of St. Michan's parish' they encountered a consumptive man who lay dying on the bare ground of a wretched cellar, 'his only covering a worn-out quilt, no fire and not an article of furniture in his damp and dreary abode'.[15] In another, a poor widow lay on a damp, earthen floor, where 'a few particles of straw were strown to serve as a bed'; 'her tattered garments and the squalid appearance of her son, a lad earning three or four shillings a week, almost the sole support of his mother and little sisters, sufficiently indicated the poverty of the whole'.[16] The relief lists give the personal details (name, address, dates, what was given and why); releasing clothes and tools from pawn, setting up a widow with a mangle, or 'apprenticing a poor lame girl to the boot-closing trade', were typical responses, and provide glimpses into the daily struggle that the poorest strata of the city's residents faced, struggling to get by on a day-to-day basis.

At the heart of the Dublin slum problem was the tenement system, itself a result of endemic poverty and the lack of opportunity for the vast bulk of the city's residents. The 'tenement cancer' spread inexorably through the city, as illustrated in Figure 15, showing the extent of the problem by 1900. Houses which were entered as 'tenements' in *Thom's official directory* are mapped; analysis of the resulting pattern must take on board the limitations of street directories as historical sources. Tenement status is likely to be masked (for example) where

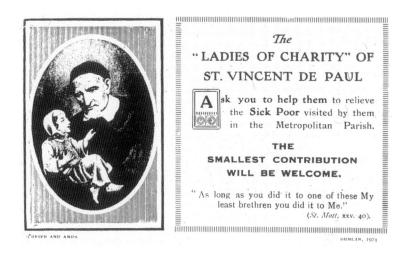

Fig. 14 **Fundraising leaflet, Ladies' Association of Charity, Dublin**

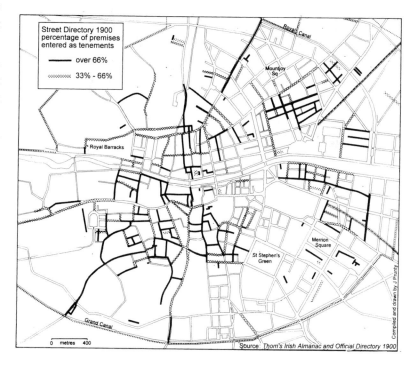

Fig. 15 **Percentage tenement housing, Dublin 1900**

a business occupies the ground floor, most blatantly along old commercial routes such as Thomas Street, Bride Street and Patrick Street (south side) or Church Street and Dorset Street (north side). The methodology employed (with limits of 33% and 66%) also comes with a health warning, as some very long streets with a large number of tenement houses may not feature as strongly as they ought. Despite these and other reservations, it does at least provide a broad-brush picture of the geography of tenement housing and its spread

Fig. 16 **Dereliction, Magenniss's court, off Townsend Street, 1913 (RSAI 29)**

by the end of the nineteenth century. Many of the smaller back lanes and courts are gone by 1900 (they feature heavily in comparable map exercises for 1850 and 1875), some because of the corporation's policy of closing premises most flagrantly in breach of sanitary regulations, others cleared to make way for rebuilding (mostly by philanthropic companies but also by church charities and the municipality) while some were lost to commercial expansion (especially around Grand Canal Basin/James' Gate/Thomas Street/Watling Street where the Guinness brewery, Power's distillery and Dublin Distillers expanded massively). Areas which are solidly tenement districts by 1850 are even more entrenched by 1900; there is rarely any upgrading residentially. On the south side these are most notably the Liberties industrial sector and stretching to the rear of the south quays; the courts behind Merrion Square, and the docklands/railway sector to the east of Trinity College. On the north side the old Ormond markets, the environs of the Royal (later Collins) Barracks, the Mecklenburgh/Montgomery Street red light district, the Sheriff Street docklands, and a number of formerly aristocratic streets most spectacularly Henrietta Street and Gardiner Street have all succumbed to tenement status. The slum geography revealed in the Civic Survey maps published 1925 (Fig. 23) confirms this inexorable downward slide, and the huge percentage of the city's housing that was unfit for anyone by then, man or beast, to inhabit.

The downside to the zealous programme of closing up unfit housing (commenced in earnest in 1879), was increasing dereliction (Fig. 16), as little rebuilding was undertaken, and those evicted were left to crowd out other poor quality tenements. Some caution should be exercised when using the corporation's meticulous published lists of houses temporarily and permanently closed up; witnesses to the 1885 housing inquiry testify that the pressure for accommodation was such that premises that had been detenanted could

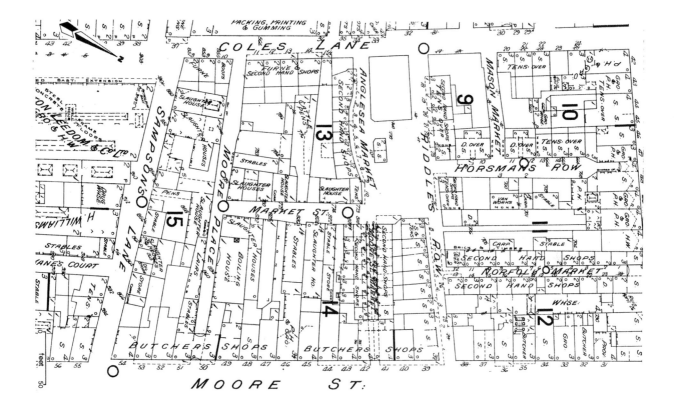

Fig. 17 **Coles Lane/ Moore Street,** *Insurance plan of Dublin, sheet 3,* **April 1926, Charles E. Goad.**

be occupied once the officials were safely out of the way, while charity records also record instances of persons with addresses in supposedly closed-up houses receiving assistance.[17]

It is when you get down to the local level, of individual courts and alleyways, that you better understand the challenges of managing the Dublin slum crisis, against the prevailing political philosophy of *laissez faire*. While (as always) everyone believes 'something should be done', who will carry the costs of effective action? The ratepayers were very reluctant to pay for costly new initiatives, and there were limits to what the corporation could do as the public health authority, once minimum sanitary standards were met. The question of slaughter house regulation illustrates this very well.

Long recognised as 'public nuisances', the licensing and inspection of slaughter houses was instigated in August 1851, one of the very first public health initiatives of the newly-reformed corporation. By 1879 there were 99 slaughter houses registered with the corporation (location, occupier's name, owner's name and home address); when these are mapped, it becomes obvious that they are an intrinsic part of the most congested districts. The south side concentrations are along Patrick Street and the appropriately named Bull Alley; in the Coombe, around Carman's Hall and Spitalfields; along Thomas Street leading west, and along Camden Street leading south; north of the Liffey the Ormond Market and Henry Street/Coles Lane (Fig. 17) are the most important concentrations, and in the vicinity of the Royal Barracks. The licensing did more to protect the slaughter house owner (who usually lived in suburban comfort), than further the cause of public health. Any owner who held a licence dated before 1849 could not be compelled to surrender it, unless under special Act of Parliament, which was not very likely. The corporation drew up more stringent regulations in 1882 (under the 1878 Public Health Act), 'for preventing cruelty therein; for keeping the same in a cleanly and healthy state; for removing filth at least once in every twenty-four hours, and requiring a sufficient supply of water'.[18] The corporation could of course purchase the licences, but at inflated prices, the bargaining power lying with the licence holder.

In what we can only agree was imaginative and forward-looking, and under pressure from the medical officers of health and the Public Health Committee, the corporation undertook to develop a model abattoir, where 'animals intended for human food could be slaughtered with the least amount of suffering, and their carcasses dressed in a cleanly manner'; it would also greatly facilitate the detection of diseased meat.[19] A site for a municipal abattoir was eventually secured, on the North Circular Road, despite worries about devaluing local properties and drawing 'a class of persons notorious for unruly and improper conduct'.[20] But there was no way that private operators could be forced to move their operations here. Rather than develop to serve the city's slaughtering needs in full, the municipal abattoir was to operate alongside over 50 private, poorly-inspected slaughter yards in traditional locations. Moore Street / Coles Lane, for example (Fig. 17), was charac-terised by closely-packed stalls, markets and second-hand shops in 1854 with some tene-ments (possibly understated, as commercial uses mask tenement status) and a large number of butchers and provision merchants. The corporation pursued a Mr. Taaffe, the owner of Taaffe's Row, in 1899, over ten houses without yards, 'built back-to-back thus excluding all light and ventilation from the rere, and seriously interfering with the circula-tion of air necessary for health'; the only sanitary provision was 'four closets placed on the opposite side of the street'. In this case the judge interrupted the hearing to visit the site for himself, while Dr. Cameron the chief medical officer for health testified that the lower stories were disused clothes shops, and that he ascended to the upper floors 'by very narrow and defective stairs', where he had 'ready and conclusive reason to appreciate the want of a proper circulation of fresh air'.[21] The corporation won this case, but that it took new powers (Mr. Taaffe was prosecuted under the Housing of the Working Classes Act 1890), and so very long before fairly minimum standards could be enforced speaks for itself. Nearby was the thriving slaughtering industry; the visiting judge could not have missed the smell, even if he did not actually enter any of these yards. The 1926 Goad insurance plan (Fig. 17) shows how butchers continued to dominate Moore Street, backed by slaugh-ter houses, pens, lairs, 'boiling house', in the closest possible proximity to second-hand clothes shops and grocers (most with tenements over), other tenement dwellings, stables and warehouses. The 'softly softly' approach of the corporation to encourage the reloca-tion of the slaughtering trade had little success. And slaughtering, in a confined, densely-populated district, had not ceased to be a 'public nuisance'.

The scale of the slum management problem and the inadequate response of the corporation may blind us to advances that were indeed made. The question might be

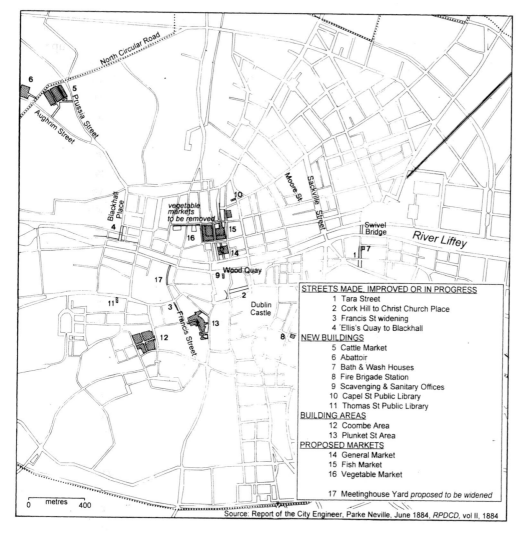

Fig. 18 **Municipal improvements, Dublin Corporation 1879–84**

STREETS MADE, IMPROVED OR IN PROGRESS
1 Tara Street
2 Cork Hill to Christ Church Place
3 Francis St widening
4 'Ellis's Quay to Blackhall
NEW BUILDINGS
5 Cattle Market
6 Abattoir
7 Bath & Wash Houses
8 Fire Brigade Station
9 Scavenging & Sanitary Offices
10 Capel St Public Library
11 Thomas St Public Library
BUILDING AREAS
12 Coombe Area
13 Plunket St Area
PROPOSED MARKETS
14 General Market
15 Fish Market
16 Vegetable Market

17 Meetinghouse Yard *proposed to be widened*

Source: Report of the City Engineer, Parke Neville, June 1884, *RPDCD*, vol II, 1884

posed: what did the corporation pride itself on? If called to account, what could the reformed corporation point out as notable successes? A report of the city engineer, Parke Neville, published in 1884, maps the 'municipal improvements' carried out since the Public Health Act came into force in 1878 (Fig. 18); all of these 'improvements', excepting only the new fire brigade station at Chatham Street, could be seen as responses to some aspect of the slum problem. Streets 'made, improved or in progress'; head the list, including the new 'Swivel Bridge' linking Tara Street with Beresford Place, and what was to be known as Lord Edward Street (1892), linking up the City Hall with Christ Church Place, and bypassing the impossibly sharp turn at Cork Hill leading to Castle Street. In the latter case, a much more extensive remodelling of the area (the 'Cork Hill and General Improvement Scheme') was planned, but abandoned, for which students of medieval Dublin city at least must be grateful, as it would have wiped out any trace of the early streetscape from Cornmarket and Back Lane to Werburgh Street, the Castle Steps and Palace Street, and northwards to Wood Quay. What the later nineteenth-century corporation managed to see through to completion was a limited number of road improvements, the erection of some fine municipal buildings (cattle market, abattoir, the Tara Street baths and wash-houses, the fire brigade station in Chatham Street, scavenging offices at Wood Quay, and very fine public libraries, the three earliest being Capel Street, Thomas Street and Charleville Mall. In the summary report of 1879 the only housing initiatives were the Coombe and Plunket street schemes; in both cases, as already outlined, the corporation merely cleared and serviced the land which was then handed over to the Dublin Artisans' Dwellings Company who built the houses and managed the estates.

The 1879 report gives the location of 'proposed markets'; behind this tentative title there is another long-running and complicated saga. Under the Dublin Improvement Act of 1849, the Lord Mayor of Dublin was empowered to reform the city markets; the 1851 Royal Commission on fairs and markets reported that the task was beyond the mayor, an officer of one year's standing, 'in the face of vested interest and established usages', and 'when unofficial persons attempt any improvement, the crippled finances and cloud of compensations to be afforded scare away all change'.[22] Proposals were drawn up in 1875 for comprehensive reforms; 'the disgusting state' in which fish was being sold by 'filthy and drunken women sitting obstructively on the footways and pavement in Pill Lane and Patrick Street' was 'a living reproach to corporate administration 24 years after the powers to right such wrongs had been invested in the Corporation'.[23] In both 1878 and 1879 the police magistrate refused to levy fines on women fish-sellers operating in Pill Lane as there was no designated market in which they could sell their wares.[24] The saga around the reform of the fish, vegetable and general markets culminated in 1894 with the erection of the magnificent covered north city markets, on the site between Mary's Lane and Old Pill Lane (realigned and widened), fittingly restored, in recent years, to mark its centenary.

Perhaps the most significant achievement of the corporation during the later nineteenth century does not lend itself to city mapping at all, and was not facilitated by public health legislation. This is the 'wholesome and abundant' supply of the 'purest soft water', under the Vartry water scheme 1863–68, replacing the unsatisfactory and insufficient supply provided by the canals and associated city reservoirs (at Blessington Street on the north side, and at James' Street Basin and Portobello Harbour on the south side). 'Few cities have obtained so fine a supply, delivered at high pressure, on such moderate terms' claimed one observer,[25] and history bears this out. It was a stunning engineering achievement and did indeed provide this city with a far superior water supply than was to be found in many other urban centres. It is good to have something we can celebrate. But the downside was the infrastructure to deliver this fresh water to homes in the poorer districts was very limited, so that ten years after its arrival complaints were made that many families were reliant for drinking water on water 'taken from the cistern intended to supply the water closet, resulting in typhoid'.[26] There was still a distance to travel.

Returning to the question of housing reform, the scale of the crisis was such that we might be surprised at the lack of public or popular support for the construction of block dwellings. The Dublin Artisans' Dwellings Company has already been introduced with reference to the two earliest schemes, the Coombe and Plunket Street. An offshoot of the Dublin Sanitary Association, the DADC has been described as a relatively energetic and efficient company, run by Protestant businessmen, and paying modest dividends to its shareholders, usually not exceeding 4%.[27] It favoured estates of small brick houses, one and two stories high, set along wide streets (Oxmantown is the most monotonous in layout), allowing free circulation of air and ample scope for sunshine to penetrate as the houses were not overlooked. The sanitary credentials were excellent –'each tenant has the satisfaction of having his own house and yard reserved to himself and family'[28] – but at such low densities it did not house anything like the number displaced. The blocks of flats built by the DADC at Buckingham Street and Dominick Street were never really popular, one witness to the 1885 housing inquiry explained that the residents 'did not like to be with so many people', abandoning them for small houses wherever possible.[29] Another witness, Dr. Cameron, was advocating a system of 'reparation' of tenement houses, whereby premises which were structurally sound (as in Henrietta Street) might be bought out by the corporation, refurbished to a high standard and let directly to the tenants, cutting out the middle man who was the real beneficiary of inflated rents. Cameron would strongly advocate the building of an outside stairs, for health and safety reasons, but knew that this would be opposed by all, 'because they think it gives the place so much of a public institution or barrack-like appearance. That is a matter of sentiment, and as you know, the people of Dublin are very much moved by sentiment.'[30] It took the Guinness Trust, renamed the Iveagh Trust in 1903, to break down some at least of this antipathy, and to demonstrate that large scale barrack buildings could be attractive and well-managed family homes. This was by far the most ambitious intervention to date in the Dublin slum story, requiring wholesale but phased slum clearance, including buying out the licences of slaughter houses, closing brothels, and re-routing a branch of the river Poddle, which complicated the engineering task in a most expensive way. The first phase of clearance led to the development of St. Patrick's Park (1897), providing a gracious setting for the national Church of Ireland Cathedral. Family dwellings were then erected in eight T-shaped blocks, each of five storeys, with a lodging house for single men facing Bride Road (1905). To complete the complex, the Iveagh Baths (1906), including male and female baths as well as a swimming pool, was erected on land facing the men's hostel, while a very large two-storied play centre, with splendid Baroque façade, faced onto St. Patrick's Park and the cathedral. Within the scheme there were high standards of construction and sanitation; this was matched by close supervision of the tenantry, facilitated by perimeter walls with gates, and the overall self-contained design. Rents ranged from 2s 6d per week (single room tenement, shared facilities) to 5s 9d (three-roomed, own laundry and toilet); these rents were still far in excess of what those most in need could afford (no more than 1s or 1s 6d per week). And the nature of Dublin's labour market, which was dominated by casual employment, could see a man or woman left without work for weeks on end, making it impossible to commit yourself to paying rent regularly at anything above the minimum.

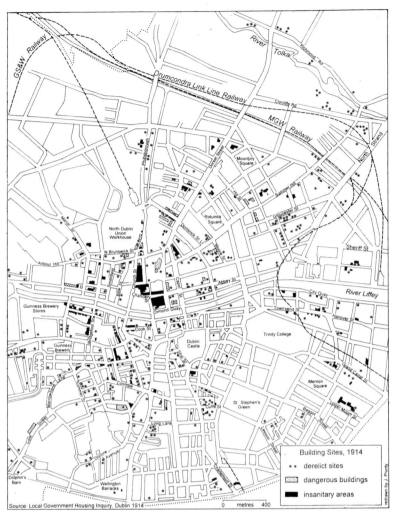

Fig. 19 **Derelict sites, dangerous buildings and insanitary areas, Dublin 1914**

The Local Government Board for Ireland commissioned a report on the Dublin slum problem in 1913, this includes the 'Darkest Dublin' photo collection housed in the Royal Society of Antiquaries of Ireland (see Figures 6, 7, 8, 16), along with a complex coloured map showing the state of dereliction (on sanitary or structural grounds) and the housing situation, redrawn here as Figures 19-20. It is accompanied by an alphabetical street list, which if used in conjunction with the published corporation lists of houses closed from 1879, and the later lists of all Dublin streets where cases of infectious diseases occurred,[31] allows quite detailed local histories to be reconstructed. The 1914 report is not in any way sensational but based on hard evidence. There was widespread dereliction and a significant number of houses condemned on structural or sanitary grounds, each carefully noted and mapped. The tables place Dublin in its UK context: 25,822 Dublin families were living in tenement houses, of whom over 20,000 families lived in one room. There were 1,560 cellar dwellings occupied. According to the 1911 census, 23% of the city's population lived in one-room tenements; the closest UK figures were Finsbury nearly 15% and Glasgow 13%.

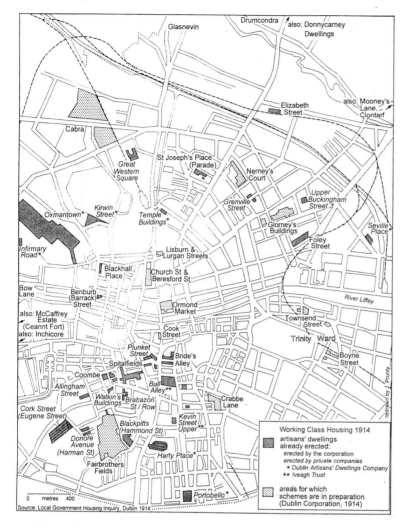

Fig. 20 **Artisans' dwellings completed/ planned (municipal and private companies), Dublin 1914.**

Within the map:

Glasnevin

Drumcondra / also: Donnycarney Dwellings

also: Mooney's Lane, Clontarf

Elizabeth Street

Cabra

Great Western Square

St Joseph's Place (Parade)

Nerney's Court

Upper Buckingham Street

Grenville Street

Oxmantown*

Kirwin Street*

Temple Buildings*

Glorney's Buildings

Seville Place

Foley Street

Infirmary Road*

Lisburn & Lurgan Streets

Blackhall Place

Church St & Beresford St

River Liffey

Bow Lane

Benburb (Barrack) Street

Ormond Market

also: McCaffrey Estate (Ceannt Fort)
also: Inchicore

Townsend Street

Cook Street

Trinity Ward

Plunket Street

Bride's Alley

Boyne Street

Spitalfields

Coombe

Allingham Street

Bull Alley**

Watkin's Buildings

Brabazon St / Row

Crabbe Lane

Cork Street (Eugene Street)

Kevin Street Upper**

Blackpitts (Hammond St)

Donore Avenue (Harman St)

Harty Place*

Fairbrothers Fields

Portobello*

0 metres 400

Source: Local Government Housing Inquiry, Dublin 1914

redrawn by J. Prunty

Working Class Housing 1914
artisans' dwellings already erected:
erected by the corporation
erected by private companies
* Dublin Artisans' Dwellings Company
** Iveagh Trust

areas for which schemes are in preparation (Dublin Corporation, 1914)

Dublin had the greatest number of one-room tenements in any British Isles city, the highest occupancy rate per room, and the highest proportion of population thus accommodated. However you reworked the statistics the answer was the same: Dublin had the worst housed urban citizenry in the British Isles in 1914.

By mapping the housing schemes completed (philanthropic and municipal), and for which plans have been drawn up, the 1914 report allows an assessment of progress to date; regrettably what progress has been made is being quickly outpaced by the continued neglect of the existing housing stock. The new schemes, welcome as they were, did little to alter the overall picture of Dublin as a slum city. But the 1914 report does mark an important stage in the slum housing debate. The report advocated nothing short of 'the complete breaking up of the tenement situation as it exists';[32] the same point was made thirty years earlier by Dr. Cameron who insisted that regardless of any improvements, where 'people cook and work in and make workshops and living rooms of their bedrooms' it is 'opposed to every sentiment of decency, besides being unhealthy. They are

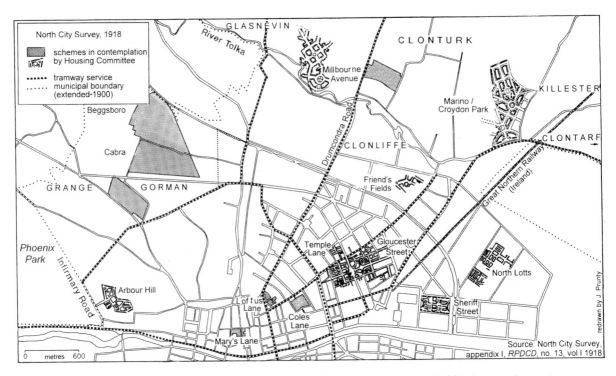

Fig. 21 **North city survey, schemes in contemplation by the housing committee, Dublin Corporation, 1918**

all breathing the same air, and a great many people have lungs more or less tainted, and no matter what the size of the room is it must be bad'.[33] By 1914 the psychological move towards eradicating, not regulating, tenement dwellings has been made, though action will be long delayed. The absolute necessity of subsidising the housing of the poorest strata of society has also been accepted by now, and there is an expectation that the corporation will take a leading role. Arguments that providing healthy housing would 'pauperise' the poor had long been countered by those closest to slum realities; Dr. Cameron argued (repeatedly), that state subsidy was already to be found in innumerable sectors, including the Queen's Colleges, without anybody raising a fuss.[34] By 1909 he could highlight that the construction of 'healthy dwellings' for rural labourers was underway, but little had yet been done to benefit the urban poor, packed into 'purlieus' where 'the sun's rays are almost or entirely unseen':

> The poor get gratuitous medical advice, old age pensions, free reading rooms, and practically free elementary education; it is only going a step farther when they are provided with healthy dwellings at the same rent as the unhealthy ones.[35]

The corporation's contribution to date had been, as we have outlined here, largely confined to the regulation and closure of insanitary dwellings and the provision of serviced sites to the DADC, along with a small number of city-centre schemes: Benburb Street flats 1887; Bow Lane 1889; St. Joseph's Place, 1896; Blackhall Place, 1895; Foley Street flats 1905; Bride's Alley flats 1911. The map of 1914 (Fig. 20) shows its ambitions on the outbreak of World War I, with plans in hand for at least ten sites.

In response to what it regarded as the unfair criticisms of the Local Government Board, Dublin Corporation commissioned its own report, in June 1917; this opens with a virulent attack on 'ill-considered and ill-informed statements' published in the press by 'irresponsible and inexperienced social reformers'.[36] From the perspective of the local historian, this report is a treasury of information on the inexorable decline into tenements of many north Dublin streets; it is also a testament to the energy being invested by the housing committee on the slum question, and on the immense possibilities opened up by the extension of the municipal boundary. Appendix A 'schemes in contemplation by the housing committee 1918', (redrawn as Figure 21) includes existing tramway services; Appendix B, is a large format colour-coded map showing land use and housing conditions (public institutions, business premises, tenements, ruins and wasteland, grass lands, cultivated lands, devastated area); it places the north city area (with a number of schemes ready to roll) within the much more hopeful context of its suburban and rural hinterland, and shows where the argument has moved.

But keeping within the pre-1900 city limits, Church Street might be taken as an example of one of the first schemes executed by the corporation. It was the collapse of numbers 66 and 67 that precipitated the 1913/14 slum enquiry; it had already featured prominently in an exposé of slum conditions run by the *Daily Nation* in 1898,[37] and in most of the earlier slum

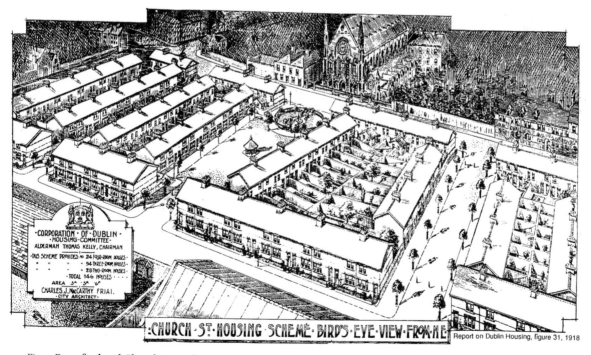

Fig. 22 **Beresford and Church Street housing scheme, Corporation of Dublin, bird's eye view from North East, 1918**

studies. It fulfilled all the criteria for total clearance, and in addition was along a prominent routeway, making it difficult to avoid. Planned in 1913, executed in amended form in 1917, this scheme involved the complete acquisition and reordering of the unit bounded by Beresford Street and Church Street, North King Street and Mary's Lane, and the erection of 146 modest self-contained artisans' dwellings, one and two storey (Fig. 22). Street widening was part of the plan, so that 'what was formerly a narrow, congested street, with dark and unhealthy alleys and passages, is now a fine open thoroughfare, forming a more fitting environment for the imposing edifice erected by the Capuchin Fathers'.[38]

The year 1918 marks a concerted policy movement towards the suburbs. The North City report, commissioned by the corporation, has already been introduced. A better-known and city-wide report is by P.C. Cowan, commissioned by the Local Government Board for Ireland to generate action on the slum housing front, as exposed so thoroughly in the earlier (1914) report. The task was to produce 'a memorandum giving some general ideas as to how a complete scheme for housing the working people in Dublin, who are said to be living in insanitary conditions, might be carried out in sections for different parts of the city, which could be taken up in rotation or according to need'.[39] A coherent master plan, but one which could be approached in stages as funds allowed, was first required. The task itself was twofold: to provide for 14,000 'new, self-contained houses of sufficient size to prevent overcrowding and the separation of the sexes, with scullery and water closet accommodation for the sole use of each family', and to remodel 3,803 first and second class tenement houses to provide suitably for 13,000 families in units of one to four rooms. Allowing for the increase in numbers in need since the 1914 report, the challenge was to provide improved housing for 41% of the city's population. This was a colossal task, 'immensely greater proportionately' than the task facing England and Wales of building 300,000 new houses as soon as the war ended.[40] Cowan advocated a new independent authority to manage housing, with drastic new powers; his report draws heavily on the theories and language of town planners and housing reformers in Britain, assuring the Irish public that the route to a bright and brave new future had been laid by 'experienced pioneers', whose 'breadth of view and invincible energy and faith' had overcome apparently insurmountable difficulties to lead to 'a safe and spacious place in the sun', quoting from Octavia Hill, 'there are two great wants in the life of the poor of our large cities which ought to be realised more than they are – the want of space and the want of beauty'.[41] A start could be made with blocks of 400 houses each in Marino, Cabra, Drumcondra, Crumlin. Cheap and rapid transit links were seen as the key to the success of the schemes, working towards an ideal day where 'healthy houses and healthy economic conditions may be found together'.[42] New housing was seen as a way of socialising the poor, breaking down the bad habits formed in the city tenements; for even if the older members are a lost cause, 'a drastic change is imperatively demanded for the sake of the children – the coming generation. The desire of working class parents to give their children a better chance than they had in their childhood is widely and deeply felt, and most young men are anxious to take their wives to bright and hopeful homes'.[43]

By the second decade of the twentieth century, the management of the Dublin slum problem has been transformed, at least in terms of ideology. The most striking difference exists between the 1876 identification of 'fever nests' and 'black spots' undertaken on behalf of the corporation by Dr. Mapother, medical officer of health, and seconded by the city engineer Parke Neville (Fig. 11), and the first integrated master plans for the eradication of the slum evil, in the surveys published after the ending of World War I, but in preparation before that. Instead of the piecemeal and cautious upgrading seen as the only possible route forward in the 1870s, by the early twentieth century the garden suburbs and town planning movements transformed the context within which the city's slum problem was to be addressed. The Civics Institute of Ireland, founded in March 1914, had among its 32 objects, studies into the means by which urban and rural slums might be 'cleared, remodelled or improved', the people rehoused in sanitary dwellings in 'healthy areas', blessed with 'playgrounds, parks, gardens, garden spaces' and allotments for vegetables. It promoted the concept of garden suburbs and garden cities, but also applied other positive aspects of this movement to existing situations, including tree-planting, 'the conversion of derelict, neglected, waste or unsightly places into gardens or flower beds or shrubberies', and 'all matters connected with the rendering beautiful the Cities and Urban and Rural areas of Ireland'.[44] But first it had to face Dublin realities, squarely.

The landmark survey produced by the Civics Institute of Ireland in 1925 provides as 'impartially and comprehensively as possible' a compendium of 'the fundamental facts concerning the City and Environs of Dublin', as the city sought to cope with the destruction caused by several years of rebellion and civil war, and takes on the role of capital of an independent Irish state.[45] In the spirit of the town-planner Patrick Geddes, it was part of the process 'survey to analysis to (eventually) a comprehensive town plan', and part of the 'great awakening' which the city needed if it was to take its place among the great capital cities of the world. The report is upbeat about the potential of Dublin, 'a city of magnificent possibilities, not even inferior to Paris, placed astride a fine river, geographically well situated, and generally of great beauty and interest'.[46] But top of the planning programme had to be the scandal where 'a high proportion of the population of Dublin starts life without hope of having what makes life worth living – a decent home' and 'children in many thousands are born into an environment which gives no fighting chance of life'.[47] Mapping revealed the extent of slum housing (Fig. 23). Its elimination was presented as a core political, economic and social issue, as well as a matter of justice in the new Ireland:

> Housing in Dublin today is more than 'a question' and more than 'a problem'
> it is a tragedy! Its condition causes either a rapid or a slow death – rapid when
> the houses fall upon the tenants, as has happened already – slow when they
> remain standing dens of insanitation.[48]

And there was no point pretending that this would be rectified 'by a brief and intensive application of collective activity'; to rehouse all those urgently in need as well as providing for the upcoming generation requires 'nothing short of perpetual construction at the

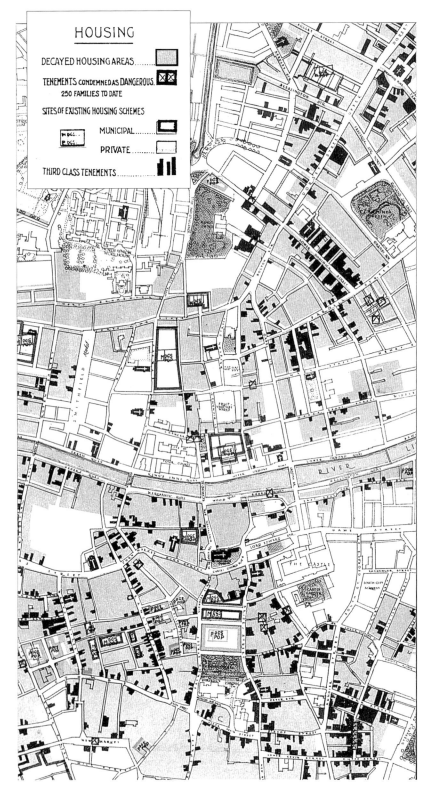

HOUSING

DECAYED HOUSING AREAS..........

TENEMENTS CONDEMNED AS DANGEROUS.
250 FAMILIES TO DATE

SITES OF EXISTING HOUSING SCHEMES

MUNICIPAL..........

PRIVATE..........

THIRD CLASS TENEMENTS..........

required rate'[49] (a quote that could be brought to the attention of central government again today). As a stand-alone document the maps of the slum geography of the city (Fig. 24) are the strongest indictment of previous half-hearted efforts, though in fairness none of the low-visibility work such as white-washing yards, cleaning out privies and closing down attics and cellars can be mapped.

The management of the Dublin city slums in the nineteenth century is a rather dark and depressing story; even in recounting it at this remove there is a feeling of hopelessness due to the scale of the problem and its intractable nature. The brightness held out by the suburban solution as articulated in the two decades before the foundation of the state is grasped eagerly even by us who are merely reflecting on historical realities.[50] As with the corporation officials of the 1920s and 1930s, we feel that there has to be a happy ending, that our fellow citizens, who have proved themselves extraordinarily resourceful, deserve to live in decent homes with decent opportunities. The Dublin story continues into the new suburbs, a new chapter with its own shadows

Fig. 23 **Central city, showing decayed housing areas (shaded), third class tenements (black) and tenements condemned as dangerous (X),** *Dublin Civic Survey,* **housing map, 192**

and many bright moments. It continues today, where the provision and management of decent housing for Travellers is but one of the challenges still to be faced. But it is good to know where we have come from, the challenges we inherited at Independence, to learn from the vision and energy of some of our forebears, and to question ourselves as citizens on how we are contributing to the betterment of life in the city we all love.

Acknowledgements

I wish to acknowledge the continued interest and support of Professor Anngret Simms, Department of Geography, University College Dublin, who supervised the PhD research upon which this lecture is based. The kind permission of the Royal Society of Antiquaries of Ireland to reproduce figures 6, 7, 8 and 16 is also appreciated.

Notes

1 For a full treatment of these matters see Jacinta Prunty, *Dublin slums 1800–1925, a study in urban geography* (Dublin, 1998, 2000).

2 On the pre-nineteenth century inheritance, where the roots of the slum problem will be found, see Edel Sheridan, 'Designing the capital city, Dublin 1660–1810', and 'Living in the capital city: Dublin in the eighteenth century', in Joseph Brady and Anngret Simms (eds.), *Dublin through space and time* (Dublin, 2001), pp 66–158.

3 See Séamas Ó Maitiú, *Dublin's suburban towns, 1834–1930* (Dublin, 2003).

4 Where more than five families occupied a first class house, each family was judged to have fourth class accommodation. Where a first class house was occupied by four or five families, each family had third class accommodation.

See *Report of the census commissioners, Ireland* (1841), p. vi.

5 F. R. Falkiner, 'Report on the homes of the poor', *Journal of the Statistical and Social Inquiry Society of Ireland*, viii, 59 (1882), p. 267 (hereafter *Stat. Soc. Inq. Soc. Jn.*)

6 Ibid., pp 263–271.

7 Parke Neville, 'Report of the city engineer to lay all necessary evidence before the Royal Commission of Enquiry into the Sewerage and Drainage System of Dublin, and their effects on the sanitary condition of the city', *Reports and printed documents of the Corporation of Dublin*, no. 184 (1879), p. 181; see also pp 180, 183 (hereafter *RPDCD*).

8 John Norwood, 'On the working of the sanitary laws in Dublin, with suggestions for their amendment', *Stat. Soc. Inq. Soc. Jn.*, vi, 43 (1873), p. 230.

9   Charles Cameron, *Municipal public health administration* (Dublin, 1914), p. 37.

10 Miss F. O'Sullivan achieved first place, and three other women were among the eight top achievers; Report of Public Health Committee for 1899, *RPDCD*, iii (1900), p. 972–3; see also the report for 1900, *RPDCD*, iii (1901), p. 406.

11 Parke Neville, 'Report of the city engineer', *RPDCD*, iii, 184 (1879), pp 164–167.

12 Charles Cameron, 'Report of the medical officer of health', *RPDCD*, i (1876), p. 106.

13 As always the outrageous awards caught the headlines. One woman who paid no rent but had a squatter's title was awarded £600; a dairy owner and a green grocer were awarded a total of £479 by the arbitrator which was increased to £1,350 by the jury. *RPDCD*, iii (1879), p. 792.

14 See Jacinta Prunty, *Margaret Aylward, lady of charity, sister of faith* (Dublin, 1999).

15 *Second annual report of the Ladies' Association of Charity of St. Vincent de Paul* (Dublin, 1853), p. 12.

16 *Tenth annual report of the Ladies' Association of Charity of St. Vincent de Paul* (Dublin, 1861), pp 6-7.

17 *Third report of HM commissioners for inquiring into the housing of the working classes (Ireland)*, 4547 (xxii), 1885; evidence of Mr. Pim, qs 22,642-22,648; evidence of Thomas Grimshaw, qs. 23,105-23,108 (hereafter *Housing inquiry, 1885*). Compare entries in the relief registers of the Ladies' Association of Charity, Dublin with corporation returns; Holy Faith Archives, Glasnevin: A/LC/36 no. 3.

18 Reported in the *Dublin Civic Survey* (Liverpool, 1925), p. 53.

19 Charles Cameron, Edward Mapother, 'Report on the means for the prevention of disease in Dublin', *RPDCD*, i (1879) pp 347–348.

20 Minutes of the North Dublin Union, Resolution, 29 Nov. 1879 (National Archives of Ireland).

21 Charles Cameron, 'Report of public health committee', *RPDCD* (1899), pp 976–977.

22 *Report of Royal Commission to inquire into the fairs and markets in Ireland*, xli (1852–3), quoted in 'Report of markets committee', *RPDCD*, ii (1886), p. 304.

23 Francis Morgan, 'Report of markets committee', *RPDCD*, no. 19 (1875), pp 3–11.

24 'Report of markets committee', *RPDCD*, ii (1886), p. 307.

25 John Norwood, 'On the working of the sanitary laws in Dublin, with suggestions for their amendment', *Stat. Soc. Inq. Soc. Jn.*, vi, part 43 (1873), p. 232.

26 'Report on the means for the prevention of disease in Dublin', *RPDCD*, i (1879), pp 345–346.

27 F.H.A. Aalen, *The Iveagh Trust: the first hundred years, 1890–1900* (Dublin, 1990), p. 8.

28 See Spencer Harty, 'Some considerations on the working of the Artisans' and Labourers' Dwellings Acts, as illustrated in the case of the Coombe area, Dublin', *Stat. Soc. Inq. Soc. Jn.*, viii, 62 (1884), p. 517.

29 *Housing inquiry, 1885*, evidence of Mr. Edward McMahon (Drumcondra), qs. 24,619–24,620.

30 *Housing inquiry, 1885*, evidence of Dr. Cameron, qs. 22,403–22,409.

31 See for example 'Report of the Public Health Committee', *RPDCD*, iii, 136 (1894), pp 56–84.

32 *Report of the departmental committee appointed by the Local Government Board for Ireland to inquire into the housing conditions of the working classes in the city of Dublin* (Dublin, 1914), p. 6.

33 *Housing inquiry, 1885*, evidence of Dr. Cameron, qs. 22,237–22,241

34 Ibid., qs. 22,298–22,301

35 *Report of the public health committee for 1909* (Dublin, 1910), p. 92.

36 'Report of the housing committee, being a survey of the north side of the city of Dublin, containing historical notes on the city's expansion north of the Liffey, illustrated by maps and other particulars, together with statistical information showing the evolution of the tenement system and an outline of the housing requirements', *RPDCD*, i, 13 (1918), pp 81–145 (hereafter *North Dublin Survey, 1918*).

37 For example, *Daily Nation*, 3 Sept. 1898.

38 *North Dublin Survey, 1918*, p. 99.

39 P. C. Cowan, *Report on Dublin housing* (Dublin, 1918), pp 3, 8.

40 Ibid. p. 12.

41 Ibid., p. 4.

42 Ibid., p. 7.

43 Ibid., p. 25.

44 'Memorandum and articles of association of the Civics Institute of Ireland Limited, under the Companies Acts 1908 and 1913, 20 March 1914', PRO: T1 11752.

45 *The Dublin Civic Survey Report, prepared by Horace T. Plunkett and the Dublin Civic Survey Committee for the Civics Institute of Ireland*, ii (Liverpool, 1925), p. 49. See Yvonne Whelan, *Reinventing modern Dublin, streetscape, iconography and the politics of identity* (Dublin, 2003).

46 *Civic Survey*, p. 5.

47 Ibid., p. 58.

48 Ibid., p. 58.

49 Ibid., p.73.

50 For a comprehensive treatment see Ruth McManus, *Dublin 1910–1940, shaping the city and suburbs* (Dublin, 2002).

Robert Emmet and Songs of Rebellion[*]

by **Nicholas Carolan**

➤-➤-➤-➤-➤ ✦ ◄-◄-◄-◄-◄

*Gilbert Lecture, January 2003

I have to thank Ms Deirdre Ellis-King, Dublin City Librarian, for the invitation to give this John T. Gilbert Annual Memorial Lecture on the topic of 'Robert Emmet and Songs of Rebellion', and also Dr Máire Kennedy, Special Collections Librarian of the City Libraries, and her staff for facilitation of the invitation in various ways. During the years that I have lived in Dublin, I have spent many hours in the Gilbert Library and have much reason to be grateful to the late Sir John Gilbert and to the Dublin Corporation that bought his magnificent collection of manuscripts, books, pamphlets, and other printed items for public use.

Irish songs of rebellion form an old and a varied tradition; they existed long before Emmet's time and they have flourished since his death. It is a tradition of which the origins and early forms are unknown, and of course it is a tradition which still continues.

By way of setting the tone for the kind of Irish songs of rebellion, or subversive songs, or patriotic songs, that we will be dealing with here – because there are many kinds of such songs – I have asked Barry Gleeson, a friend who is providing our live illustrations tonight and to whom I am greatly obliged, to sing a famous nineteenth-century patriotic song of anonymous authorship: 'By Memory Inspired'.

Track 1 **'By Memory Inspired', Barry Gleeson**

It seems likely that the very earliest songs of rebellion sung on this island were songs on a local scale, songs which operated at inter-familial or inter-tribal or inter-regional levels. But in speaking about songs of rebellion with reference to Robert Emmet we are necessarily talking about songs of recent centuries which have a national as well as a possible local consciousness.

You will know that the question of just when a national political consciousness arose in Ireland is a matter of debate among historians. Many would agree that concepts of nationality really began to develop among the Irish in the 16th century as the Tudor reconquest of Ireland began to get under way with its incendiary alien elements of race, religion and language.

But even then older loyalties were hard to shake off. When a poet and harper is said to have sung a song to persuade Silken Thomas Fitzgerald to rebel against Henry VIII in 1534, he appealed to the young man's sense of family pride, rather than to his national feelings.[1]

The Elizabethan poet Edmund Spenser, author of *The faerie queene*, worked as an official in the royal service in Ireland. He recorded some of his observations of Irish life in his prose dialogue of the 1590s *A veue of the present state of ireland*, and he said with reference to songs of rebellion:

> There is among the Irish a certain kind of people called the bards... whose profession is to set forth the praises and dispraises of men, in their poems and rhymes... their verses are... usually sung at all feasts and meetings by certain other persons whose proper function that is... these Irish bards are for the most part... far from instructing young men in moral discipline ... but whomsoever they find to be most licentious of life, most bold and lawless in his doings, most dangerous and desperate in all parts of disobedience and rebellious disposition, him they set up and glorify in their rhymes, him they praise to the people, and to young men make an example to follow... tending for the most part to the hurt of the English, or maintenance of their own lewd liberty ...[2]

So, major themes of Irish songs of rebellion are already in evidence there in the late 1500s: praise of the rebellious individual as an admirable exemplar, the pursuit of Irish liberty, and opposition to English power within Ireland.

The songs that Spenser refers to were of course in the Irish language – he speaks elsewhere of having them translated for him – and there is a long and a rich tradition of such songs in Irish dealing with the whole matter of Irish politics as seen essentially from a Gaelic and Catholic perspective. We have songs in Irish which incite rebellion, lament the sorry state of Ireland, look for help from abroad and expect it, extol the Catholic cause and denigrate the Protestant; we have songs which refer to a variety of prominent individuals from James I and Cromwell to Sarsfield and the O'Neills, and events from the Boyne and Limerick to the introduction of the Penal Laws and White Boy disturbances. And these are just from the century before Emmet's time. After his birth in 1778 the Irish-language tradition was still relatively strong up to the Great Famine: we have songs referring to the 1798 Rebellion, the Act of Union, Daniel O'Connell and Catholic Emancipation, the Tithe War, Repeal. But the songs of Robert Emmet, and indeed Robert Emmet himself, do not belong to the Irish-language political tradition, except in a very peripheral way, so, important as the Irish-language tradition is in its own right, it does not really concern us here tonight.

The songs of Robert Emmet belong instead to Ireland's English-language tradition of songs of rebellion, obviously a tradition which developed later than that of the Irish. The earliest known such songs were of religious content and were in existence at least by the 1590s, when Dublin Castle proclaimed a list of imports which began with Papist vestments and also included 'books, ballets [and] songs', for the importing of which a fine or imprisonment would be incurred.[3] Ballad sheets were actually being published in Dublin from at least the 1620s, and some of these early sheets were also politically subversive.[4]

Candidates are the Williamite 'Boyne Water' commemorating the victory at the Boyne in 1690 and the Jacobite 'The Blackbird' which appeared after the unsuccessful Scottish rising of 1715 and which seems to be of Irish authorship.[5] There was some early-ish political ballad publishing in Cork also: 'An Elegy on... James Cotter' of about 1720, for instance, arises from the celebrated execution of a prominent Catholic in the period of the Penal Laws.[6] And an outpouring of songs provoked from the merchant classes and their lyricists by the introduction of Wood's Halfpence in the early 1720s could be seen as a specialised class of Irish songs of rebellion. By and large these songs in English reflect the concerns of the colony in Ireland rather than the colonised.

By Emmet's time, such early intimations of national consciousness in Irish and English, which had encompassed only the concerns of one side or the other of the population, had developed to include – in theory at least, if not usually in practice – Protestant, Catholic and Dissenter. The Irish political songs which are most likely to have had a strong influence on the young Emmet are the many songs of the late 18th century which dealt with questions of national freedom and democratic governance, and which were inspired by such seminal events as the American War of Independence (which began in 1775), the foundation and rise of the Volunteer movement from 1777, the establishment of Grattan's Parliament (which sat from 1782), and especially the outbreak of the French Revolution in 1789. The great printed collection of such radical songs was *Paddy's resource*, the United Irishmen collection which appeared in several popular editions from the mid-1790s, and which reflected all these political developments. (Fig. 1) From it, to represent the genre, this is a snatch of 'The Carmagnole' sung in 1993 by the Kerry singer Tim Dennehy. The carmagnole was a short French jacket associated with the Jacobin cause.

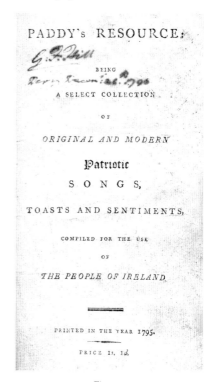

PADDY's RESOURCE:

BEING

A SELECT COLLECTION

OF

ORIGINAL AND MODERN

Patriotic

SONGS,

TOASTS AND SENTIMENTS,

COMPILED FOR THE USE

OF

THE PEOPLE OF IRELAND

PRINTED IN THE YEAR 1795.

PRICE 1s. 1d.

Fig. 1

Paddy's resource, [Dublin] 1795.

(Dublin City Public Libraries)

Track 2 **'The Carmagnole', Tim Dennehy**

Great Liberty... patriots... sons of Freedom... foes confounded... tyrants shaking... victory... This and many similar songs echo the concerns of the young and maturing Robert Emmet.

Having put Emmet in song context to this degree, it is time now to approach more closely to the man himself.

The salient facts of his life are clear enough, and have been recently presented in a new 2002 biography by Patrick M. Geoghegan, to which I am indebted.[7]

Robert Emmet was born in privileged circumstances, a few hundred yards away from this building, in St Stephen's Green in 1778. He was the seventeenth and final child of Dr Robert Emmet Senior and his wife Elizabeth Mason, who were both originally from the Cork area, with Tipperary and other connections. Dr Emmet was the State Physician for Ireland, and was well connected by birth. One of his cousins was Lord Lieutenant for Ireland in the 1780s, and another became the first British Consul-General to the United States in 1785. A more distant cousin was William Pitt the Younger, the British Prime Minister from 1783. Robert Emmet Junior was the fifth child of the name to have been born to the couple, and was one of only three brothers and one sister to survive infancy. He attended Samuel Whyte's famous school on Grafton Street – where Bewley's now is and where a younger fellow-pupil was Thomas Moore, destined to become Ireland's national poet. Emmet – like Moore although in different ways – was a precocious and highly idealistic child: he excelled at oratory, mathematics and the sciences. He was early exposed to radical views: his father was a strong 'Irish patriot' and sympathised with the American revolutionaries; William Drennan was a family friend; his older brother Thomas Addis Emmet, a doctor and lawyer, became a prominent leader of the United Irishmen and, following years of imprisonment in Scotland from 1798, would spend the rest of his life in exile on the Continent and in the United States.

Robert Emmet entered Trinity College at the age of 15, and Thomas Moore was again a fellow-student and friend. Both were supporters of the United Irishmen. In a familiar anecdote Moore later recalled a prophetic occasion in their college years when he was playing over to Emmet melodies from Edward Bunting's recently published collection of harp airs *A general collection of the ancient Irish music* of 1796. Emmet was listening in reverie, but when Moore played a martial-sounding air 'The Little Red Fox' he started up and exclaimed passionately 'Oh, that I were at the head of twenty thousand men marching to that air'.[8] This is that air, 'The Little Red Fox' (or as we would know it better from the song Moore later wrote to the air, 'Let Erin Remember'), played in the 1920s by the then new No 1 Army Band conducted by Colonel Fritz Brase. Emmet's dream of Irish soldiers marching to this air became at least partly true.

Track 3 **'Let Erin Remember', or 'The Little Red Fox', No 1 Army Band**

So even as a student Emmet was contemplating leading men into battle. There is just one difficulty with the story: the air does not appear in the Bunting volume of 1796, or indeed in any other early known printed source of the period. Attempts have been made to rationalise the error by saying that the martial air in question was 'The Foxe's Sleep', which does appear in the volume. But that is the air to which Moore wrote a song for Emmet, 'When He Who Adores Thee', and which, as you will hear in a few moments, is a languishing rather than a martial air. Their fellow Trinity student and fellow United Irishman the flute player Edward Hudson, who was very musical, has been suggested as a source,[9] but it seems as likely that the highly musical Moore could have heard it from his Irish-speaking father from Moyvane, Co Kerry, or from the general tradition. 'An Maidrín Rua' or 'The Little Red Fox' is still sung today after all. But, at any rate, there is no reason to doubt the essential truth of the anecdote: that Moore as a student played this martial air and his fellow-student Emmet was memorably affected by it.

It is a pity that it is not one of Bunting's harp tunes of 1796 – it would make a better story, because the harp of course was a symbol of the United Irishmen: when Emmet was still a student in Trinity College he designed a seal for the southern directory of the United

Irishmen which incorporated a harper and harp engraved on an emerald.[10] (And, incidently, both Moore and Sarah Curran played the harp.) In addition, the story as told would have given us an early connection between Emmet and the United Irishman Thomas Russell, a leading participant in rebellion with Emmet in 1803. Bunting's volume would not have come into existence, at least at that time, if it were not for Russell who, in the mid-1790s, had actually pushed the work through to completion, as the secretary of the Belfast Society for the Promotion of Knowledge which had funded Bunting's work.[11]

Emmet excelled in his studies in Trinity College and was an outstanding orator, destined like his brothers for a distinguished career at the bar when politics intervened. He was secretary of one of the illegal committees of the United Irishmen within the college, and, after the arrest of his brother Thomas Addis for planning rebellion, he decided to leave the college rather than obey regulations which proscribed the organisation. He was then expelled, in April 1798, and he more or less went on the run. He seems to have joined the Directory of the United Irishmen, although there is no evidence that he took an active part in the 1798 rebellion. He became involved however with those planning the next rebellion, and ensuring that it would not be affected by informers.

During this period Emmet wrote several poems which appeared in radical newspapers. These were not for singing – Anne Devlin said about Emmet that he sometimes hummed a tune, but that he was no great singer.[12] However one of Emmet's best poems, 'Arbour Hill', which was inspired by the graves of executed 1798 rebels in Dublin, was set to music about fifty years ago by the late Leo Maguire of the Walton's programme of radio fame. There are no recordings of it that I know about, but we do have a notation of the tune, thanks to Terry Moylan who published it recently.[13] A colleague in the Irish Traditional Music Archive, Joan McDermott, kindly agreed to record it for use in this lecture. This is as close as we can come to a song *by* Robert Emmet.

Track 4 **'Arbour Hill', Joan McDermott**

A callous judge with hands dyed in blood... memories for ever blest... endless fame... These are things on Emmet's mind about 1800. And, strangely, the callous judge of the song was Lord Norbury who would a few years later sentence Emmet to death.

After the passage of the Act of Union in June 1800 Emmet was sent as secretary of a secret United Irishmen delegation to France, where he remained until 1802, having meetings with the French about a possible invasion of Ireland and studying military tactics and the science of explosives. In 1801 he had meetings with Napoleon Bonaparte, the first consul, of whom he had a very poor opinion. It is odd to think of these two, who feature prominently in the Irish song tradition, actually meeting.

There is an intriguing sighting of what may be Robert Emmet in France in a United Irishmen song published in Dundalk in 1802. It is an old version of what later became one of the most popular Irish songs ever: 'The Wearing of the Green'. The old version is called 'Green on My Cape', and it is a very corrupt and fragmented text and not really singable. It has never been recorded that I know of, and indeed could not be recorded as it stands, but it begins (sings)

I'm a man that's going to travel, and must quit my native land,
There's an oath sworn [out] against me, in my country I can't stand...

The scansion falls apart then, but the speaker leaves Dublin, goes to Wexford, finds a ship's captain and crew who are United sympathisers, is brought across to Flanders, and then goes to France.

And this then is the relevant verse (sings):

In Brest I met E – t who took me by the hand,
And asked me for I – d and how did it now stand,
Such a poor distressed [nation] you never [have] seen,
They hang men and women for wearing of the green.
    For wearing of the green, for wearing of the green,
    They hang men and women for wearing of the green.[14]

Now, the name that I take as Emmet is actually represented in the text by a capital E, a long dash and a final t (just as Ireland in the next line is represented by a capital I, a long dash and a final d), so I suppose it is possible that some name other than Emmet is meant, although I cannot think what, or that the Emmet in question is Thomas Addis Emmet, although as far as I can establish be was not in France as early as 1802 and Robert was. So Robert Emmet was possibly the forerunner of Napper Tandy in the more popular version of the song developed by Dion Boucicault in the early 1860s.

Emmet's story after his return to Ireland in late 1802 is well known: he was invited to assist in a new scheme for rebellion and was assigned a prominent role in the secret preparations; his father died and left him a legacy which he dedicated to these preparations; he met and fell in love with Sarah Curran, the twenty-year-old daughter of the prominent lawyer John Philpot Curran; depots for arms were rented at strategic points in the city, and rockets and other military items were prepared; Emmet lived incognito in a house in Rathfarnham where he was looked after by Anne Devlin, niece of the Wicklow insurgent Michael Dwyer; the rebellion began on 23 July 1803 but was inadequately prepared, and soon disintegrated in confusion and random bloodshed – the most prominent victim was Lord Kilwarden, a privy councillor who was unlucky enough to be passing by in his coach; the outbreak was easily suppressed; Emmet and some of his men escaped to Rathfarnham and then to the Wicklow mountains; a month later Emmet was captured in Harold's Cross by Major Sirr, town major of Dublin; a month later again he had been found guilty of treason at a trial presided over by Lord Norbury, and without delay he was hanged, and then beheaded, opposite St Catherine's Church on Thomas Street on 20 September 1803. He met his death bravely at the age of twenty-five, but there was no public outcry.

It is more than probable that we would not be here tonight had Emmet not been asked, at the end of his trial, if he had any reason to give why the judgement of death and execution should not be passed against him according to law. The speech he gave from the dock in reply, with interruptions by Norbury, has resounded through the centuries and is the single most important reason why Emmet is remembered today as a great Irish patriot. It is a long speech, but this is the famous last minute of a version of it, as delivered by Mícheál Mac Liammóir in the 1950s.

Track 5 'Emmet's Speech from the Dock', Mícheál Mac Liammóir

As G.K. Chesterton said, Emmet made an epitaph of the refusal of an epitaph.[15] Versions of Emmet's speech from the dock have been re-delivered innumerable times over the last two hundred years and in a great variety of circumstances: at private and public political gatherings, on the stage from the years immediately after his death, on commercial recordings in Irish-America from the early 1920s, on radio and television, and so on. I remember the speech as played in character and in costume in the fit-ups in Drogheda, Co. Louth, about 1960. Versions have been printed innumerable times, and remind us indeed that performances of historic speeches and historical recitations were always the companions of songs of rebellion in the tradition.

Although there are quite a number of Irish songs commemorating Emmet and his associates or at least referring to them, the Swiss scholar Georges-Denis Zimmermann, who examined some 12,000 Irish broadside songs from the period 1780 to 1900 for his masterly Ph.D. thesis of 1965,[16] found that no *contemporary* 1803 broadside ballads exist commemorating Emmet's rebellion (song broadsides being the single-sided sheets of song texts which were sold on Irish streets for a penny or halfpenny or less from the 1600s to the 1960s).[17] I cannot contradict this finding, and I think that it is an interesting one. Historians are rightly wary of ballads as historical sources, but ballads do often reflect historical reality or at least refract it. Clearly Emmet's rebellion was not seen as important enough in its own time for the writing of songs; it was not a rebellion for which there was a ballad-buying public; it was a skirmish, a 'row in the town'. Most people, on all sides, disapproved of it. Its symbolic importance for Irish nationalists would only grow gradually over the next century or so, and its elements of youth, social position, personal nobility and courage, self-sacrifice, doomed love, failure and death, would increase in power in the course of the nineteenth century and reach their apotheosis possibly in the 1916 rebellion.

However, not too long after Emmet's death, in 1804, a collection of songs entitled *The Patriot's vocal miscellany, or A collection of loyal songs* was published in Dublin, and in it is a song entitled 'Rebellion', which attacks Emmet's uprising. It was written by an anonymous loyalist and, significantly, is dated 24 July 1803, the day after the rebellion. No music is printed in the volume, but tunes are specified for the songs, and, oddly, for this particular one a tune with a garbled title in Irish is given: 'Cree ne Failaght', which may mean 'Croí na Féile' (The Heart of Hospitality) or 'Croí na Fáilte' (The Heart of Welcome). No such tune can now be found at any rate, so I can only quote some verses of this very first song referring to Robert Emmet and his rising:

Dire Rebellion, see, preparing / In the gloomy well of night,
And her hopeless banners rearing, / 'Gainst the king and people's right.

Imp of hell, how unsuspected, / Hast thou sprang to light again;
Rushing on the unprotect'd / With thy worse than tyger train!

Save us, heav'n! see mild Kilwarden / Bleeds beneath the monster's fangs!
Mercy shuts the gate of pardon / As she views the martyr's pangs...

See the rebel horde disperses, / Baffled in their dire intent —
Praise to God for all his mercies! / May our cruel foes repent![18]

So, an instant, and rather literary, loyalist song reaction penned the day after the rebellion. It is interesting to see the word 'martyr' already in play, and applied to Kilwarden.

Emmet's friend Thomas Moore is actually the first person to be credited with the production of a song which sides with Emmet, a song which also begins to preserve the nationalist version of his public memory.

Moore had the highest regard for Emmet and, although their ways parted after Emmet was expelled from Trinity, Moore stood by the friendship. Just four years after Emmet's execution, in 1807, he wrote for the first number of his highly successful *Irish melodies* two songs which commemorated Emmet but which would hardly have endeared Moore to the members of the gentry and nobility to which the volume was dedicated, had they properly understood them. The first, 'Oh! Breathe Not His Name',[19] is inspired by Emmet's wish that his epitaph not be written. The singer is Jane Cassidy of Belfast about 1995.

Track 6 **'Oh! Breathe Not His Name' (air: The Brown Maid), Jane Cassidy**

Moore's second Emmet song is 'When He Who Adores Thee'.[20] (Fig. 2) It has been suggested that this may have been inspired by the memory of Lord Edward Fitzgerald rather than that of Emmet, and it may, but it is frequently sub-titled 'Emmet to Ireland', and certainly in terms of public perception, it is an Emmet song.[21] The singer here is Margaret Burke-Sheridan in 1944.

Track 7 **'When He Who Adores Thee' (air: The Foxe's Sleep), Margaret Burke-Sheridan**

Four years later, in 1811, Moore was again commemorating Emmet in the fourth number of the *Irish melodies* by writing 'She is Far from the Land',[22] a song about Sarah Curran and her memories of Emmet. The singer here is John McCormack in 1911.

40 **When He who Adores Thee.**
(Emmet to Ireland.)

THOMAS MOORE. *Air—"The Fox's Sleep."*
Slow, and with feeling. *(Codladh an tsionnaigh.)*

When he who adores thee has left but the name Of his
fault and his sor-row be-hind, Oh! say, wilt thou weep when they
dark-en the fame Of a life that for thee was re-
sign'd? Yes, weep, and however my foes may condemn, Thy
tears shall ef-face their de-cree; For Heav'n can wit-ness, tho'
guilty to them, I have been but too faithful to thee.

With thee were the dreams of my earliest love,
Every thought of my reason was thine;
In my last humble pray'r to the Spirit above,
Thy name shall be mingled with mine!
Oh! bless'd are the lovers and friends who shall live
The days of thy glory to see;
But the next dearest blessing that heaven can give
Is the pride of thus dying for thee!

56

Fig. 2 **'When He Who Adores Thee' from *The Irish Song Book*, ed. Alfred Perceval Graves, London 1905. (Dublin City Public Libraries)**

Track 8 **'She is Far from the Land' (air: Open the Door), John McCormack**

With these three melancholy and highly influential songs by Thomas Moore, a stage has been set and notes sounded which will occur and re-occur in the song commemoration of Emmet.

Broadside ballads are notoriously difficult to date: they appear usually without even a publisher's name, not to mind a date of publication. There is a small number of 19th-century Emmet broadsides, and of these the earliest seems to be one entitled 'My Emmet's No More'. (Fig. 3) It was in print in 1836,[23] but it probably belongs to the two opening decades of the century. Its composition seems to have been influenced by a popular poem of about 1800, 'The Exile of Erin', and its register of language and its historical perspective are far more literary than the normal broadside ballad. But it did appear commonly on ballad sheets and it survived strongly into song books of the 20th century. It has not been recorded however, and it does not seem to have survived in oral tradition, so Barry Gleeson will recreate it now. The air which is specified for the song on many of the sheets is the 18th-century air 'Savourneen Deelish'. This actually exists in several versions, and we have chosen one close to a version used by Thomas Moore for another of his songs.[24]

Track 9 **'My Emmet's No More', Barry Gleeson**

Not surprisingly, Emmet, the rebel committed to military action, does not figure in the songs of the O'Connell movement, but a song of the 1830s, probably made by the ballad composer and street singer Michael Moran of the Liberties, alias Zozimus, shows that some memory of Emmet's rebellion lived among Zozimus's Dublin street audience and formed part of the whole 1798 sequence in its thinking. The song is a satire attacking a retired Dublin member of the yeomanry who took part in suppressing the 1798 rebellion, and it begins:

> At the dirty end of Dirty Lane
> Lived a dirty cobbler, Dick McClane,
> His wife lived in the old king's reign,
> A stout old Orange woman;
> On Essex Bridge she strained her throat,
> And 'six a penny' was her note,
> And Dicky wore an old red coat
> That he got in the yeomen.

The song goes on to make fun of Dicky's actions in Wexford and Dublin, all of them cowardly, all of them attacks on women and animals. It continues, and this is the relevant verse:

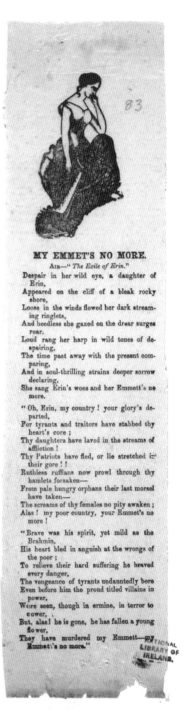

MY EMMET'S NO MORE.

AIR—"*The Exile of Erin.*"

Despair in her wild eye, a daughter of
   Erin,
Appeared on the cliff of a bleak rocky
   shore,
Loose in the winds flowed her dark stream-
   ing ringlets,
And heedless she gazed on the drear surges
   roar.
Loud rang her harp in wild tones of de-
   spairing,
The time past away with the present com-
   paring,
And in soul-thrilling strains deeper sorrow
   declaring,
She sang Erin's woes and her Emmett's no
   more.

"Oh, Erin, my country! your glory's departed,
For tyrants and traitors have stabbed thy
   heart's core ;
Thy daughters have laved in the streams of
   affliction !
Thy Patriots have fled, or lie stretched in
   their gore ! !
Ruthless ruffians now prowl through thy
   hamlets forsaken—
From pale hungry orphans their last morsel
   have taken—
The screams of thy females no pity awaken ;
Alas ! my poor country, your Emmett's no
   more !

"Brave was his spirit, yet mild as the
   Brahmin,
His heart bled in anguish at the wrongs of
   the poor ;
To relieve their hard suffering he braved
   every danger,
The vengeance of tyrants undauntedly bore
Even before him the proud titled villains in
   power,
Were seen, though in ermine, in terror to
   cower,
But, alas! he is gone, he has fallen a young
   flower,
They have murdered my Emmett—my
   Emmet's no more."

Fig. 3 **'My Emmet's No More'**
(Courtesy National Library of Ireland)

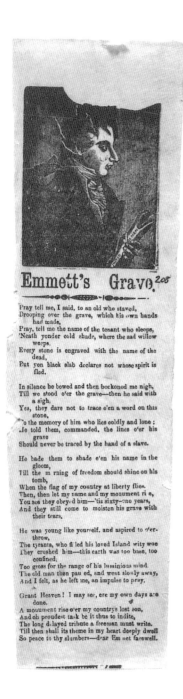

Fig. 4 'Emmet's Grave' (Courtesy National Library of Ireland)

When Kilwarden drop'd in Thomas Street,
A crop'd-eared dog he [Dicky] chanced to meet,
He tip'd him a brace of balls so sweet,
Mistaking him for a Roman;
At the Weavers' Hall upon the Coombe,
When tyranny was in its bloom,
Many a Croppy met their doom
From lame duck Drury's yeoman.[25]

So, some memory of Emmet's rebellion remained with a nationalist Dublin song audience in the 1830s.

While Emmet was admired to some extent by the Young Irelanders, he does not appear as the subject of any of their numerous songs, although one often reprinted poem, 'Emmet's Death', appears in their famous 1845 anthology *The spirit of the nation*. The poem is interesting in showing that basic elements of the Emmet story – his trial and his doomed love – survive almost half a century after his death, although in a more combative and dramatic way than in the melancholy songs of Moore. The first verse is:

He dies today! said the heartless judge,
Whilst he sate him down to the feast;
And a smile was upon his ashy lip
As he uttered a ribald jest.
For a demon dwelt where his heart should be,
That lived upon blood and sin;
And oft as that vile judge gave him food
The demon throbbed within.

Then there is a verse about Emmet's jailor, and then the last verse is:

He dies today! thought a fair, sweet girl —
She lacked the life to speak;
For sorrow had almost frozen her blood,
And white were her lips and cheek.
Despair had drunk up her last wild tear,
And her brow was damp and chill;
And they often felt at her heart with fear,
For its ebb was all but still.[26]

While it is not my subject, I will just say in passing that there seem to be more poems written on the theme of Robert Emmet than there are songs. One of them however, 'Miss Curran's Lament over the Grave of Robert Emmet', by Dr Madden, the biographer of Emmet and the

United Irishmen, must have been written in the hope that it might be sung because it begins:

> The joy of life lives here, Robert Aroon,
> All that my soul held dear, Robert Aroon,
> Spouse of my heart, this shrine,
> This long-lost home of thine,
> Entombs each hope of mine, Robert Aroon.[27]

This was obviously written with the song 'Eibhlín a Rún' in mind, although I doubt if it ever was sung popularly.

Most popular Emmet songs, apart from 'My Emmet's No More' and Thomas Moore's songs, seem in fact to be later than the mid-19th century, although we still have problems about their precise dating. The earliest of these seems to be a ballad sheet decorated by a woodcut of Robert Emmet and entitled 'Emmet's Grave'. (Fig. 4) No melody survives for it, and, although one source specifies that it be sung to the air 'Wolfe Tone's Grave',[28] it does not fit the air that we would know by that name. But interestingly, from an internal reference, it seems to have been written in 1864. If so, it has to be reckoned as a ballad of the Fenian period, and it is interesting also to remember that the Fenians modeled themselves to an extent on the United Irishmen. The point of the song is to encourage the achieving of Irish freedom in order that Emmet's epitaph may be finally written, and the verses can be read as an incitement to rebellion after a period of inactivity. So, more than sixty years after his death, Emmet's rebellion was again becoming politically relevant.

There is a second undated ballad sheet 'Emmet's Farewell to His Love' (Fig. 5) which uses the same woodcut, the same decoration, and the same typeface as 'Emmet's Grave', and is clearly the work of the same publisher. This must also be taken therefore as a ballad of the Fenian period.[29] It is definitely a song because, remarkably, it has been recorded at least twice in recent years from elderly traditional singers. The fact that one of these was recorded in the extreme north of the Inishowen peninsula in Donegal and the other on the extreme west coast of Clare suggests that the ballad was widespread as well as long-lived. The singer in Clare was the late Tom Lenihan of Miltown Malbay who learned it from an Irish-American songbook of about 1900 in which the ballad sheet had been reprinted.[30] The singer in Donegal, whom we are going to hear, was the late Maggie McGee of Derry and Inishowen who probably learned it from her parents. Recorded in 1993, in street-ballad style, it is what used to be called a come-all-ye.

Track 10 **'Emmet's Farewell to His Love', Maggie McGee**

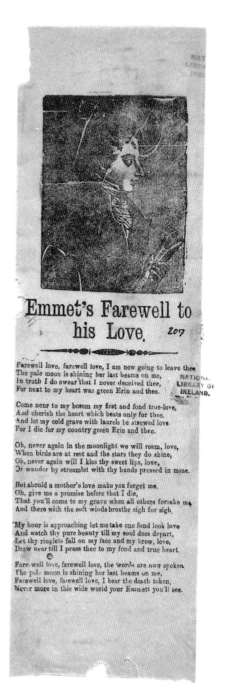

Fig. 5 **'Emmet's Farewell to His Love'**
(Courtesy National Library of Ireland)

There is an Irish-American songster, *The love of the shamrock songster*, compiled by the popular entertainer J.K. Emmet and published in Cincinnati in 1882, and, interestingly, the only Robert Emmet songs it contains are Moore's songs and 'My Emmet's No More'. So it seems that these other Emmet songs of the 1860s, which we know were published as street ballads, were not yet generally known to the Irish in America by 1882 (although they were by the end of the century). This is in spite of Emmet's power as an icon in Irish America and the strength of Fenianism there.

By the late 19th century and the turn of the 20th, no more Emmet songs had appeared, but his name was appearing regularly in lists of patriots featuring in nationalist songs. For example, this is from *Harding's Dublin songster* of the period:

> Brave Emmet, Fitzgerald and Grattan
> Have died in defense of the tree,
> While Shiel and O'Connell predicted
> That the plant would see Ireland free.[31]

And on a Boer War broadside of 1900 we get:

> And soon, my boys, we all shall see on Ireland's soil again
> Our dashing, dauntless, John McBride with all his fighting men.
> They'll raise the flag of Emmet, Tone, and Mitchell up once more,
> And lead us in the fight to drive the tyrant from our shore.[32]

There were many such appearances. According to Zimmermann, by about 1900 the favourites in such lists in nationalist songs were Robert Emmet and O'Donovan Rossa.[33]

As we come towards the end of this presentation, many of you will be thinking, what about *the* Robert Emmet song, the song we would all think of first if asked to come up with an Emmet song. I mean of course the Dublin street song which we now call 'The Bold Robert Emmet' (Fig. 6) or simply 'Robert Emmet', the song that more than any other has moulded our perception of Emmet. And the reason it has not been mentioned until now, as you will have guessed, is that it is a song not of Emmet's time, or indeed not even probably of the 19th century, but a song of the period of the Emmet centenary – it seems to been written about 1900. It was published, as a broadside song in come-all-ye style and entitled 'The Last Moments of Robert Emmet', by the Dublin ballad printer PCD Warren, and is sometimes attributed to a ballad composer Tom Maguire.[34] As it is *the* Emmet song of our own time – very popular in the ballad revival of the 1960s and again in the North of Ireland over the last three decades – I have asked Barry Gleeson to sing it for us.

Track 11 **'Bold Robert Emmet', Barry Gleeson**

Although that song has been the dominant Emmet song since its first appearance, the tradition of Emmet song and poetry did not end with it. Apart from odd 20th-century outcroppings of Emmetry in songs about Hibernian marching bands and football teams named after the patriot, the prolific Co Meath songwriter and publisher Brian O'Higgins, 'Brian na Banban', for instance, wrote and published, in the 1930s I think, a poem, possibly a song, in Irish about Emmet which began 'Ná greanntar leac dom is ná cantar m'fheartlaoi...' (Let not my memorial stone be inscribed nor my funeral lamentation be sung...),[35] and in 1940 a Séamus Ó Maoildhia published in Dublin an Irish-language translation of 'The Bold Robert Emmet' beginning 'Tá an cath anois thart is na buachaillí buailte...'.[36] In our own time, the Dublin dancer and musician Paddy Bán Ó Broin wrote a song called 'Young Emmet', popular in the 1960s,[37] which in its performance style here brings us to the accompanied pub ballad of recent decades.

Track 12 **'Young Emmet', Abbey Tavern group, Howth, Co. Dublin**

In final summary I would say that the entire range of Irish songs of rebellion – in Irish and English – is a very wide one, so wide that in concentrating here on Emmet I could only hint at it. The Emmet songs belong to a certain area of its spectrum. Apart from the one loyalist example quoted, they belong of course to the Green rather than to the Orange. In the Green

87.—BOLD ROBERT EMMET

The strug-gle is ov-er the boys are de-feat-ed, Old Hung, drawn and quartered, sure that was my sentence, But Ire-land's sur-round-ed with sadness and gloom, soon I will show them no coward am I, My We were de-feat-ed and shame-ful-ly treat-ed And crime is the love of the land I was born in, A I, Ro-bert Em-met a-wait-ing my doom.} he-ro I lived and a he-ro I'll die. CHORUS Bold Robert Emmet, the darling of E-rin, Bold Robert Emmet will die with a smile, Farewell com-panions both loy-al and dar-ing, I'll lay down my life for the Em-er-ald Isle.

Fig. 6 **'Bold Robert Emmet'** from *Irish street ballads,* **collected by Colm O Lochlainn, Dublin 1939 (Dublin City Public Libraries)**

camp they do not at all belong to the Scullabogue school of political song-writing – songs which can be sectarian, hate-filled, bloodthirsty, ignoble – but they belong to the broad stream of idealistic nationalist songs which emphasise the admirable traits of patriotism exemplified in Emmet's own life. There is a highly literary type of Emmet song – not just Moore's – and there is a more vernacular street-ballad type. In both we find the strong element of pathos which unifies the Emmet songs, and which again arises from Emmet's own story. Art imitates life, although not slavishly.

As you have heard tonight, the Emmet songs, of whatever kind, are either about Emmet centrally or they refer to him peripherally. You have heard snatches of both kinds, and we'll finish with one from Barry Gleeson that falls somewhere between both: a fairly modern song, written by the Dublin songwriter Norman Reddin, probably in the 1920s,[38] and referring to Emmet as one of 'The Three Flowers'.

Track 13 **'The Three Flowers', Barry Gleeson**

Acknowledgements

I would like finally to thank Barry again on our behalf, and to thank also various people who have helped me with the subject, among them Terry Moylan, Nuala O'Connor, Ríonach uí Ógáin, Maeve Carolan, Frank Harte and Tom Munnelly, and especially my colleagues in the Irish Traditional Music Archive who have assisted in various ways: Joan McDermott who sang 'Arbour Hill', Glenn Cumiskey who made the sound transfers, Maeve Gebruers who prepared the sheet of facsimiles which has been distributed, and Orla Henihan who is recording the proceedings.

N.C

In the course of 2003, the above lecture was also delivered by Nicholas Carolan and Barry Gleeson to the Folklore of Ireland Society, Dublin; the Old Drogheda Society, Co. Louth; and Arklow Historical Society, Co. Wicklow; and as a public lecture at Ballyfermot Public Library, Dublin; Newry Arts Center, Co. Down; and Inchicore Arts Festival, Kilmainham Gaol, Dublin. It also formed the basis of a programme for the anniversary of Robert Emmet's rebellion on the RTÉ Radio 1 arts series *Rattlebag*.

Notes

1 Mary Hayden and George A. Noonan, *A short history of the Irish people* (Dublin, 1921), p. 197.

2 Edmund Spenser, *A view of the present state of Ireland*, ed. W.L. Renwick (Oxford, 1970), pp 72–4.

3 Hugh Shields, *Narrative singing in Ireland* (Dublin, 1993), p. 43.

4 Shields 1993, p. 43.

5 Georges-Denis Zimmermann, *Songs of Irish rebellion: political street ballads and rebel songs 1780–1900* (Dublin, 1967), p. 121.

6 Shields 1993, p. 44.

7 Patrick M. Geoghegan, *Robert Emmet: a life* (Dublin, 2002). Since this lecture was first delivered I have become further indebted to new studies of Emmet: to Ruán O'Donnell's *Robert Emmet and the rebellion of 1798* and *Robert Emmet and the rising of 1803* (both Dublin and Portland, Oregon, 2003) and to Marianne Elliott's *Robert Emmet: the making of a legend* (London, 2003).

8 Thomas Moore, *Memoirs, journal and correspondence of Thomas Moore* (London, 1853), p. 58. Moore actually refers to the melody anachronistically as 'Let Erin Remember the Day [*sic*]'.

9 W.F. Trench, *Tom Moore: a lecture* (Dublin, 1934), p. 43.

10 Geoghegan 2002, p. 70.

11 Colette Moloney, *The Irish music manuscripts of Edward Bunting (1773–1843): an introduction and catalogue* (Dublin, 2000), p. 148.

12 Geoghegan 2002, p. 134.

13 Terry Moylan, *The age of revolution in the Irish song tradition 1776 to 1815* (Dublin, 2000), p. 114.

14 Zimmermann 1967, pp 167–70. *Pace* O'Donnell 1 2003, p. 254, there is no evidence that it was written by James Garland of Lurgan, Armagh.

15 G.K. Chesterton, *The crimes of England* (London, 1915), p. 51. I am obliged to Maeve Carolan for this reference.

16 Geneva 1966 (published as at note 5 above, republished Dublin, 2002).

17 Zimmermann 1967, p. 40.

18 *The Patriot's vocal miscellany*, pp 68–9.

19 Thomas Moore, *A selection of Irish melodies no I* (Dublin, 1807), p. 4.

20 Moore, *Irish melodies no I*, p. 5.

21 Elliott 2003, pp 117–9, details the effect a translation of this song had on the composer Hector Berlioz.

22 Thomas Moore, *A selection of Irish melodies no IV* (Dublin, 1811), p. 7.

23 See Elliott 2003, pp 129–31. It was published that year in a chapbook *The life, trial and conversations of Robert Emmet, Esq.* (Dublin, 1836). An American songster J.K. *Emmet's love of the shamrock* (Cincinnati, 1882 - see below) attributes the song to a Harry Osborne, but this was doubtless a commercial ploy of some kind.

24 ''Tis Gone and Forever'.

25 'Dicky in the Yeoman', Zimmermann 1967, pp 218–20. The approximate dating given is that of Zimmermann. O'Donnell 2 2003, p. 251, considers it much earlier, because of the people named in it.

26 *The spirit of the nation*, ed. C.P. Meehan, second ed. (Dublin, 1882), pp 215–7. [First published 1845].

27 *The Emmet song book* (Dublin, 1903), p. 6.

28 *Harding's Dublin songster*, new series, vol. 2 (Dublin, n.d.), p. 334.

29 A Dublin periodical publication of the late 19th century, *Harding's Dublin songster*, claims that the song was written specifically for it by a James Nicholson (*Irish country songs & street ballads collected by P.J. McCall*, vol. 7, 14, a scrapbook in the National Library of Ireland), but this too seems a later commercial ploy.

30 See Tom Munnelly ed., *The Mount Callan garland* (Dublin, 1994), pp 64–6.

31 'Ireland's Liberty Tree', *Harding's Dublin songster*, new series, no. 32, probably second half of the 19th century: Zimmermann 1967, pp 255–6.

32 'John McBride's Brigade', Warren broadside (Dublin, *c*.1900): Zimmermann 1967, p. 293.

33 Zimmermann 1967, p. 66.

34 Zimmermann 1967, p. 292. The Robert Emmet website (www.emmet1803.com) improbably identifies him with Tom Maguire (1892–1993), a member of the Irish Volunteers and the 1921 Dáil. The song is attributed to an Andy Lee and copyrighted to its publisher William W. Delaney in a [1915] New York Irish-American song book *Delaney's Irish song book no 5*, but this is doubtless a commercial ploy of some kind.

35 *National songs, ballads & recitations* (Dublin, n.d.), p. 67.

36 Séamus Ó Maoildhia, *Dánta & amhráin* (Dublin, 1940), pp 44–5.

37 *Songs of Dublin*, ed. Frank Harte (Skerries, 1978), p. 55.

38 Issued July 1932 on Beltona 78 no 564, sung by Dublin tenor Gerard Crofts.

1 Arbour Hill

Robert Emmet

No rising column marks the spot
Where many a victim lies;
But Oh!, the blood which here has streamed
To Heaven for justice cries,
It claims it on th' oppressor's head
Who joys in human woe,
Who drinks the tears by misery shed
And mocks them as they flow.

It claims it on the callous judge,
Whose hands in blood are dyed,
Who arms injustice with the sword,
The balance throws aside.
It claims it for his ruined isle,
Her wretched children's grave;
Where withered Freedom droops her head,
And man exists – a slave.

O Sacred Justice! Free this land
From tyranny abhorred;
Resume thy balance and thy seat –
Resume – but sheathe thy sword.
No retribution should we seek –
Too long has horror reigned;
By mercy marked may freedom rise,
By cruelty unstained.

Nor shall a tyrant's ashes mix
With those our martyred dead;
This is the place where Erin's sons
In Erin's cause have bled.
And those who here are laid to rest,
Oh! Hallowed be each name;
Their memories are for ever blest –
Consigned to endless fame.

Unconsecrated is this ground,
Unblest by holy hands;
No bell here tolls its solemn sound,
No monument here stands.

But here the patriot's tears are shed,
The poor man's blessing given;
These consecrate the virtuous dead,
These waft their fame to heaven.

- Terry Moylan, *The age of revolution in the Irish song tradition 1776 to 1815* (Dublin, 2000), 114–5

2 Rebellion

Written the 24th July, 1803.
Air: 'Cree na Failaght'

Dire Rebellion, see, preparing,
In the gloomy veil of night,
And her hopeless banners rearing,
'Gainst the king and people's right.

Imp of hell, how unsuspected,
Hast thou sprung to light again;
Rushing on the unprotect'd
With thy worse than tyger train!

Save us, heav'n! see mild Kilwarden
Bleeds beneath the monster's fangs!
Mercy shuts the gate of pardon,
As she views the martyr's pangs.

Save us, heav'n! the tumult thickens!
Savage shouts the air resound –
Massacre his fury quickens –
Mangled victims strew the ground.

Valour, gen'rous and undaunted
Grasps his sword with eager hand,
Flies where'er his aid is wanted,
Terror chills the rebel band.

Forward! Hearts of sterling value!
Let the red-wing'ed vengeance fly –
Sound your Sov'reign's standard rally!
See – the blood-stain'd rebels fly.

See the rebel horde disperses,
Baffled in their dire intent –
Praise to God for all his mercies!
May our cruel foes repent!

- *The Patriot's vocal miscellany: or A collection of loyal songs* (Dublin, 1804), pp 68–9

3   Oh! Breathe Not His Name

Thomas Moore

Oh! breathe not his name – let it sleep in the shade,
Where cold and unhonoured his relics are laid;
Sad, silent, and dark, be the tears that we shed,
As the night-dew that falls on the grass o'er his head.

But the night-dew that falls, though in silence it
    weeps,
Shall brighten with verdure the grave where he
    sleeps,
And the tear that we shed, though in secret it rolls,
Shall long keep his memory green in our souls.

- *Irish melodies by Thomas Moore*, (London, 1854), p. 5

4   When he, who adores thee

Thomas Moore

When he, who adores thee, has left but the name
Of his fault and his sorrows behind,
Oh! say, wilt thou weep, when they darken the fame
Of a life that for thee was resign'd?

Yes, weep, and, however my foes may condemn,
Thy tears shall efface their decree;
For Heaven can witness, though guilty to them,
I have been but too faithful to thee.

With thee were the dreams of my earliest love;
Every thought of my reason was thine;
In my last humble prayer to the Spirit above,
Thy name shall be mingled with mine.
Oh! blessed are the lovers and friends who shall live
The days of thy glory to see,
But the next dearest blessing that Heaven can give,
Is the pride of thus dying for thee.

- *Irish melodies by Thomas Moore*, (London, 1854), pp 5–6

5   She is Far from the Land

Thomas Moore

She is far from the land where her young hero sleeps,
And lovers around her are sighing;
But coldly she turns from their gaze and weeps
For her heart in his grave is lying.

She sings the wild songs of her dear native plains,
Every note which he lov'd a-waking;
Ah! little they think, who delight in her strains,
How the heart of the minstrel is breaking.

He had liv'd for his love, for his country he died,
They were all that to life had entwin'd him;
Nor soon shall the tears of his country be dried,
Nor long will his love stay behind him.

Oh! make her a grave where the sunbeams rest
When they promise a glorious morrow;
They'll shine o'er her sleep, like a smile from the
    West,
From her own lov'd island of sorrow.

- *Irish melodies by Thomas Moore*, (London, 1854), pp 47–8

6 My Emmet's no more

Despair in her wild eye, a daughter of Erin
Appeared on the cliff of a bleak rocky shore,
Loose in the winds flowed her dark streaming
    ringlets,
And heedless she gazed on the dread surge's roar,
Loud rang her harp in wild tones of despairing,
The time pass'd away with the present comparing,
And in soul-thrilling strains deeper sorrow
    declaring,
She sang Erin's woes, and her Emmet's no more.

Oh, Erin, my country! your glory's departed,
For tyrants and traitors have stabb'd thy heart's
    core,
Thy daughters have laid in the streams of affliction,
Thy patriots have fled or lie stretched in their gore!
Ruthless ruffians now prowl through thy hamlets
    forsaken –
From pale hungry orphans their last morsel have
    taken –
The screams of thy females no pity awaken,
Alas! my poor country, your Emmet's no more!

Brave was his spirit, yet mild as the Brahmin,
His heart bled in anguish at the wrongs of the poor;
To relieve their hard sufferings he braved every
    danger,
The vengeance of tyrants undoubtedly bore,
Even before him the proud villains in power
Were seen, though in ermine, in terror to cower,
But, alas! he is gone, he has fallen a young flower,
They have murdered my Emmet, my Emmet's no
    more.

- 19th-century ballad sheet, n.d., n.p.

7 Emmet's Grave

Pray tell me, I said, to an old [man] who stayed,
Drooping over the grave, which his own hands had
    made,
Pray, tell me the name of the tenant who sleeps,
'Neath yonder cold shade, where the sad willow
    weeps,
Every stone is engraved with the name of the dead,
But yon black slab declares not whose spirit is fled.

In silence he bowed and then beckoned me nigh,
Till we stood o'er the grave – then he said with a sigh,
Yes, they dare not to trace e'en a word on this stone,
To the memory of him who lies coldly and lone;
He told them, commanded, the lines o'er his grave
Should never be traced by the hand of a slave.

He bade them to shade e'en his name in the gloom,
Till the morning of freedom should shine on his
    tomb,
When the flag of my country at liberty flies,
Then, then let my name and my monument rise,
You see they obeyed him – 'tis sixty-one years,
And they still come to moisten his grave with their
    tears.

He was young like yourself, and aspired to o'erthrow,
The tyrants, who filled his loved island with woe
They crushed him – this earth was too base, too
    confined,
Too gross for the range of his luminous mind.
The old man then paused, and went slowly away,
And I felt, as he left me, an impulse to pray.

Grand Heaven! I may see, ere my own days are done,
A monument rise o'er my country's lost son,
And oh proudest task be it thus to indite,
The long delayed tribute a freeman must write.
Till then shall its theme in my heart deeply dwell
So peace to thy slumbers – dear Emmet, farewell.

- 19th-century ballad sheet, n.d., n.p.

8 Emmet's Farewell to His Love

Farewell love, farewell love, I'm now going to leave
    you,
The pale moon is shining her last beams on me.
In truth I do swear that I never deceived thee;
For next to my heart was green Erin and thee.

Come near to my bosom, my first and fond true love,
And cherish the heart which beats only for thee.
And let my cold grave with green laurel be strewed,
    love,
For I die for my country, green Erin, and thee.

Oh, never again in the moonlight we'll roam, love,
When birds are at rest and the stars they do shine.
Oh never again will I kiss thy sweet lips, love,
Or wander by streamlet with thy hands pressed in
    mine.

But should another love make you forget me,
Oh give me a promise before that I die?
That you'll come to my grave when all others
    forsake me,
And there with the soft winds breathe sigh for sigh.

My hour is approaching, let me take one fond look,
    love,
And watch thy pure beauty till my soul does depart;
Let thy ringlets fall on my face and my brow, love,
Draw near till I press thee to my fond and true heart.

Farewell love, farewell, the words are now spoken,
The pale moon is shining her last beams on me.
Farewell, love, farewell, love, I hear the death token,
Never more in this wide world your Emmet you'll
    see.

- 19th-century ballad sheet, n.d., n.p.

9 The Last Moments of Robert Emmet

The struggle is over, the boys are defeated,
Old Ireland's surrounded with sadness and gloom;
We were betrayed and shamefully treated
And I, Robert Emmet, awaiting my doom.
Hung, drawn and quartered, that was my sentence,
But soon I will show them no coward am I;
My crime was the love of the land I was born in,
A hero I lived and a hero I'll die.

Chorus
Bold Robert Emmet, the darling of Erin,
Bold Robert Emmet will die with a smile;
Farewell! companions, both loyal and daring,
I'll lay down my life for the Emerald Isle.

The barque lay at anchor awaiting to bring me
Over the billows to the land of the free;
But I must see my sweetheart for I know she will
    cheer me,
And with her I will sail over the sea.
But I was arrested and cast into prison,
Tried as a traitor, a rebel, a spy;
But no one dare call me a knave or a coward,
A hero I lived and a hero I'll die.

Hark! The bell's tolling, I well know its meaning,
My poor heart tells me it is my death knell;
In come the clergy, the warder is leading,
I have no friends here to bid me farewell.
Good-bye, old Ireland, my parents and sweetheart,
Companions in arms, to forget you must try;
I am proud of the honour, it was only my duty –
A hero I lived and a hero I'll die.

- Ballad sheet, published Warren, Kilmainham,
  Dublin, n.d.

10 Riobaird Emmet

Tá an cath anois thart is na buachaillí buailte,
Tá brón agus buaidhreadh ar Éirinn mar seo,
Feall a chuir síos sinn – nár náireach an choir í! –
'S mise, Riobaird Emmet le bás fhághail de'n chroich.
'Sí an bhreith atá tabhartha mé chrochad 's mé
      sgláradh,
Acht bhéarad le rádh dóibh nach cladhaire bocht mé,
An grádh thug mé d'Éirinn, 'sí sin mo choir-se,
Acht laoch a bhéas ionnam go dteighidh mé 'sa gcré.

Curfá
Ó, Riobaird bocht Emmet, mac múirneach na
      hÉireann,
A fuair bás mar an naoidheanán a béarthaí aréir,
Slán libh, a cháirde a bhí dílis is dána,
Táim sásta le bás fhághail do m'Oileán Glas féin.

Tá soitheach ar ancoir le m'árdhughadh chun bealaigh
Siar treasna na mara chuig tír atá saor,
Acht caithfidh mé a dhul chuig mo ghrádh bán le sgéala
Go gcasfar le chéile sinn lá éicint aríst;
Acht tóigeadh is caitheadh isteach mé i bpríosún,
'S mar déanfaidhe le spiadóir 'seadh d'fhéachadar mé,
Acht níor fhéadadar cladhaire ná cluanaidhe thab-
      hairt orm,
Mar laoch a bhéas ionnam go dteighidh mé 'sa gcré.

Tuigim cé an fáth a bhfuil an clog úd dá bualadh,
Tá mo chroidhe bocht dhá thuar gurab é sgéal mo
      bháis,
Seo isteach an phearsa eaglaise 's an coiméaduidhe i
      n-éinfheacht,
'S gan duine ann le bhféadfainn fiú 'Slán leat' a rádh;
Ó, beannacht le Éirinn, mo mhuinntir 's mo chaoin-
      shearc,
'S mo chomráduidhthe dílse a sheas dom chomh tréan:
Acht bród atá orm, 'sé mo dhualgas a rinneas,
Agus laoch a bhéas ionnam go dteighidh mé 'sa gcré.

- Séamus Ó Maoildhia, *Dánta agus amhráin*,
  (Dublin, 1940), pp 44–5

11 The Three Flowers

Norman G. Reddin

One time when walking down a lane
When night was drawing nigh,
I met a *cailín* with three flowers,
And she more young than I.
"Saint Patrick bless you, dear," said I,
"If you'll be quick and tell
The place where you did find these flowers
I seem to know so well."

She took and kissed the first flower once
And sweetly said to me:
"This flower comes from the Wicklow hills,
Dew wet and pure," said she
"Its name is Michael Dwyer—
The strongest flower of all,
But I'll keep it fresh beside my breast
Though all the world should fall."

She took and kissed the next flower twice,
And sweetly said to me:
"This flower I culled on Antrim hill,
Outside Belfast," said she.
"The name I call it is Wolfe Tone—
The bravest flower of all,
But I'll keep it fresh beside my breast,
Though all the world should fall."

She took and kissed the next flower thrice,
And sofly said to me:
"This flower I found in Thomas Street,
In Dublin fair," said she.
"Its name is Robert Emmet,
The youngest flower of all,
But I'll keep it fresh beside my breast
Though all the world should fall."

Then Emmet, Dwyer and Tone I'll keep,
For I do love them all,
And I'll keep them fresh beside my breast
Though all the world should fall."

- Ballad sheet, n.d., n.p.

12 Young Emmet

Paidí Bán Ó Broin

In Green Street courthouse in eighteen and three
Stood young Emmet the hero true and brave—
For fighting the tyrant, his country to free,
And to tear from her brow the name of slave.

Chorus
There are still men in Ireland both loyal and true
Who remember her patriots with pride;
And with God's help, young Emmet—
We'll still give to you the epitaph unwritten since
you died.

The verdict was 'Guilty', the sentence was death,
And in Thomas Street the tyrant's work was done
But young Emmet smiled as he drew his last breath
For he knew the fight for freedom would be won.

Alone and defiant he stood in the dock
While Lord Norbury, the hanging judge, looked
down;
Against his false charges he stood firm as a rock,
Yet another Irish martyr to the crown.

• Frank Harte, *Songs of Dublin*, (Skerries, 1978), p. 55

13 By memory inspired

By Memory inspired
And love of country fired,
The deeds of Men I love to dwell upon;
And the patriotic glow
Of my spirit must bestow
A tribute to O'Connell that is gone, boys, gone!
Here's a memory to the friends that are gone.

In October Ninety-Seven,
May his soul find rest in heaven!
William Orr to execution was led on;
The jury, drunk, agreed
That Irish was his creed,
For perjury and threats drove them on, boys, on.
Here's the memory of John Mitchel that is gone!

In Ninety-Eight, the month July,
The informer's pay was high,
When Reynolds gave the gallows brave McCann;
But McCann was Reynolds' first,
One could not allay his thirst,
So he brought up Bond and Byrne that are gone,
boys, gone.
Here's the memory of the friends that are gone!

We saw a nation's tears
Shed for John and Henry Sheares,
Betrayed by Judas Captain Armstrong.
We may forgive, but yet
We never can forget
The poisoning of Maguire that is gone, boys, gone;
Our high star and true apostle that is gone!

How did Lord Edward die?
Like a man, without a sigh;
But he left his handiwork on Major Swan!
But Sirr, with steel-clad breast
And coward heart at best,
Left us cause to mourn Lord Edward that is gone,
boys, gone.
Here's the memory of our friends that are gone!

September Eighteen-Three
Closed this cruel history,
When Emmet's blood the scaffold flowed upon;
O had their spirits been wise
They might then realise
Their freedom – but we drink to Mitchel that is
gone, boys, gone.
Here's the memory of the friends that are gone!

• Terry Moylan, *The age of revolution in the Irish
song tradition 1776 to 1815* (Dublin, 2000), pp 122–3

TRACK LISTING FOR CD ON INSIDE BACK COVER

1 'By Memory Inspired', Barry Gleeson, 2003*

2 'The Carmagnole', Tim Dennehy, 1993

3 'Let Erin Remember', or 'The Little Red Fox', No 1 Army Band, n.d. [late 1920s]

4 'Arbour Hill', Joan McDermott, 2003*

5 'Emmet's Speech from the Dock', Mícheál Mac Liammóir, n.d. [c. 1957]

6 'Oh! Breathe Not His Name' (air: The Brown Maid), Jane Cassidy, n.d. [c. 1995]

7 'When He Who Adores Thee' (air: The Foxe's Sleep), Margaret Burke-Sheridan, 1944

8 'She is Far from the Land' (air: Open the Door), John McCormack, 1911

9 'My Emmet's No More', Barry Gleeson, 2003*

10 'Emmet's Farewell to His Love', Maggie McGee, 1993

11 'Bold Robert Emmet', Barry Gleeson, 2003*

12 'Young Emmet', Abbey Tavern group, Howth, Co. Dublin, n.d. [1960s]

13 'The Three Flowers', Barry Gleeson, 2003*

   * Recorded by Jackie Small, ITMA

CD edited by Nicholas Carolan

Tracks 1, 4, 9, 11, 13 © the performers
Tracks 2, 3, 5, 6, 7, 8, 10, 12 © as per publication

For permission to publish tracks from existing commercial recordings on this CD, Dublin City Public Libraries and the Irish Traditional Music Archive are greatly obliged for their generosity to Tim Dennehy (Track 2, from *A winter's tear,* Cló Iar-Chonnachta CICD 087, Galway, 1993), to Jane Cassidy and Maurice Leyden (Track 6, from *Mary Ann McCracken 1779–1866,* Ashgrove Music ASH 004, Belfast, n.d.), and to Jimmy McBride (Track 10, from *An hour of song from Maggie McGee and Dan McGonigle,* Inishowen Traditional Singers' Circle ITSC 002, Donegal, 1993). It has not been possible to trace other copyright holders, but any such copyright holders whose rights have been inadvertently breached should contact the publishers.

CD manufactured by Trend Studios, Dublin

℗ © this compilation Dublin City Public Libraries in association with the Irish Traditional Music Archive

℗ © 2004

'Such Happy Harmony'*

Early twentieth century co-operation to solve Dublin's housing problems

by **Ruth McManus**

✦

*Gilbert Lecture, January 2004

I am delighted and honoured to have been invited to give this seventh lecture in honour of Sir John T. Gilbert. The story I want to share with you tonight is one which I hope will inspire us all on this wintry evening, telling as it does of how a relatively small number of dedicated citizens made an important contribution to the well-being of the people of Dublin. I will begin by outlining some of the problems which faced the city in the first two decades of the twentieth century, before turning to the extraordinary story of co-operation which played a significant part in their solution.

The city of Dublin that Gilbert knew in his lifetime was undergoing significant change. The second half of the nineteenth century had seen much of the upper and middle class

Fig. 1 **City centre** Early twentieth century postcard (Joe Brady collection)

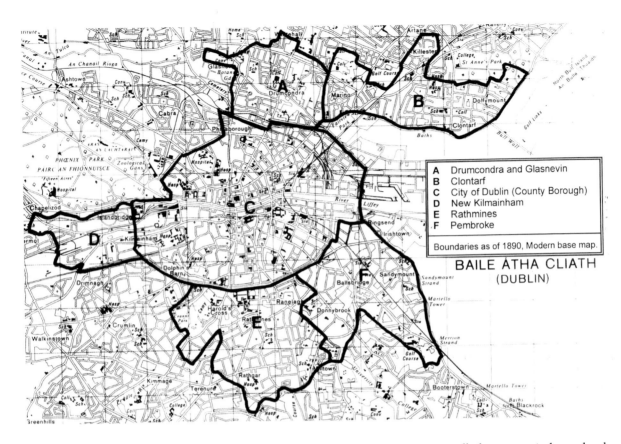

A	Drumcondra and Glasnevin
B	Clontarf
C	City of Dublin (County Borough)
D	New Kilmainham
E	Rathmines
F	Pembroke

Boundaries as of 1890, Modern base map.

BAILE ÁTHA CLIATH
(DUBLIN)

Map 1

Townships

Location of townships around Dublin (from Joseph Brady and Anngret Simms (eds), *Dublin through space and time,* Dublin, 2001)

population moving out of the Dublin Corporation controlled area to independently governed suburban townships such as Rathmines and Pembroke[1] [MAP I]. Not only were they leaving the physical dereliction and unhealthy squalor of the city for a new suburban lifestyle, but they were also leaving behind their obligations to pay taxes to the city. This loss of revenue from the rates meant that the city authorities were in an increasingly difficult position, trying to cope with an ever-worsening slum problem with dwindling resources.

The move to the suburbs had implications other than a reduction in the Corporation's revenues. Most of you are probably familiar with the distressing characteristics of the city by the time of Gilbert's death in 1898, which were discussed in a lecture by Jacinta Prunty in this series.[2] The former residences of upper and middle class families were subdivided into tenements housing several families and let at high rents to the working classes. Given an acute demand for accommodation, there was little or no incentive for landlords to improve or rebuild their property. Widespread poverty was linked to a weak local economy, where high numbers of unskilled workers depended on casual labour and had a very low rent paying capacity.[3] Slums were in evidence throughout the city, with a high proportion of the population living either in tenements or in tiny cottages in courts and alleys which were hidden behind the main streets. The high proportion of people living in single rooms was a particular problem, with more than 20,000 families living in one-room tenements in 1913, about 78% of all tenement dwellers. This unhealthy overcrowding was

Fig. 2 **Late 19th century postcard of Poole St** (Joe Brady collection)

Fig. 3 **Magenniss's Court, off Townsend Street, 1913** (from the Darkest Dublin collection, Royal Society of Antiquaries of Ireland)

one of the key explanations of high death rates in the city.

The second decade of the twentieth century was a particularly troubled one for the city. The year 1913 saw huge labour unrest, culminating in a lock-out of workers who were members of the Irish Transport and General Workers' Union. The success of Larkin's union was said by many to relate to the impoverished conditions of the workers. In an editorial towards the start of the lock-out, even the generally conservative *Irish Times* acknowledged that: 'If every unskilled labourer in Dublin were the tenant of a decent cottage of three or even two rooms, the city would not be divided into two hostile camps.'[4] A letter to that same newspaper questioned whether the employers could be sure 'that their children would not learn to throw bottles at the police if society had condemned them to the reeking nursery of the tenement house.'[5] The urgency of the housing situation was highlighted with the collapse of two tenement houses in September 1913. Following a huge public outcry, the Local Government Board for Ireland set up a committee to 'Inquire into the Housing Conditions of the Working Classes in the City of Dublin'. The evidence presented illustrated the nature and scale of the problem, as well as previous efforts which had been made to provide working class housing by the local authority and by philanthropic organisations. Conditions in the tenements were quite shocking. Out of a total of 5,322 tenements, over one-fifth had only one toilet (closet) for every twenty to forty people. The report of the inquiry suggested that the housing problem was getting worse.[6]

Table 1: **Key findings of the 1913 Housing Inquiry**

House Classification	Description	Number of People
First Class	'structurally sound'	27,052 persons
Second Class	'decayed or so badly constructed',	37,552 persons
	'approaching the borderline of unfit for habitation'	
Third Class	'unfit for habitation and incapable of being rendered fit'	22,701 persons

Source: *Housing Inquiry* (1914)

In common with other British cities, a number of attempts had been made to deal with Dublin's slum problem on philanthropic lines in the Victorian period. Among the most notable achievements were those of the Dublin Artisans' Dwellings Company (DADC), founded in 1876, and the Guinness (later Iveagh) Trust.[7] The combined efforts of Dublin Corporation and various philanthropic groups and individuals, such as Lord Meath, had provided 5,271 dwellings by 1913, amounting to almost 19% of the city's housing stock. However this was insufficient to meet the city's needs.[8] The inquiry showed that 60,000 people in the city needed to be re-housed, a huge task made all the more difficult by the political turmoil of the time.[9] A further £3.5 million would be required to provide the 14,000 dwellings which were urgently needed to relieve congestion and to close tenements which were unfit for habitation.[10] One of the main questions raised by the inquiry, therefore, was where these 14,000 or so new dwellings were to be built. Overall, the committee of inquiry came out strongly in favour of suburban housing, a view which was supported by a number of influential witnesses to the inquiry.[11]

Some important points were raised at the inquiry by Patrick Geddes, Scottish town planner, ecologist, philosopher and social thinker.[12] He stressed the importance of citizen participation, especially of the poor who were, in his words, 'all too often treated as if they were mere passive creatures to be housed like cattle'. Co-operation between public authorities, private organisations and individuals, with an emphasis on self help, could help to solve the housing problems of the poor. He believed that improvements in living conditions would enable people to help overcome their impoverishment, and he made a particularly strong case for a social mix in housing schemes. The existing practice of segregating two-roomed dwellings from larger dwellings, was 'not only mistaken, wasteful, and costly, but even injurious' and inevitably created future slums. Economically and morally, it was important to combine as many types and scales of dwelling as practicable in each scheme and neighbourhood. As we shall see, these ideas were relevant to the solutions adopted in the 1920s and 1930s.

Of course, the obvious question to ask is, if the situation was demonstrably so terrible, why was nothing done? The answers lie beyond the scope of this particular talk, but relate to a lack of political will, limited financial resources and bad timing. The report of the inquiry was published in 1914, when the Great War pushed local concerns temporarily off the agenda. Despite the evident horrors of the Dublin slums, the Government in Westminster refused to provide the preferential interest rates which would have enabled local authorities to build working-class housing in Irish urban areas. It has been suggested that this reluctance to intervene related more to conditions in England than to problems in Ireland. If the Government provided funds to remedy the problems of the Dublin slums, surely other city authorities would demand similar treatment for their own poverty-stricken populations.[13] A series of increasingly desperate pleas to the Government was ignored. Even the Chief Secretary for Ireland and President of the Local Government Board acknowledged the severity of the problems: 'There can be no mistake that the state of things which now exists is horrible and intolerable'.[14] Eventually the Chancellor of the Exchequer provided a small amount of money in April 1917 for some emergency schemes.[15]

Rather than being the start of a new assault on the slums, then, the Housing Inquiry simply provided a marker which illustrated the continuing deterioration of conditions following the outbreak of the First World War. The number of working-class dwellings required to meet the housing emergency was continually increasing, as in-migration compounded the city's problems. One thousand tenements were closed between 1914 and 1919, but this did not necessarily imply an improvement in living conditions. Of the 4,150 families displaced by these closures, 3,563 had, in the words of Lambert McKenna, 'gone to intensify the congestion of the still standing 6,735 tenement houses, or have been packed into small single houses throughout the city'.[16] Something clearly had to be done.

The 1919 Housing (Ireland) Act was the vehicle intended to tackle the nationwide post-war housing shortage and included extensive new powers and responsibilities.[17] However, due to the difficult political situation, only 800 houses had been built in the country under the act by 1921. This was partly due to a stand-off between the official Local Government Board for Ireland which was responsible for housing matters and an increasingly powerful 'Local Government Department' which had been established by the underground Dáil Éireann in 1920 and which was competing with the existing Local Government Board for the allegiance of the Irish local authorities. It is not surprising, given such circumstances, that there had been a complete hiatus in Dublin Corporation building between 1918 and 1921, and just 162 houses were completed between then and 1925.

This, then, is the background to a fascinating chapter in the city's history. A Church of Ireland clergyman, David Henry Hall was instrumental in the foundation in 1920 of a co-operative type organisation, the St. Barnabas Public Utility Society, which not only built working-class housing for the local population but managed to bring together an unlikely combination of people invested with civic spirit to inspire two decades of co-operative house building nationwide.

Assigned to St. Barnabas parish, East Wall, in July 1918, Hall had encountered some of the worst conditions in the city, as reflected in a death rate of 46 per 1,000 within the parish, well above the city average of 18 per 1,000.[18] The parish was in a heavily industrialised zone, surrounded by canals, railways and docks (Map 2, p.10). Overcrowding was severe yet there was also considerable dereliction. Seán O'Casey grew up in this area and it seems that the reality of life in the tenements of this parish was often as grim as his fictionalised accounts. In one case, Hall found 84 children living in a single house on Commons Street, in another, a family of five living in a room just nine feet by six (c. 2.7 metres x 1.8 metres). Faced with extreme poverty and appalling housing conditions, Reverend Hall actively began to search for some way of aiding his parishioners in a practical way.

Hall's decision to tackle the housing problems of the parish could not have come at a worse time. Both building materials and labour were in short supply, building costs had soared and the political situation was unstable. Hall entered into his earliest building activities against the advice of everyone with experience of the difficulties of post-war building, apparently with no prospect of success. Nevertheless, he resolved to do his best to improve the situation.

It is not clear where Hall got the idea of forming a co-operative self-help housing organisation, known as a public utility society. In England, where the movements for housing reform, garden city development and modern town planning were closely intertwined, housing societies were being used to provide housing for members on a co-operative basis. Known both as 'co-partnership tenant societies' and 'public utility societies', they had been involved in developments at Hampstead, Bournville and Letchworth, all heralded as examples of the best in modern town planning. A series of reports in England had noted some of the additional benefits of erecting housing using public utility societies, including enhanced relationships between tenant and owner, the better quality of the housing, and the ability to 'build homes not just houses'.[19] Similar self-help housing movements also existed in most European countries. The idea that public utility societies might be used to help Dublin's housing problems had been floated at least as early as 1914, although the first legislation to specifically mention such societies in an Irish context was not passed until 1919.[20] This empowered local authorities to promote and assist any public utility society which aimed to provide working-class housing.

So, enough of the background. We know that in August 1919 Hall attended a meeting at which speakers promoted the concept of forming utility societies to build working people's cottages. From then on, Hall never ceased in researching the issue and working to get land on which to build. Eventually he acquired a site of about three-and-a-half acres (c. 1.4 hectares) for £700 freehold. By December 1919 he had called a parish meeting at

Fig. 4
David Henry Hall, (1873–1940)
(from Arthur Garrett, *In ages past, the story of North Strand Church Sunday and day schools*, Dublin, 1985, p.33)

which an architect from the Local Government Board explained the construction of houses 'suitable for working people' and Hall himself explained what he had learned about the working of a public utility society. On foot of this meeting it was decided to form the St. Barnabas Public Utility Society which was formally registered as a Friendly Society on 9 January 1920, with Hall as Honorary Secretary. Eight people were listed as members of the committee of management, five of whom later became residents of the new scheme.[21] According to Hall, 'the whole scheme was initiated and carried on as a piece of pure citizenship'.[22] The initial aim was to build a garden suburb of 40 semi-detached houses, with a portion of ground to each house. The organisation was affiliated to the Garden Cities and Town Planning Association in London, which is significant in terms of the desire to produce a model 'garden suburb'. A prospectus was issued, with £9,000 loan stock at 5% and 1,000 shares of £1 each.

This, the first such society in Ireland, was intended to improve living conditions in the area, so as to 'render happy the lives of many who were existing under conditions too awful to be described'.[23] There was no financial motivation, rather it 'was meant to be a Christian endeavour to meet and correct some of the appalling housing conditions of Dublin'.[24]

Through a combination of loan stock and issuing shares, Hall raised 25% of the cost of the first scheme, with the remainder to be loaned by the Government. The ten initial houses would cost £10,700 to build, which is an indication of the high costs of building at this time. An experimental method of walling which required very little skilled labour was used, proving 'most expeditious'. Local Fairview firm J. & R. Thompson was contracted to build the houses. It is undoubtedly indicative of Hall's character that Thompson was persuaded to undertake the job in the first place. When Thompson asked Hall what money he had, the latter replied 'none', but explained that the Government would provide a loan for 75% of the capital if the society raised 25% first. Demonstrating great faith in Hall's fund-raising abilities, Thompson agreed to make a start when Hall had raised the first £1,000. Raising the money was not an easy task, but Hall was a determined individual and went canvassing, preaching charity sermons and appealing through the press in order to raise the initial £1,000.[25] In the first week, Hall called on over 300 people and he eventually got the first £1,000 at a time when insurrection was likely. Looking back, Hall later described how 'sixty-seven gallant ladies invested in the scheme, when even the Rotary Club failed to support it!'[26]

The first ten houses had characteristics of the early 'garden suburbs', including a low density cul-de-sac layout. Each house had three bedrooms and an indoor bathroom, as well as a garden. A recreation ground for children was also planned. Another ground-breaking feature was the experimental design, to plans by Messrs Batchelor & Hicks, which were 'selected by the women'. Each house had been 'so economically planned, under the supervision of the wives, that the woman can work the house conveniently'.[27] There were six houses which had five rooms, at a rental of £65 per annum each, and four four-roomed houses, at an annual rental of £58 10s. Tenants paid the rent on a weekly basis,

part of which went toward the purchase of their homes. That portion was invested in gilt-edged securities and thus yielded a return which was also placed to the benefit of the purchasers. The society aimed to enable members of the working class to purchase a comfortable home of their own over a twenty year period, through a combination of tenant purchase and shares in the society. For every pound which was subscribed, the tenant received a £1 share in the society. For each year's occupation the capital value of each share owned by the tenant increased by £1, so that if a tenant put in five shares and left after ten years, the society would purchase the shares for £50, besides having paid the tenant a dividend of 5% yearly on the shares. Many of the tenants invested what savings they had in the loan stock, while some paid in weekly instalments along with their rent, so that they were steadily increasing their capital in their own homes.

This purchase scheme was novel in an Irish context, although similar mechanisms had operated in Britain. By a gradual process, ownership was transferred from non-tenant shareholders who took the main risk initially, to the tenant shareholder who would hopefully become the ultimate owner. Hall believed in making every person pay for their house, but succeeded in devising a means of making it possible for payment to be made gradually, so that eventually the tenant would become full owner of the house. He felt that 'deep in man's nature there is ingrained a contempt for that which can be secured without labour. That which a man gains by the strength of his own right hand is more prized by him than all the philanthropic sops that a generous public has in its gift'.[28]

Providing for the needy was an important concern, but equally important was the promotion of the public utility concept to others. Therefore, the society issued an open invitation to 'all interested in Dublin housing' to inspect the building scheme. Attendees at the opening ceremony in June 1921 included the local Roman Catholic parish priest, P.C. Cowan and staff of the Local Government Board Housing Committee, representatives of local employers and various other dignitaries. This coming together of so many varied interests prompted the *Church of Ireland Gazette* to observe that 'it was a happy feature that a Church of Ireland rector should have assisted his men to gather such a number of the important elements of Irish life together in such happy harmony'.[29] The Lord Mayor, Laurence O'Neill, echoed this view, saying that it was particularly pleasant 'to find ladies and gentlemen of different degrees and forms of thought and religion gathered together with the one common object of benefiting their fellow citizens', expressing the hope that this scheme would be 'a beacon of light, the influence of which would spread throughout their beloved land'.[30] In laying the name-stone of the society, the Lord Mayor specifically thanked Hall 'for the splendid patriotic services he had rendered to the locality, and indeed, by his example, for the whole city', as the housing of the working classes was a subject that must concern everyone.

The first ten houses at St. Barnabas Gardens were occupied from December 1921 and the society began to obtain revenue from the rents. This enabled the society to pay its first dividend in May 1922. A second phase of twenty-six houses was planned for a two and a half acre (c. 1 hectare) site but was again dependent on raising investment through 6% loan stock. With this money, with many donations and with support from Dublin Corporation, which installed the necessary water mains free of charge and made a grant equivalent to the rates on the first 36 houses for a ten year period, these houses were built from March 1922 to April 1923 at a cost of £20,421. Rents for the houses started at 25 shillings per week, so only skilled artisans were really in a position to pay them. However, the cost per house was being continually reduced as building costs were falling with a stabilisation in political conditions and greater availability of materials. The builders hoped to reduce the cost per

house to £700, so that it would be nearer the 'economic level of rent' at £1 weekly. Initially these new roads were named Utility Road and Utility Gardens (now Strangford Road and Strangford Gardens). By the 1924 AGM, Hall could report that the society was well on its feet, and expected to pay back £1,000 capital yearly until the 36 houses were completely bought out in 21 years' time.[31]

Fig. 6
Utility Gardens
(now Strangford
Gardens)
(photo by Ruth
McManus)

The building scheme also provided much-needed local employment for building workers, a fact which boosted the whole community and gained support from many varied sources. A favourite anecdote of Hall's indicates the level of goodwill which surrounded his scheme. When the chimney of the first house was completed, the workers put up a red flag, as was customary, to indicate their desire for refreshment. Tradition held that money should be given to the workmen for a 'treat'. Most reluctantly, dreading the possibility of a strike, Hall handed a small sum of money to the foreman. However, the workers had asked the foreman to tell him 'that they recognised our hard effort in raising money, that they were grateful for the work while so many were idle, and they would take no money, but only asked for more work!'[32] Hall was generous in his praise for the workmen both for their co-operative spirit and their attempts to work faster.

Hall seems to have been the sort of person who could get the best out of anyone. He secured the goodwill of a huge number of persons and bodies, including the Builder's Federation, the Ministry, Dublin Corporation, the operatives in the building trade, 'to an extent which shows how much the disinterested service of one's fellow-men appeals to all sorts and conditions of men'.[33] Hall's drive and enthusiasm were such that he succeeded in building houses at a reasonable cost at a time when almost no building operations were taking place.[34] That Hall could galvanise so many different people into action was undoubtedly one of his greatest feats.

Although the St. Barnabas Public Utility Society was associated with the Church of Ireland parish of that name, from the start it was very much an ecumenical undertaking, something which was all the more remarkable given the troubled times in which it operated. All denominations were present among the shareholders and prospective tenants. There was also very real tenant control over the society through a tenant-dominated management committee which managed the houses and approved tenants. Tenants were taken 'as they came', once they had satisfied the requirements of the Tenants Committee. In the first 36 houses, 15 families were Protestant and 21 were Catholic. Most were foremen or skilled workers, given the necessarily high rents of the scheme.

A recreation ground was provided with a hard tennis court, open space and sandpit. Over time, Lady Ardilaun was to present gifts of three tennis courts, a 'pavilion' (a Nissen hut) and a piano for the enjoyment of the tenants. People from as far away as Delgany and Athlone donated plants, including shrubs, thorn hedging and fruit trees, for the gardens. Hall was delighted with the way that these added to the character of the area, and there was an annual competition for the best gardens. Residents too had fond memories of this period and the remarkable community spirit which evolved.[35]

By mid-1924, the St. Barnabas Society had acquired more land and was preparing to build again. The 62 five-roomed houses at Seaview Avenue and Crescent Gardens were described as being for 'better class workmen' and had a bath, hot water and gardens. At £550, they were £40 cheaper than the least expensive of the Dublin Corporation houses which had neither bath nor hot water. At the final St. Barnabas scheme the houses were smaller, with 73 four-roomed houses built. By building smaller houses, the reach of the society was extended to those with lower incomes. Again J. & R. Thompson Ltd. erected the houses, at a cost of £449 each. It is also worth noting that the auditors report in 1926 showed that no rents were in arrears, suggesting that the tenant's own selection process was effective and that the tenants took greater responsibility for their homes than might have been the case in a public housing scheme.

Although the initial output was small, this first public utility society was extremely important in providing an example which others were to follow. The public utility society concept gradually spread across the country, due in no small part to Hall's tireless promotion of the idea, and organisations were founded in both rural and urban areas.[36] While the Civics Institute of Ireland soon took in hand all of the materials relating to the formation of public utility societies, it was to Hall that people tended to turn for practical guidance. He was involved in a direct and advisory capacity with the establishment of many of the early societies, including the Linenhall Public Utility Society and Dublin Commercial Public Utility Society. Through his encouragement, the Church Representative Body took loan stock in a number of societies. In 1932 Hall joined with the Roman Catholic parish priest of Finglas in the formation of St. Canice's Public Utility Society.

The second active society in Dublin was also promoted by a person driven by an almost missionary zeal for housing and planning reform. E.A. Aston was involved in the Greater Dublin Reconstruction Movement, the Dublin Citizens' Association and the Housing and Town Planning Association of Ireland. At the 1913 Housing Inquiry he had called for the development of 'plantations for city workers in convenient rural areas'.[37] These ideas were put into practice when the Killester Public Utility Society was registered in June 1921 with the aim of carrying out 'co-operative building and management of suburban housing upon modern "garden suburb" principles'.[38] It built houses at Vernon Avenue and Castle Avenue. The society's solicitor was J. Vincent Brady, another staunch supporter of housing reform, author of *The future of Dublin – practical slum reform* (1917), and witness at the Housing Inquiry in 1913.

It was really from the mid-1920s that the concept of the public utility society became prominent, with the return of more settled political conditions and the introduction of new legislation. Fixed sum grants and rates' remissions were introduced for all housing which conformed to certain specifications. Under the 1925 Housing Act, public utility societies were given grants of £60, £80 and £100 respectively for three-, four- and five-roomed houses. This 1925 Housing Act was a milestone in that it enabled the provision of State grants to public utility societies at the same rate as grants to local authorities. In other words, for every house built by a public utility society, that organisation would receive the same level of grant aid as a local authority. This was a deliberate policy to encourage people to join such societies, which it was believed would be 'of great assistance in house production' and indeed, the attractive measures stimulated the formation of a large number of societies.[39]

A further important impact of the 1925 Housing Act was that it enabled local authorities to work in closer co-operation with the public utility societies, by giving the former a role in land provision and site preparation for public utility societies. Most of the activity at this time was in the Dublin region. In March 1929, of the 961 houses completed by public utility societies in the Irish Free State to date, some 631 were in Dublin County Borough, and almost 86% in a Greater Dublin area which included the neighbouring urban districts.[40] This focus on Dublin was largely due to the favourable approach taken by Dublin Corporation, which clearly recognised the value of these organisations. The Corporation gave additional loans and a remission of rates on a sliding scale over a nineteen year period, as well as making serviced sites available to societies. From 1922 to 1927, public utility societies built 9% of all the housing erected in Dublin.

At a State level, the continuing favourable terms afforded to public utility societies throughout the 1920s and 1930s suggest that the Government was anxious to encourage what was sometimes termed 'assisted private enterprise'.[41] A circular from 1932 went further in explaining why this was the case, with reasoning reminiscent of that which Geddes had used to the Housing Inquiry almost 20 years previously: 'it is felt that it is only by the co-operation of all sections of the community that the conditions under which so many of the inhabitants of our cities and towns live can be effectively remedied'.[42] In a second spurt of activity following the 1932 Housing Act, fifty-two new public utility societies were approved nationally in a twelve month period, so that by the end of 1933, there were 125 registered societies in Ireland, making a significant contribution to the housing stock.

As I have already suggested, one of the most significant features of the public utility societies in Dublin is their close relationship with the Corporation. This had already begun at the St. Barnabas schemes, where the Corporation provided rates' remissions and installed the water mains free of charge. From the mid-1920s, most public utility societies were building on land developed by, and leased from, Dublin Corporation. Indeed, the approval of this semi-private form of construction went so far that when the Cabra (Annamoe Road) Compulsory Purchase Order was being made, the inspector suggested that the Corporation should consider developing the site 'and leasing it to private persons and Public Utility Societies for the erection of a better type of house than the Corporation would themselves build'.[43]

We have already seen that the housing activities of Dublin Corporation had been hampered for a long time by lack of funding. This desire to build a 'better type of house' mentioned above was a persistent one during the 1920s. The first major scheme under the new Free State regime, the Marino Garden Suburb, was intended as 'a model one', but again the Housing Committee was checked by financial constraints. As a result, the committee decided to let the main frontages of the scheme to private builders, whose plans would be subject to Corporation approval. This was seen as a means of providing the desired 'superior class of dwelling' within existing financial constraints.[44] From March

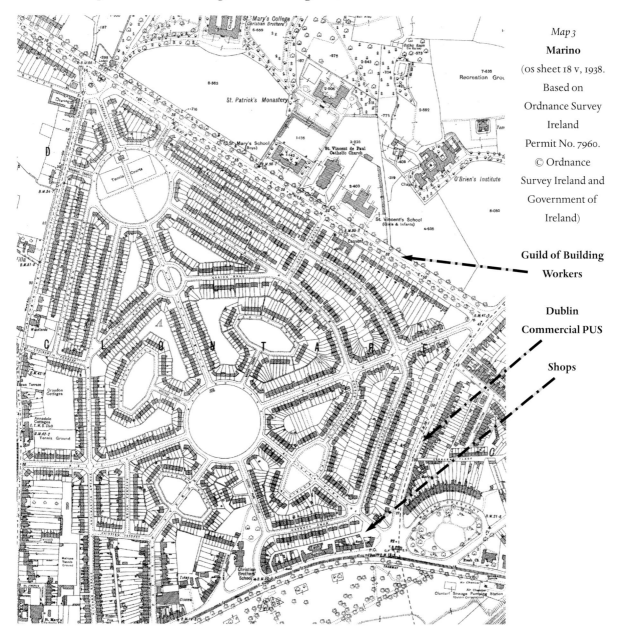

Map 3
Marino
(os sheet 18 v, 1938.
Based on
Ordnance Survey
Ireland
Permit No. 7960.
© Ordnance
Survey Ireland and
Government of
Ireland)

Guild of Building Workers

Dublin Commercial PUS

Shops

Fig. 7

DCPUS houses, Marino, Malahide Road frontage

(photo by Ruth McManus)

Fig. 8

Daly's shop, Marino frontage at Fairview

(photo courtesy of G. & T. Crampton Ltd)

1925, then, leases were granted for residential shops facing Fairview Strand. Each site was developed by the owner in accordance with the City Architect's designs.[45] The policy of reserving serviced sites on Corporation schemes for development by others was to become an important strategy for the next decades, facilitating the growth of the public utility society movement.

The first body to lease sites at Marino for house building was the Dublin Commercial Public Utility Society, which planned to build twelve houses at the Malahide Road, at an average cost of £750 each.[46] As these houses were to be built in accordance with the provisions of the Housing (Building Facilities) Acts, the society would receive a Government grant of £100 per house, with a further £100 from Dublin Corporation. The first year's ground rent payable under these leases was also remitted. It is again clear that the scheme was very much a co-operative venture. The society's 1926 annual report noted the 'valuable help and assistance' of Senator Farren, Reverend Hall, the Town Clerk, the Dublin Commissioners, the Corporation Housing Department, the Local Government Board Housing Department and the Central Housing Council of the Civics Institute.[47]

The first two leases along the north-eastern boundary of Marino, at Griffith Avenue, were granted in 1927 to the Guild of Building Workers (Dublin and District) Ltd. The guild was also a public utility society, which had been registered urgently at the behest of the same Senator Farren who had assisted the Dublin Commercial Public Utility Society. Its ten members were all delegates from trade unions and the guild had been established to

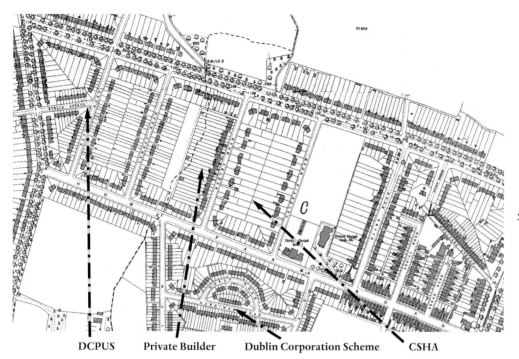

DCPUS   Private Builder   Dublin Corporation Scheme   CSHA

Map 4
**Reserved areas,
Drumcondra**
(os sheets 14 xv,
and 18 iii, 1938.
Based on
Ordnance Survey
Ireland
Permit No. 7960.
© Ordnance
Survey Ireland and
Government of
Ireland)

Fig. 9
**Below: Dublin
Corporation
houses,
Drumcondra
scheme**
(photo courtesy of
G. & T. Crampton
Ltd)

undertake 'building and construction other than for the society's own requirements', employing an average of fifty-eight people. In practice, this included the construction of housing for other utility societies, such as twelve brick houses 'of a superior type' for the Dublin Commercial Public Utility Society.[48] It would seem, then, that the guild took the co-operative principle a step further, by enabling the co-operative housing societies to contract their construction work to a co-operative builder.

Dublin Corporation was clearly pleased with the success of the 'reserved areas' idea at Marino, and initiated a similar process for the Drumcondra housing area in 1928, with a more extensive area of land. In the privately developed section of the Drumcondra Scheme, builders could take advantage of State and municipal grants, while all roads and underground services were constructed by the Corporation free of expense to the lessees.[49] This provided a considerable incentive to build on these sites, with easy sale practically guaranteed thanks to the availability of cheap mortgages under the Small Dwellings Acquisition Acts.

Fig. 10 & 11

Comparing the Civil Service Housing Association houses (top), with houses built by private speculative builder Louis Kinlen on Bantry Road

(photos by Ruth McManus)

One might ask whether there was any material difference between the kind of housing being built by private speculators and that offered by public utility societies, since both operated in 'reserved areas'. The first plots leased at Drumcondra were leased to the Civil Service Housing Association and to a private developer, Louis Kinlen. In both cases the lessees intended that the houses provided by them would come within the terms of the Housing Acts, 1925-26, so that they would qualify for State and municipal grants. Further leases were granted to the Dublin Commercial Public Utility Society and to the Saorstát Civil Service Public Utility Society. So, all of these houses had to conform to similar requirements, in order to qualify for the grants. Yet, if we look at the layout and style of the houses, it is immediately apparent that there were differences in the approach adopted by the public utility societies and by the private speculator. Whereas the Kinlen houses are to a rather non-descript design and appear almost squashed into the available site, the utility society has clearly employed an architect and provided a much more spacious layout. This focus on design, quality of materials and workmanship had been seen as a hallmark of the public utility societies which had been operating in Britain. Indeed, one report observed that such societies had 'provided cottages and small houses considerably in advance of the hitherto accepted standard for the class of property, not only as regards quality of construction, but in a still more marked degree in the quality of the design'.[50]

Certainly, the Dublin-based public utility societies employed some of the best-known architectural firms to design their houses. The Dublin Commercial Public Utility Society houses at Mobhi Road were built to plans prepared by Messrs McDonnell, Dixon and Downes. The Civil Service Housing Association dwellings at Whitehall were to plans by Rupert Jones who also designed expensive private houses in Mount Merrion. These five-roomed concrete houses built at Whitehall cost £660 each.

Returning to Drumcondra, the Saorstát Civil Service Public Utility Society was active in house-building on Clare Road to designs by Messrs Hargreave & Horner, MRIAI, of Grosvenor Square, Rathmines. The nineteen houses were built to high specifications. Each house had both drawing and dining rooms, hall (with verandah), kitchen, three bedrooms, water closet and bath, as well as a garage. Such specifications were a world away from even the best of the Corporation's 'parlour' houses. By 1932 the society had ninety-seven tenants and had also undertaken building schemes at Beaumount and Milltown.

Thanks to the co-operation of Dublin Corporation, public utility societies could

Fig. 12

Civil Service Housing Association housing on Home Farm Road.

(photo courtesy of G. & T. Crampton Ltd)

benefit from the reduced costs of serviced sites either by spending the money saved on higher quality houses, or by charging less for its houses than the speculative builder operating on non-serviced sites. Thus, public utility society houses often proved to be a better value alternative to 'private' houses, and could remain competitive in the housing market. In many cases they did not actively assist the poorest members of the working classes, but they did extend the possibility of home ownership to workers who might otherwise not have been able to purchase their own homes. This was often done through a tenant purchase scheme (as had been the case at the St. Barnabas houses). The Dublin Commissioners recognised that the societies were serving a useful role in providing houses for people with small capital and tried to facilitate them by making the maximum advances prescribed by the Small Dwellings Acquisition Acts,[51] a form of local authority-assisted mortgage lending for people of limited means.

That there was a need for such housing was evident. The Dublin Commercial Public Utility Society management committee report for 1928 noted with some satisfaction that there were a large number of applications for the society's houses, because 'the society is appealing in a remarkable way to many hundreds of people who desire to take the initial step towards home ownership'.[52] When two contracts totaling 184 houses were completed at Drumcondra and Malahide Road, 'over a hundred surplus applications were received'.

Generally the societies did not build the houses themselves, but contracted builders to erect houses which were then sold or rented. The builders of public utility society schemes were generally well-respected companies such as G. & T. Crampton Ltd., one of Dublin's top building companies, again highlighting the quality of such undertakings. The boost which these contracts provided to the building trade was also important. For example, the

The Dublin Commercial Public Utility Society contracts in 1928 provided employment for over 800 men for more than a year 'during a period when increased employment in the building trade was badly needed'.[53]

Quite a few societies catered for civil servants, a tendency which can be traced to the fact that the grants offered by the State gave preferential treatment to civil servants, who were entitled to build larger houses than everyone else while still qualifying for housing grants.[54] A range of occupations was represented among the tenants of other public utility schemes. For example, the occupants of houses in Parnell Road and Arbutus Avenue which had been built by the Harold's Cross Public Utility Society included a merchant, brewery official and tailor. Some public utility societies were established to assist a particular interest group, such as the Dublin Municipal Public Utility Society, which was controlled by the Irish Local Government Officials' Union, or the self-explanatory Tram and Omnibus Workers' Public Utility Society. Some employers found that assisting in the development of public utility societies was a way of ensuring adequate housing for their workers. Thus, the Linenhall Public Utility Society received support from two local firms, Messrs J. Jameson & Sons and Messrs Maguire & Patterson Ltd. Among those taking loan stock in the Rathmines Public Utility Society were Messrs W. & R. Jacob & Co and Messrs Robert Roberts & Co.[55]

A degree of philanthropy was evident in at least some of the public utility societies operating in the 1920s and 1930s, such as the Holy Child Housing Society which built ten flats at Temple Lane/Hill Street. Even where public utility societies catered for a better class of worker, it could be argued that their work brought more general benefits, by allowing the local authority to focus on housing the most needy.

As the city boundary was extended after 1930, Dublin Corporation availed of new suburban lands for building purposes and it continued to apply the 'reserved areas' model. For example, the Corporation developed an eleven acre (c.4.5 hectares) site at Kimmage under a Relief Grant in the early 1930s, and then specifically invited offers from public utility societies to build houses for sale in this area, known as Larkfield. The tenders accepted were from the Building Operatives Public Utility Society, the Post Office Public Utility Society and the Dublin Commercial Public Utility Society.[56] The area centres on Larkfield Avenue.

From 1932 there was a shift in Government housing policy. A new Housing Act changed the circumstances under which public utility societies operated, with a special provision[57] encouraging the societies to provide housing for letting in urban areas. The Dublin Commercial Public Utility Society was the first society to produce houses for rent under the 1932 Act. The foundation stone of its seventh scheme was laid by Seán T. O'Kelly in June 1932. This was the first to include a combination of housing for rental and housing for purchase, divided between the Mobhi Road/Griffith Avenue frontages and Stella Avenue and Rathlin Road. The contrast between the two house types is noticeable, with the houses built for rental being smaller and less attractive than the houses built by the same organisation for sale. Nevertheless, the committee of the society considered the rents to be 'very low' at 17s. 6d., 16s. 6d. and 16s. per week. Each house had five rooms and a kitchenette, gardens front and rear, and 'every modern convenience'.[58] More than 500

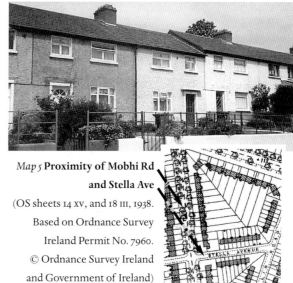

Fig. 13 & 14
**Above: DCPUS houses on Mobhi Road, for sale, and on
Stella Avenue (right) for rental** (photos by Ruth McManus)

Map 5 **Proximity of Mobhi Rd
and Stella Ave**
(OS sheets 14 xv, and 18 iii, 1938.
Based on Ordnance Survey
Ireland Permit No. 7960.
© Ordnance Survey Ireland
and Government of Ireland)

applications were received for the houses, showing that there was a definite need for quality rented accommodation in the city.

The flexibility of the public utility society concept meant that it provided a perfect vehicle for activity by quite contrasting social groups: dreamers, planners, philanthropists, employers, trade unionists, politicians and clergymen. Many women found a role in the organisation of public utility societies. Several early societies followed Hall's ecumenical example, such as the previously-mentioned St. Canice's Public Utility Society in Finglas, and the Carlow Public Utility Society.

One of the public utility societies to cater for a special interest groups was the Nua Ghaedhltacht Átha Cliath Teo., formed by a group of Irish-language speakers in 1924. The objects were 'to establish and maintain a community of Irish speakers', with eligibility for membership based on either being a native speaker of the Irish language or having passed the first exam for the Fáinne. However, difficulties arose in carrying out the scheme in accordance with the terms of the lease once the first ten houses had been built.[59] As a result, Dublin Corporation stepped in and developed the remainder of the land (29 acres, c. 11.7 hectares) which it owned in the area for housing purposes. The developed sites were leased from 1930, mostly to other public utility societies, including the Civil Service Housing Association, Saorstát Civil Service Public Utility Society, State Servants Public Utility Society, St. Mobhi Public Utility Society and Post Office Public Utility Society, however the name 'Gaeltacht Park' survived.[60]

The development at Gaeltacht Park illustrates the mutually-beneficial relationship between Dublin Corporation and the public utility societies. To the Corporation, the role of land developer rather than builder was attractive. It provided a means of rapidly developing the City Estate at little cost to itself, while reducing the housing shortage and boosting the city coffers with a steady income from ground rents. The leasehold system of development, as at the 'reserved sites', gave the Corporation a degree of control over the type of houses being built. Thus, for example, the local authority could specify the use of slate roofs at Gaeltacht Park, a preference which, due to costs, it was unable to insist upon in its own schemes.

One of the highlights of the public utility society movement in the eyes of observers was the opportunities it provided for 'public spirited investment'.[61] Cowan had strongly promoted co-partnership in an address given in 1916, claiming that 'the system happily combines the benefits of wholesale dealing and management with elements which foster self-reliance and secure the active co-operation of the tenants in maintaining their houses and their surroundings in good order. Some of its cardinal merits are ... that it encourages and develops manly conduct and good citizenship'[62] (!)

Not all of the schemes that I have mentioned lived up to these ideals, of course, but the potential was there. The St. Barnabas scheme certainly was formed along the lines promoted by one author, who stated that 'the whole motive of forming and carrying on these societies has been the idea of social service and the stimulation of co-operative endeavour. Its advocates claim that ... it provides an opportunity for securing not only houses but homes'.[63] One society which closely followed Hall's model was the Linenhall Public Utility Society which built 63 four- and five-roomed houses at the site of the former Linenhall Barracks.[64] These houses, in miniature garden suburb layout complete with cul-de-sac, contrast sharply with the neighbouring 'bylaw style' Corporation-built housing. This particular society had much in common with Hall's St. Barnabas Public

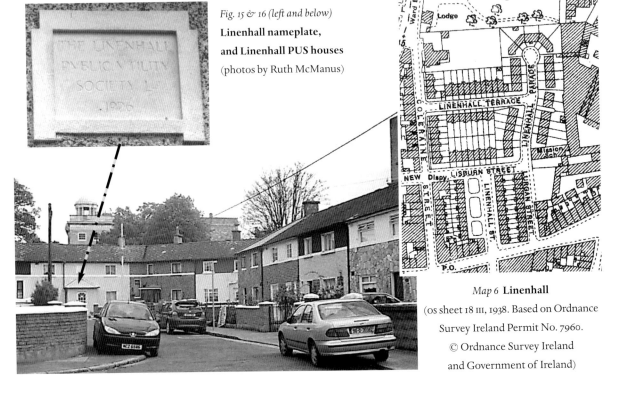

Fig. 15 & 16 (left and below)
Linenhall nameplate,
and Linenhall PUS houses
(photos by Ruth McManus)

Map 6 **Linenhall**
(os sheet 18 III, 1938. Based on Ordnance
Survey Ireland Permit No. 7960.
© Ordnance Survey Ireland
and Government of Ireland)

Utility Society. It was also founded following a meeting of parishioners in January 1926, and operated along similar lines.[65]

The Charlemont Public Utility Society stands out as one of the societies which reflected Hall's vision and which responded to the deteriorating slum problems of the 1930s. Bringing together feminists, public servants, trade unionists, academics and doctors, the society's members comprised a virtual 'who's who' of Dublin philanthropy – people of divergent backgrounds who were united by a common desire to do something 'in a personal way' to tackle Dublin's slum problem. They included Dr Collis (later celebrated for his work following the liberation of Belsen) and Helena Molony (a well-known activist for women's suffrage, revolutionary and trade unionist). The society was not just focused on bricks and mortar, but aimed to work on the social problems bound up with the actual housing problem. The initial building of what was to later become known as ffrench-Mullen flats consisted of 37 flats, including a range of sizes from two to four rooms. Each flat had its own bath and kitchenette, while there were washing and drying rooms, garages for perambulators and an ample, safe playground for children. Others attempting to tackle the worst of the slums included the Family Housing Association and the Old Belvedere Housing Society, both of which reconditioned existing tenements in the 1930s.

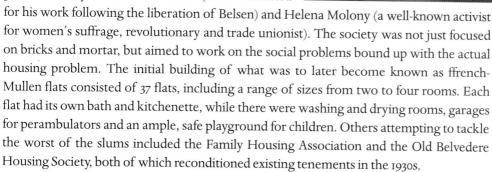

Fig. 17
Charlemont PUS flats
(photo by Ruth McManus)

The scale of building by individual public utility societies may appear relatively small, but in the context of the time their impact was much larger than the modern observer would expect. In the year ended 1929, the Dublin Commercial Public Utility Society could report that it had provided 212 new houses since May 1926, a total which made the society the largest house-building organisation in the Free State, with the exception of Dublin Corporation. In the five years from 1933 to 1938, fifteen public utility societies operated in Dublin, building a total of 1,878 houses.[66] The majority of their developments were on the edges of Dublin Corporation's housing areas, on sites which had been serviced as part of the local authority schemes but which had been reserved for better quality housing. Like their 1920s counterparts, the 1930s public utility societies benefited from the Corporation's housing schemes and were closely linked to them. Indeed, the success of public utility societies was reliant on various different forms of co-operation, involving the Dublin Corporation; individual members, tenants and investors; builders and architects; the State and associated bodies including the Local Government Board and the Department of Local Government.

Fig. 18
David Henry Hall
(from *The Irish Times*, Dublin, 28 February 1940, p.11, courtesy of *The Irish Times*)

What can we learn from the past? This evening I have tried to focus on some of the positive developments of the 1920s and 1930s, when efforts were made to improve living conditions and increase home ownership in innovative ways, with individuals from across the religious divide working together, contributing to shaping our city by building new, quality housing and providing much needed employment. The history of the public utility society movement in Ireland is largely unwritten, yet much could be learned from such organisations at this time of renewed interest in public-private partnerships and alternative forms of housing tenure. Perhaps we can take our cue from Canon Hall and his perseverance, remembering that with the right motivation and sense of citizenship, we can achieve what seems to be impossible. He made a meaningful contribution to the housing situation in Dublin, not least by showing that ordinary people could become involved and could make a real difference. Drive, determination, citizenship and goodwill could achieve much, even where only a handful of individuals were involved. Let us take heart and use these lessons in making new resolutions about solving the city's problems today.

Acknowledgements

Special thanks to G. & T. Crampton Ltd for permission to reproduce the photographs which appear here as figures 8,9,and 12, and to Ordnance Survey Ireland for permission to use maps 2 to 6, (Ordnance Survey Ireland Permit No. 7960).

I would like to acknowledge the continued support of Dr. Joe Brady, Geography Department, UCD, who supervised the Ph.D. research which forms the basis of this lecture. I would also like to thank Professor Anngret Simms for her encouragement and advice over many years, and Professor Philip J. Ethington for his comments on an early draft of this lecture. Without the excellent research facilities and supportive staff of the Dublin City Library and Archives Services, the research presented here could not have been undertaken. Special thanks to Dr Mary Clark, City Archivist, and to Dr Máire Kennedy, Special Collections. This work draws on research at the National Archives in Kew, made possible by funding from the Research Committee of St. Patrick's College, Drumcondra.

Notes

1 The nature of the suburban townships is explored in some detail by Séamas Ó Maitiú, *Dublin's suburban towns, 1834–1930* (Dublin, 2003). A discussion of aspects of Dublin life in the nineteenth and early twentieth centuries can be found in Joseph Brady and Anngret Simms (eds) *Dublin through space and time* (Dublin, 2001).

2 Jacinta Prunty, *Managing the Dublin slums, 1850–1922* (Dublin, 2004). Considerable research on the city's problems during this period has been undertaken by, among others, Jacinta Prunty, *Dublin slums 1800–1925, a study in urban geography* (Dublin, 1998), Mary Daly, *Dublin: the deposed capital, a social and economic history 1860–1914* (Cork, 1984), J.V. O'Brien, *Dear dirty Dublin, a city in distress, 1899–1916* (Berkeley, 1982). Kevin C. Kearns provides a very readable account of life in the tenements in his book *Dublin tenement life: an oral history* (Dublin, 1994).

3 'The wages of unskilled labourers are rarely more than £1 per week; many earn only from 15s. to 18s. weekly. Even when the labourer is a sober man, and has a small family, he cannot enjoy much comfort on the higher rate of wages. When he is of the inferior order, has a large family, and precarious employment, it is easy to imagine his deplorable condition', Sir Charles A. Cameron, *Reminiscences* (Dublin, 1913), p. 166.

4 Editorial, *Irish Times*, 4 September 1913, p. 6.

5 E.A. Aston, letter to the *Irish Times*, 3 September 1913.

6 *Report of the Departmental Committee appointed by the Local Government Board for Ireland to inquire into the housing conditions of the working classes in the city of Dublin* [Cd 7273], H.C. 1914, xix.

7 The Dublin Artisans' Dwellings Company provided about 3,300 working-class dwellings in the period prior to 1913, which was more than twice what Dublin Corporation had achieved during the same period. The work of the Guinness Trust, the only major housing trust to operate in Dublin, is described in detail by F.H.A. Aalen in *The Iveagh Trust, the first hundred years, 1890–1990* (Dublin, 1990). This general area is explored further by Aalen in two papers, 'Approaches to the working class housing problem in late-Victorian Dublin: the Dublin Artisans' Dwellings Company and the Guinness Trust' in R.J. Bender (ed.) *New research on the social geography of Ireland, Mannheimer Geographische Arbeiten*, 17 (Mannheim, 1984), pp 161–90, and 'The working-class housing movement in Dublin, 1850–1920' in M.J. Bannon (ed.), *The emergence of Irish planning 1880–1920* (Dublin, 1985), pp 131–88.

8 Although the Dublin Corporation Public Health Committee claimed that the Corporation had 'done our best according to our means' (*Reports and printed documents of the Corporation of Dublin*, 1914, no. 120, p. 177), in the thirty years

since the first local authority housing scheme in Dublin, a total of 1,385 families had been re-housed in twelve schemes.

9 Simply closing the unfit dwellings would, on its own, have led to further overcrowding, because there was nowhere else for the people to go (*Report of inquiry*, 1914, 2, pp 18–25).

10 Even with extensive renovation of existing tenements, a minimum of 13,958 new dwellings was required.

11 These included the City Architect, Charles MacCarthy and the Dublin Citizens' Association which stated that its ideal was the (self-contained) 'suburban house for the working man' (*Report of inquiry*, 1914, p. 160, para. 4200).

12 Geddes gave evidence to the inquiry on behalf of the Women's National Health Association, an organisation committed to the eradication of tuberculosis and other diseases.

13 This point is explored by F.H.A. Aalen in 'Public housing in Ireland, 1880–1921', *Planning Perspectives*, 2, (1987), pp 175–9. Such special rates applied to agricultural cottages because Ireland's rural housing problem was held to be unique, whereas it was claimed that similar concessions would be sought by other cities in the United Kingdom. Ironically, then, by 1914 Ireland's rural labourers were among the best housed of their class in Western Europe, while there had been almost no improvement in the plight of the urban slum dwellers. As late as 1921, it was reported that 48,000 cottages had been provided in rural Ireland since 1883, with a total expenditure of £8.5 million, whereas under the Urban Housing Acts only £2.5 million pounds had been spent and just 10,000 houses built (*Irish Builder*, 1921, p. 325).

14 Quoted in *Reports and printed documents of the Corporation of Dublin*, 1916, 35, p. 349.

15 It provided for Spitalfields (1st section), McCaffrey Estate, St. James's Walk, Fairbrother's Fields and Crabbe Lane.

16 Lambert McKenna, 'The housing problem in Dublin', *Studies*, 8 (1919), p. 283.

17 This 1919 legislation marked a change of attitude from the mid-nineteenth century *laissez-faire* approach, because for the first time, the responsibility to provide adequate housing was placed squarely on the shoulders of the local authorities, who now had a duty to prepare schemes for provision of housing to be carried out within a specified time limit. The Local Government Board would provide an annual subsidy.

18 The current death rate in Ireland is just 8 per 1,000, based on 2003 figures from the Central Statistics Office.

19 National Archives, Kew: RECO 1/580: Memorandum on Public Utility Societies by Ewart G. Culpin, 15/10/17. See also Keith K. Skilleter, 'The role of public utility societies in early British town planning and housing reform, 1901–36', *Planning Perspectives* (1993), pp 125–65.

20 Only two public utility societies in Dublin, the St. Barnabas and Killester, took action under the 1919 provisions, building a total of forty-four houses.

21 National Archives of Ireland, Registry of Friendly Societies, St. Barnabas Public Utility Society, R 1520.

22 *Church of Ireland Gazette*, 8 July 1921, p. 423.

23 *Irish Builder and Engineer*, 17 April 1920, p. 273.

24 *Church of Ireland Gazette*, 8 February 1924, p. 87. Indeed, an obituary in the *Church of Ireland Gazette* stressed that Hall's motives were those of a true churchman and that, although it brought him to prominence, his housing scheme was not the main business of his life. 'The building of houses was due to the need for creating conditions more conducive to mental, moral and spiritual health, and in their building there were more prayers than bricks' (*Church of Ireland Gazette*, 1 March 1940, p. 101).

25 Hall was a man of perseverance, as exemplified by the tale of his pursuit of one 'dilatory Local Government Board architect' to the top of the Custom House to get him to send in his report of the inspection of the houses in 1921. According to Hall, the man in question was very quick to do it ever after! (D.H. Hall, 'The beginning of Irish Public Utility Societies, a human story' in *Irish Builder*, 21 April 1934, p. 329).

26 Hall, 1934, p. 329.

27 D.H. Hall, 'The Church and housing', in *Church of Ireland Gazette*, 25 March 1920, p. 196.

28 Editorial, 'The building parson', *Church of Ireland Gazette*, 6 June 1924, p. 344.

29 *Church of Ireland Gazette*, 8 July 1921, p. 423.

30 *Church of Ireland Gazette*, 8 July 1921, p. 423.

31 Registry of Friendly Societies, St. Barnabas Public Utility Society, R 1520.

32 D.H. Hall, 'The need for houses', *Church of Ireland Gazette*, 8 February 1924, p. 88.

33 Editorial, 'The building parson', *Church of Ireland Gazette*, 6 June 1924, p. 344.

34 In paying tribute to Hall, the 1924 Church of Ireland Synod described how 'he worked quietly and unostentatiously at the problem of ill and insufficient housing which he found at his own door, in his own parish. He has contended alone with disappointments and seemingly insuperable difficulties that would have cast down a man of inferior mettle. He has won through' (*Church of Ireland Gazette*, 6 June 1924, p. 344). A measure of the esteem in which he was held, his parishioners presented him with a gift of a motor car.

35 A. Garrett, *From age to age, history of the parish of Drumcondra, North Strand, St. Barnabas* (Dublin, 1970), p. 138.

36 To learn more about the national situation, see 'The role of Public Utility Societies in Ireland, 1919–40' in Howard B. Clarke, Jacinta Prunty, and Mark Hennessy (eds) *Surveying Ireland's past: multidisciplinary essays in honour of Anngret Simms* (Dublin, 2004), pp 613–38.

37 *Report of inquiry*, 1914.

38 Registry of Friendly Societies, R 1694, letter.

39 Thus, in 1925 there were only four such societies, whereas at the end of 1927 there were sixteen societies and during 1928, thirteen further societies were registered, with proposals for 190 houses across the country (Registry of Friendly Societies, Registrar's Report for 1928; Department of Local Government and Public Health, *second report 1925–27*, 1928).

40 A further seventy-three houses were built in the County of Dublin, fifty-seven in Blackrock Urban District, thirty-four in Rathmines and Rathgar Urban District, thirteen in Howth Urban District, ten in Dún Laoghaire Urban District, six in Pembroke Urban District.

41 *Third report of the Department of Local Government and Public Health, 1927–1928* (Dublin, 1929).

42 Department of Local Government and Public Health, *Report 1931–32* (1933), Appendix XXVIII.

43 *Reports and printed documents of the Corporation of Dublin, 1932*, p. 70.

44 Ruth McManus, 'Public utility societies, Dublin Corporation and the development of Dublin, 1920–1940' in *Irish Geography*, xxix (1996), pp 27–37.

45 *Reports and printed documents of the Corporation of Dublin, 1925*, p. 64.

46 Each house was to have a frontage of 35 feet (*c*.10 metres), with an average depth of 100 feet (*c*.30 metres), and the ground rent was to be £6 p.a. for each plot, over and above rates and taxes.

47 Registry of Friendly Societies, R 1739, Dublin Commercial Public Utility Society, 1926 Annual Report.

48 Registry of Friendly Societies, R 1739.

49 *Reports and printed documents of the Corporation of Dublin, 1928*, p. 171.

50 National Archives, Kew: RECO 1/482, Bryce Leicester, Report on Public Utility Societies and Housing, December 1917, p. 53.

51 A loan equivalent of 75 % of the amount of the accepted tender would be advanced by the Commissioners under the Small Dwellings Acquisition Act in respect of each house. This would ensure that the houses could be easily sold, as purchasers would avail of these mortgage facilities.

52 Registry of Friendly Societies, R 1739, Dublin Commercial Public Utility Society management committee report for 1928.

53 The Dublin Commercial Public Utility Society No. 3 contract for fifty houses at Griffith Avenue was followed quickly by a No. 4 contract for 134 houses at Home Farm Road, Griffith Avenue (western section) and Malahide Road, Clontarf.

54 Under the 1934 legislation, maximum floor area for houses qualifying for the grants was 1,000 square feet (*c*.93 square metres), whereas civil servants could build a 1,500 square foot (*c*.140 square metre) house and still avail of the grants.

Civil servants could also promise steady employment and guaranteed ability to repay mortgage or tenant purchase agreements.

55 Registry of Friendly Societies, R 1743, Linenhall Public Utility Society; R 1788, Rathmines Public Utility Society.

56 *Reports and printed documents of the Corporation of Dublin, 1933*, p. 38.

57 Under Section 5 (I, i) of the new legislation.

58 Registry of Friendly Societies, R 1739, Dublin Commercial Public Utility Society.

59 *Reports and printed documents of the Corporation of Dublin, 1929*, p. 48.

60 Further details of the Gaeltacht Park scheme can be found in Ruth McManus, 'Public utility societies, Dublin Corporation and the development of Dublin, 1920–1940' in *Irish Geography*, xxix (1996), pp 27–37.

61 National Archives, Kew: RECO 1/482, Bryce Leicester, Report on Public Utility Societies and Housing, December 1917.

62 National Archives, Kew: RECO 1/606: Pamphlet: The Difficulties of the Housing Problem and Some Attempts to Solve It. The presidential address of P.C. Cowan, DSc, MinstCE, Chief Inspector LGBI to the Engineering and Scientific Association of Ireland, 31/1/16, p. 14.

63 National Archives, Kew: RECO 1/580: Memorandum on Public Utility Societies by Ewart G. Culpin, 15/10/17, p. 2.

64 The former site of the Linenhall Barracks had been acquired from Dublin Corporation at an annual rent of £126 and Messrs Collen Bros had been awarded the contract at a cost of £30,500. (Registry of Friendly Societies, R 1743, Linenhall Public Utility Society).

65 Indeed, in 1940, the Annual Report of the Linenhall Public Utility Society mentioned that 'in common with many in Dublin the members learned with much regret of the sudden death of Canon D.H. Hall BD, their president. It was due to Canon Hall's suggestion and initiative that the Society was started, and his advice and guidance was invaluable at the first. The reform of housing in Dublin owes much to his zeal and driving power.' (Registry of Friendly Societies, R 1743, Linenhall Public Utility Society).

66 The most active of these was Associated Properties Ltd. (the re-constituted Dublin Commercial Public Utility Society), accounting for 1,296 houses, or just under 70% of the total figure. Other significant house builders were the Dublin Building Operatives' Public Utility Society; Post Office Public Utility Society, which operated in Kimmage, Merville Avenue and later at Lansdowne Park; Civil Service Housing Association; National Housing Society and St. Mobhi Public Utility Society, which built on Sundrive Road, part of the Crumlin reserved area.

Seventeenth-century Dubliners and their books*

by **Raymond Gillespie**

✦

*Gilbert Lecture, January 2005

Books were important in the life of Sir J.T. Gilbert. He bought books, read them and cared for them in his own library that now forms the core of the Dublin City Library's Gilbert Library.[1] He also wrote books, most notably his *History of the city of Dublin,* and was interested in the history of printing and publishing as evidenced by the many references to printers in his history of the city. This was a trait that he shared with many who had lived in Dublin before him. Two hundred years before Gilbert's death some Dubliners had amassed collections of books that, by the standards of their own day, equalled his. William Molyneux, scientist, author and political pamphleteer, claimed in a 1694 account of his family, with due modesty

> my library consists of but a few volumes (I think at present not much above one thousand) but they are such as are choice and curious on those subjects wherein I delighted, chiefly mathematical and philosophical and miscellanies. I have likewise a good collection of common law books and amongst each kind of these there are some volumes scarcely to be met with.[2]

Again the early eighteenth-century dramatist Richard Steele recalled that when he was growing up in Dublin his guardian 'had a pretty large study of books'. It was Steele's task to dust the books each week and so he was obliged to take every book from its shelf. As he observed

> I thought there was no way to deceive the toil of my journey thro' the different abodes and habitations of these authors but by reading something in every one of them and in this manner to make my passage easy from the comely folio in the upper shelf or region, even through the crowd of duodecimos in the lower. By frequent exercise I became so great a proficient in this transitory application to books that I could hold open half a dozen small authors in my hand, grasping them with as secure a dexterity as a drawer doth his glasses and feasting my curious eye

155

with all of them at the same instant. Through these methods the natural irresolution of my youth was much strengthened, and having no leisure, if I had the inclination, to make pertinent observations in writing I was thus confirmed a very early wanderer.[3]

In the late 1690s the newly appointed archbishop of Dublin, Narcissus Marsh, was assembling another large collection at his palace at St Sepulchre that would, in time, become the first public library in Ireland. On a smaller scale William King, vicar of St Werburgh's, in the 1680s had a library of some 649 titles.[4] The oriental scholar Dudley Loftus had a much smaller library with only 56 titles but this represents a highly specialised collection.[5]

A century earlier books were perhaps rather less in evidence in Dublin. Among the seventeenth-century records of the Tholsel court we can catch glimpses of books and their owners in lists of goods compiled for various reasons. In 1638 Eleanor Luttrell, widow, was found to own '23 old books great and small' valued at £1. A few months later John Gilpin had six popish books valued at 4s. A number of 1638 inventories contained only a Bible or service book while Lady Alice Hamilton boasted fourteen books but most owned only one or two.[6] In greater households there may well have been larger collections but it is possible only to glimpse them. The sixteenth-century library of the Dubliner Richard Stanihurst seems to have been significant and it was used by the Jesuit Edmund Campion in compiling his history of Ireland in 1570.[7] Many of the same works cited by Campion, and indeed by Richard Stanihurst in his history of Ireland, reappear in a Dublin manuscript compilation of the late sixteenth century, the Book of Howth.[8] From this we may infer at least part of their reading interests. In the writings of Stanihurst and Campion, in the middle of the sixteenth century, history and law are clearly predominant with standard English chronicles, including those of Robert Fabian and Edward Hall, Randulf Higden's *Polychronicon* and the historical work of Roger Hovenden, as well as histories by Hector Boece and John Major on Scotland, being listed as sources.

Something of the range of books that one might expect to find in a gentleman's house may be seen in the comment of Patrick Plunket, a student in the Irish college at Douai who was implicated in a plot to smuggle Catholic books into Ireland in 1610. The mayor of Chester discovered the books which Patrick claimed were 'certain books of history, philosophy and other science'.[9] While this was clearly untrue Patrick's dissembling does suggest the range of books which a young man of the upper social rank would expect to encounter in an Irish house.

One hundred years earlier still, in the early part of the sixteenth century books were even rarer in Dublin. Print was then a very recent invention and printed books were still a novelty in the city. Some of the major religious houses around Dublin had the wealth necessary to allow them to enjoy the novelty of printed books in their libraries. John Bale, bishop of Ossory, certainly saw some printed books among the possessions of the religious house at Kilmainham and in 1505 the canons of the Augustinian house of Christ Church seem to have appropriated two books on canon law from the estate of the late dean of St Patrick's, John Aleyn.[10] Parishes, too, may have been early into the market for printed books. By 1503/4 the parish church of St Werburgh in Dublin had acquired a printed missal, presumably from England, although it also continued to pay for manuscript copies of liturgical works.[11] However there was some market among private purchasers in Dublin for the new fangled toy of printed books. By 1545 the Dublin stationer, James Dartas, was already importing a wide range of printed works for retail in Dublin.[12] Indeed by the 1540s London printers may even have been producing books specifically for the Dublin market.[13]

Over the course of the sixteenth and seventeenth centuries those who lived in Dublin became progressively more involved in the world of books. It might be objected that the examples of book owners that I have given reflect those with the wealth to buy books and the leisure both to learn to read them and to put that learning into practice. However the technology of printing which made those books had a much wider impact, especially in the later seventeenth century. Government used print, in the form of procla-mations, to explain how subjects were to behave and Dublin Corporation followed suit. By the 1560s Dublin Corporation was making use of the printing press on *an ad* hoc basis to

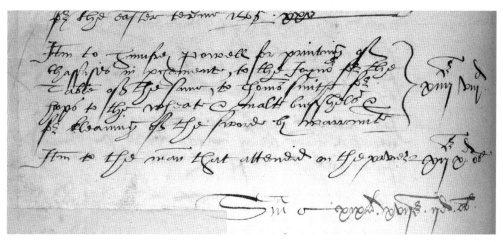

Payments by the Dublin City Assembly to Humphrey Powell, king's printer, for printing assize tables in 1565. (Dublin City Archives, Treasurer's account books, 1540–1613. Dublin City Library & Archive. © Dublin City Council)

produce a wide range of administrative documents. In 1681 John Ray was appointed as printer to the city, producing administrative documents such as court schedules and mayoral proclamations.[14] By the 1680s Dublin alone would absorb 600 copies of a mayoral proclamation, such was the demand for print.[15] Coffee houses in the city were also places where merchants and others could encounter printed newsletters and other ephemera. Political and commercial news circulated together. Indeed in 1679 the Irish lord lieutenant, the Duke of Ormond, unable to find copies of an address to the English parliament, which he was assured had been printed, asked that a search be made among the Dublin booksellers 'and coffee houses where such things possibly may be kept'.[16] Certainly in 1686 the Dublin coffee houses were said to be 'stuffed with news letters'.[17] Such communal reading made sense in the case of high-priced manuscript newsletters and imported printed newsletters since the cost could be spread widely. For those who could not read there were others who could read for them. In 1678, for instance, it was claimed that newsletters were opened and read publicly in the post house.[18] Again in more intimate surroundings the Dublin butcher Hugh Leeson, for instance, recorded how he had been converted by having the Bible read to him by his wife.[19]

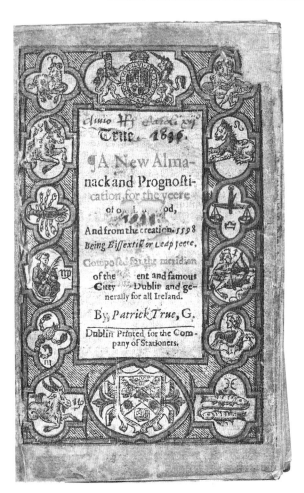

Patrick True's Almanack for 1636. Printed by the London Stationers' Company after they had become king's printer in Ireland. The royal arms at the top of the page proclaims their official status. (Dublin & Irish Collections: Dix Collection. Dublin City Library & Archive)

Clearly those who lived in early modern Dublin grew accustomed to the new technology of print and it increasingly permeated their lives. Books and printed ephemera became much more common. By the beginning of the eighteenth century bookshelves had replaced boxes as a way of storing whatever books one might own. But how did one acquire books in this world? In Dublin printing was initiated and promoted by government. The first printer, Humphrey Powell, had come from London where he had issued some ten books between 1548 and 1550. In 1550 he was given £20 by order of the privy council in London to establish himself in Ireland and on the title page of his first Irish book he described himself as 'king's printer', an office probably created by the government to regulate the trade.[20] His initial production was the first Edwardian Book of Common Prayer, issued presumably in line with the government's desire to promote reformed religion. Over the early seventeenth century the trade was monopolised by the king's printer who was also used to control what could be produced in Ireland.[21] For most of that period the office was held by the London Stationers' Company. In the later seventeenth century the print trades within Dublin expanded considerably. In 1670 printers and stationers organised themselves, with others, into the guild of St Luke. The guild increasingly assumed the role of deciding what would be published in the city and vouching for its authenticity.[22] The number of printers at work in Dublin increased in the 1680s and again in the 1690s.[23] This commercial expansion was reflected in a significant growth in the volume of material from the Dublin presses in the latter half of the seventeenth century.

Some were scathing about the world of print in Dublin. One visitor to the city in 1699, James Verdon of Market Dereham in Norfolk, complained 'they have, moreover, a printing house which, I must own, is no great glory for them because they seldom print anything but news and tickets for funerals'.[24] However, the total number of items produced in the 1660s was ten times that printed in the 1610s. By the 1690s the Dublin presses were producing almost twice as many items a year as they had been thirty years earlier. Of course such a comparison based on counting items is rather misleading since by the 1690s the presses were used for a much wider range of ephemeral items, such as tickets for funerals, which tend to inflate the estimates of production.[25] Some of this expansion is accounted for by government business and reprints of English works but a growing part of the activity of the press was explained in other ways. The number of locally conceived and produced books, for instance, grew steadily. In the 1690s, for instance, the Dublin presses were being utilised by religious controversialists in a way that had not been done earlier in the century. William King, dean of St Patrick's cathedral and later bishop of Derry, used print to attack Catholics in the 1680s and also Presbyterians in the 1690s and his work provoked spirited replies from both parties.[26]

For all this the vast bulk of the books available in Dublin came there as a result of trade mainly from England. It is possible to trace something of the trade through the Bristol and Chester port books. In the 1630s the Stationers' factor William Bladen was active in importing books to Ireland through Chester. In 1632, for instance, he probably imported over twenty hundredweight of books, some bound and some unbound, to meet his bookselling requirements in Dublin.[27] However the king's printer was not the only person prepared to sell books in Dublin. In 1614 the London stationer John Gwillam imported ten hundredweight of books into Dublin and in 1634 John Stepney and Michael Spark, both London stationers, imported two hundredweight of books each.[28] These were once-off shipments and may be regarded as speculative with a few London dealers testing the market with the consent of the Stationers'. That they did not continue with the shipments suggests that they found the Irish business unprofitable or uncongenial. By 1630, however a few Dublin based merchants were showing some interest in the book trade. John Watson, whose goods were appraised in 1638, had among his stock playing cards, bone lace, silk, buttons, cloth and 6 'primer books'.[29] William Crawford, a general merchant, imported a dozen grammars from Chester in 1641 and another Dublin merchant, Bartholomew Droppe, shipped 40 pounds of books from Chester to Dublin in the same year. One other merchant shipped fifteen hundredweight of books in 1639 and 1640.[30] By the 1690s, of imports of books worth about £2,900 a year into Dublin, £2,500 came from England and Scotland.[31] There was a smaller trade with continental Europe. In the late 1680s, for instance, two Dublin Catholic booksellers, James Malone and Christopher Jans, were importing missals and breviaries from the Antwerp firm of Plantin-Moretus into Dublin.[32] Most books were bound after being imported and some book dealers, such as John Gwillam, are also described as binders.[33] The trade seems to have been a profitable one since seven bookbinders can be identified in Dublin in the first half of the seventeenth century, before the guild of St Luke was established.[34]

Initially, at least, general merchants were the main booksellers and this probably continued into the late seventeenth century in the case of schoolbooks and other cheap books. In 1694, for example, Isachar Wilcocks, a Dublin Quaker grocer, had among the stock of his shop five dozen hornbooks, valued at a shilling a dozen, and over 600 primers.[35] The Chester port books for the late seventeenth century show a number of Dublin general merchants who imported books on one or two occasions.[36] Such men were of limited long term significance for the development of the book trade. In Dublin what might be recognised as professional booksellers began to become established by the 1630s. In 1637 John Crooke, a London trained printer, established a bookselling partnership in Dublin with his brother Edmond, Thomas Allot and Richard Sergier. John probably only settled in Dublin in 1639. All their stock was printed in London and imported. In 1639 John Crooke shipped almost eighty hundredweight of books, both bound and unbound, to Dublin from Chester and almost 15 hundredweight the following year, a much higher quantity than the king's printer William Bladen.[37] The position of their shop close to the centre of political power and patronage, probably in Castle Street near the gate of Dublin Castle, may be significant for the development of the print trade. It may also be important that they sold the plays of the English playwright James Shirley, attracted to Dublin by the development of a vice-regal court under the patronage of Lord Deputy Wentworth, Earl of Strafford.[38] The emergence of a fashionable centre in the city, of which book buying was a part, certainly provided considerable incentive to the development of the print trades.[39] Certainly by 1641 Crooke and Sergier could claim that they, for the previous five years, had run a stationer's shop 'well furnished with marte and English books', which implies they drew their stock from a wide range of sources, which they then sold 'at such rates as formerly this kingdom was not supplied withal'.[40] In terms of bookselling this was the way of the future.

In the late seventeenth century the trade of bookselling grew enormously. The number of booksellers in the city quadrupled.[41] We know something about these business men because of the advertisements which they printed in the books they published, and also through the trade records which tell us what sort of books they imported. Perhaps the most striking feature of the Dublin trade is the dominance of a few booksellers. On the basis of the port book evidence in 1680, for example, the top four booksellers, Eliphal Dobson, James Malone, William Mendy and Samuel Helsham, accounted for almost two-thirds of the trade. The individuals and proportions recorded in the port books varied slightly over time but the general pattern of a trade in a few hands seems to apply throughout the period. In the port books for the 1690s this pattern is repeated with fewer booksellers overall but two or three being predominant.[42]

In part this seems to be the result of some degree of specialisation. In contrast to those who dealt in imports, the Crooke family, as king's printers, imported little over the 1680s presumably because most of what they sold had been produced by their own press. On the other hand, Patrick Campbell imported considerable quantities of books yet his name does not appear as a bookseller in any Dublin printed work in the 1680s, although he does feature in the 1670s and 1690s. Again William Mendy produced nothing but imported a good deal. By contrast Joseph Ray, a printer himself, imported little but is named in a large number of Dublin imprints. Other printers in the same category are William Winter, William Weston and William Norman who imported little. The correlation is not perfect. There are a number of booksellers who both imported a good deal and who also feature as

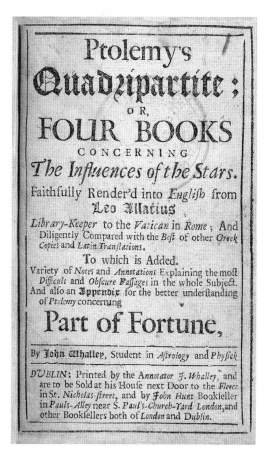
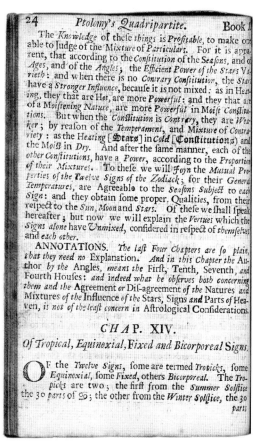

Ptolemy's *Quadripartite*, a treatise on astrology, edited by the printer and seller of patent medicines John Whalley.

Whalley funded the printing of this through pre-publication subscriptions.

(Dublin & Irish Collections: Gilbert Library. Dublin City Library & Archive)

A prospectus from Robert Ware's *Hunting of the Romish fox*, soliciting subscriptions for Robert Ware's *History of the city of Dublin*. The work was completed but never published, presumably due to lack of subscriptions. The manuscript is now in Armagh Public Library.

(Dublin & Irish Collections: Gilbert Library. Dublin City Library & Archive)

booksellers on the imprints of Dublin published works. The most significant of these are Samuel Helsham, Eliphal Dobson, John North and Joseph Howes. This evidence suggests that there was a hierarchy of booksellers in Dublin. The largest dealers handled a wide range of books, both domestic and imported, and had markets extending well beyond the city.[43] A few, probably four or five, monopolised most of the import trade which made them significant players. Some of these men may also have acted as wholesalers supplying imported works to smaller booksellers. Samuel Helsham, for instance, seems to have acted as an agent, selling on to other booksellers copies of works which he imported.[44] Finally, there were those who dealt in locally-produced works or retailed imported works possibly acquired from wholesalers.[45]

It is possible to get a sense of what these varying types of booksellers might have offered to the inhabitants of late seventeenth-century Dublin. Some consumers were critical of the stock of the Dublin bookshops. The book collector and later archbishop of Dublin, Narcissus Marsh, complained in 1689 that he could not obtain the books he wanted in Ireland 'our booksellers being rather to be called sellers of pamphlets than booksellers'. By 1706 he claimed the situation had not improved noting 'nor are our booksellers shops furnished any thing tolerably with other books than new trifles and pamphlets and not well with them also'.[46] Marsh was a demanding book buyer who assembled a large and rather specialised library and his views cannot be taken as representative of the needs of the more modest purchaser.

It is clear however that the thinness and unpredictability of the Irish market meant that forecasting demand, and hence deciding on stock levels, was difficult. Printers, for instance, produced widely varying lengths of run based on unpredictable demand. In the early part of the century the run of a scholarly work, such as a volume by Archbishop Ussher, might be of the order of 1,000 to 1,500 copies. Cautious booksellers, such as Samuel Dancer in the 1660s might produce only 500 copies of a play which quickly sold out and a reprint was called for.[47] In a different league was Charles II's 'Gracious declaration', which formed the basis of the Restoration settlement, of which 9,000 copies were produced in Dublin but even this was not enough for an insatiable market demanding to know the shape of the future. Copies were quickly retailing at two shilling each, well above their normal price as supply failed to meet demand.[48] Like printers, booksellers could not afford to tie up capital for long periods of time by holding on to unsold stock. Rather than import occasional large cargoes of books the Dublin book importers tended to ship regularly in small quantities. During the 1680s the larger importers, such as Helsham, Dobson, North or Campbell, might ship between six and eight cargoes a year from Chester in an effort to keep markets supplied. In some respects this meant that books published in London would reach Dublin more quickly than if the trade had been conducted with larger, more infrequent cargoes. However, some works published in England could be slow to get to Dublin in quantity and if sufficiently popular could sell out quickly. When Edmund Borlase's history of the rising of 1641 was first published it was much in demand in Dublin and quickly sold out with Sir John Temple paying 'perhaps ... something above the common rate that it is sold at' in his anxiety to get a copy.[49] Similarly when the controversial memoirs of the Earl of Castlehaven appeared in 1681 in London it took some time for it to reach Dublin, the Duke of Ormond having to import his own copy. When it did arrive it sold out almost immediately.[50]

Fluctuating demand and sometimes thin markets meant that the booksellers worked at a range of levels. At the lower end of the scale, William Winter, who imported nothing in his own name but who appears in a number of imprints as a bookseller, advertised his wares in one of his books in 1685 (appendix 2, no. 3).[51] Most of what Winter advertised were small works. A large amount of stationery, including pre-printed forms were offered for sale such as forms of indentures, bonds of arbitration, letters of attorney, bonds for debt and various types of processes. Moving through the scale there were pamphlets for legal work including Richard Bolton's *Rules for a grand juror*, reprinted from his larger handbook for justices of the peace. There were also sets of instructions for keeping manorial courts. Also included were the steady sellers: a selection of schoolbooks and two popular chapbook romances, the *Seven wise masters* and *Don Bellianis of Greece* which had presumably been purchased from importers. Other steady sellers such as Bibles and Books of Common Prayer also appear on the list. In the class of small books there were 'the choice of the best collection of plays in this kingdom'. Winter also claimed that there was 'a good choice of histories, novels and romances to be sold or lent at reasonable rates' suggesting that he also operated a lending library. He also dealt in second hand books. In this list there is little that appears in contemporary library lists as being deemed worthy of preservation by their owners. There were only five books of substance in stock, all of which were Dublin printed. Three, Robert Ware's *Foxes and firebrands*, Richard Lawrence's *The interest of Ireland in its trade and wealth stated* and Edward Wetenhall's *Judgement of the comet*, had appeared that year and were presumably in local demand. The remaining two were law books, an edition of the Irish statutes and Richard

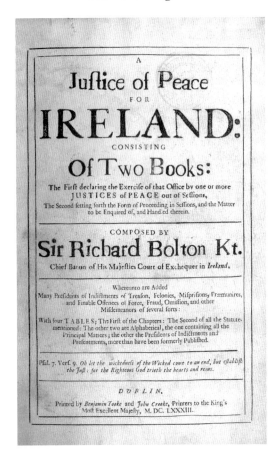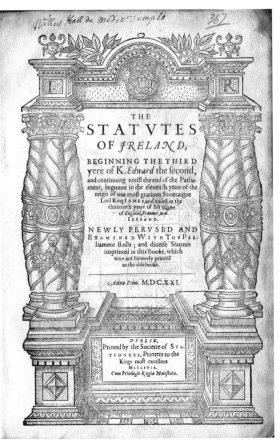

Richard Bolton's handbook for justices of the peace and his edition of the Irish statutes are good examples of the use of print by government to ensure that local officials were aware of government needs and legal requirements.

(Dublin & Irish Collections: Gilbert Library. Dublin City Library & Archive)

Bolton's manual for justices of peace which were probably bought by country gentlemen acting as JPs.

By contrast a 1688 advertisement for books sold by William Norman and Eliphal Dobson presents a rather different picture (appendix 2, no.4).[52] Dobson was a significant importer of books during the 1680s and Norman appears in Dublin imprints on eighteen occasions in the same decade. In this list there is some overlap with the contents of Winter's advertisement, including Bibles and Books of Common Prayer, Richard Bolton's edition of the Irish statutes and his manual for justices of the peace and Richard Lawrence's *Interest of Ireland*. Works such as these were the staple of the trade and are also characteristic of Samuel Helsham's bookselling business in the 1680s.[53] The other twelve titles are different to the sort of stock which Winter had. All are imported and they include the sort of works that would happily have graced a gentleman's library. The stock was largely devotional and confutational but there was also one recent scientific work, by William Molyneux, for sale along with a biography of the Earl of Rochester by Dr Burnett.

Book dealers did not have a complete monopoly on how books circulated around the city. In the case of William Molyneux, whose Dublin library we have already encountered, friends sent him works difficult to obtain elsewhere. An English member of the

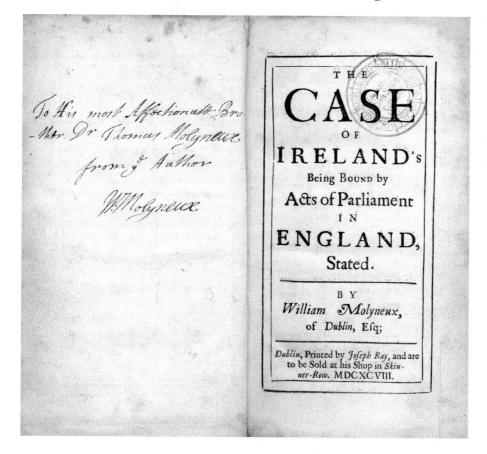

Giving books as gifts was an important way in ensuring that one's work moved in the right circles. Here William Molyneux has presented a copy of his work to his brother, Thomas, with a suitable inscription. (Dublin & Irish Collections: Gilbert Library. Dublin City Library & Archive)

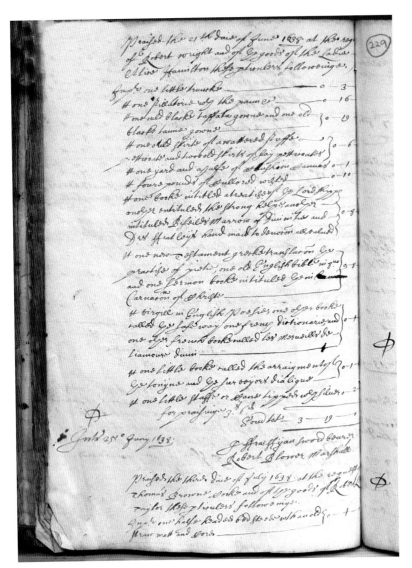

Royal Society, Robert Plot, happily sent copies of his books to Molyneux, and when, in the 1680s William's brother, Thomas, went to university at Leiden he kept his brother William supplied with scholarly gossip and books from across Europe.[54] William returned the compliment by presenting copies of his book to his friends. Furthermore the borrowing and lending of books helped broaden minds and augment collections. Both Luke Challoner, one of the first fellows of Trinity College, Dublin, and the early-seventeenth-century archbishop of Armagh, James Ussher, opened their libraries to their friends. Some of these were clerical borrowers either in Dublin or in Trinity College itself but there were a number of lay friends who also borrowed works on politics, history, geography and medicine and a few who borrowed devotional works.[55] In yet other cases institutional libraries, though not that of Trinity College, might be opened to a wider world. At the

Manuscript list of the books of Lady Ann Hamilton (see p.22, appendix 1).

(Dublin City Archives C1/J/2/4, p.228. Dublin City Library & Archive. © Dublin City Council)

beginning of the century the cathedral library of Christ Church, Dublin, for instance, seems to have lent its books to a wide range of people, presumably from its congregation.[56] Others were more closed affairs. The Jesuit house at Back Lane in Dublin in the 1630s had a library, some of the books of which now survive in Marsh's Library, but this was for the use of the students in the college. How they acquired their collection is unclear but in Drogheda the Franciscans had built up a library in the early seventeenth century from donations.[57]

Over the early modern period, therefore, the supply of books improved immensely with the emergence of professional booksellers. More and more people wanted to own books, as evidenced by the accumulation of collections of books. But what did they want to own and how did they use them? Here the evidence is rather thin but such as we have is remarkably consistent. Religion was a core element of the book trade. In a city which was increasingly Protestant in the late seventeenth century booksellers' advertisements urged Bibles, New Testaments, Books of Common Prayer and Psalters on purchasers. Moreover they also offered a range of devotional reading. Lady Alice Hamilton, in Dublin in the 1630s, had fourteen books, almost all religious, and all best sellers of a godly variety (appendix 1). These included Lewis Bayly's *The practice of piety* (then in its thirty-sixth edition), Nicholas Byfield's *The marrow of the oracles of God* (in its tenth edition), John Hayward's *The strong helper* and Daniel Fealtey's *Ancillia pietatis or the handmaid to private devotion* (then in its sixth edition).[58] Of particular importance was Lewis Bayly's *The practice of piety*. This was popular with Church of Ireland readers throughout the seventeenth century and the godly accomptant general James Bonnell was deeply affected by Bayly's work which he read in Dublin as a young man.[59] *The practice of piety* was particularly influential in the early part of the seventeenth century. Its moralistic tone together with prayers for use on particular occasions ensured its popularity. In the latter half of the century Bayly's work was edged out by a more modern text, *The whole duty of man,* which explained to an individual his duty not only to God but to neighbours and superiors also, suggesting a rather different view of social organisation.

In one case we can see something of such godly readers at work. In the middle of the 1660s James Barry from Dublin, then a youth of fifteen, began to take religion seriously as a result of reading the Bible. Brought up in the Church of Ireland he turned to books as a way of revealing God's will. He observed 'I became very bookish, looking into almost every book where ever I came to try whether I could meet with any help which might forward me in my new trade of religion'. Daily he retreated into seclusion to read and meditate on what he read. His stock of reading matter included most of the classic devotional works of the early seventeenth century. He soon found a copy of Richard Baxter's *Call to the unconverted,* 'the which I did no sooner open but its title page invited my fancy to make choice of it for my chief companion ... the more oftener I read it the more I was enamoured with it'.[60] Barry's reading has all the marks of the godly reader at work with his immersion in a text which was read frequently and slowly, new insights being found on each reading. The impact of his reading was dramatic, since comparing the spiritual models he found in the reading with his own experience, he drew the conclusion that he could no longer remain within the Church of Ireland. Despite being urged by a bishop to read *The whole duty of man* as a statement of the church's theological and social position he had found no comfort there and defected to Independency.

In the case of Catholicism it is more difficult to find evidence for readers at work. In the early part of the century most Catholic books had to be smuggled into Ireland but in 1688, as the Jacobite revanche moved towards its zenith, the Dublin Catholic bookseller William Weston advertised the titles which were available in his shop in High Street (appendix 2, no. 5).[61] It seems likely that this represents a consignment of books brought to Dublin by Weston in 1688. He had certainly imported politically dubious works from a London bookseller in the recent past and in 1684 he also imported quantities of books on his own account through Chester.[62] The books which Weston offered were the sort of books that the clergy read and wished the laity to read also. Copies of some are to be found in the libraries of clergy. Bishop Daton of Ossory, for instance, possessed a copy of Dominique Bouhours' *Christian thoughts for every day in the month* which was on Weston's list while Bishop Wadding of Ferns owned Henry Turberville's *Abridgement of Christian doctrine* and W.C.'s *A little manual of the poor man's daily devotion.*[63] One of Weston's offerings, C.J.'s *A net for the fishers of men,* was so appreciated by one Irish Franciscan that he copied the entire text into his commonplace book.[64] Other clergy expressed their approbation for the sort of books that Weston held by distributing copies of the same works to their flock in an effort to promote piety. Bishop Wadding handed out 144 copies of Henry Turberville's *Abridgement of Christian doctrine,* 1,200 copies of Pedro de Ledesma's *Christian doctrine,* at least three dozen copies of Dominique Bouhours' *Christian thoughts for every day in the month,* copies of *The most devout prayers of St Bridget* as well as 'little books of the Mass' which may correspond to a book in Weston's stock entitled *The mysteries of the holy Mass.*[65]

In broad terms three of the titles on Weston's list can be described as doctrinal, one as confutational and the remaining thirteen as devotional works. Of these thirteen, three were concerned with what might be described as public devotions, in particular commentaries on the Mass, while the remaining ten were prayer books for private use. There is some overlap between these two groups as prayer books often contained commentaries on the Mass or prayers for use before or after Mass. Even allowing for this overlap the main thrust of Weston's stock was towards books of private devotion. Such books helped to shape the devotional world associated particularly with the reforms of the Council of Trent. Works such as Turberville on doctrine, usually known as the Douai catechism, or that of Ledesma, were intended to ensure that belief was underpinned by an understanding of the doctrines of Catholicism. Turberville's work, for instance, expounded the creed, the commandments, the precepts of the church, the sacraments, the four last things, and the works of mercy. Early modern Irish Catholics were becoming increasingly familiar with such works. Diocesan synods enjoined priests working in Ireland to acquire such catechisms and to use them in educating their flock. Weston's stock was also intended to shape practice. Both Turberville's work and W.C.'s *A little manual of the poor man's daily devotion* offered detailed commentaries on the Mass, including an explanation of the ornaments and ceremonies used at Mass and a commentary on the actions of the priest from his entrance on the altar. They also included prayers for use before and after Mass but not during Mass as had been customary before. Now the world of print guided the reader through the actions of the Mass and they were expected to follow and understand the symbolism of those actions rather than perform their own devotions by reciting traditional prayers during the liturgy.

To understand the role which books, such as those stocked by Weston, were intended to play in the promotion of devotion it is necessary to understand not only the texts but the ways in which they were read. Some insight is provided by the texts themselves. One of the works on Weston's list, *Christian thoughts for every day of the month*, carried a preface which explained how it was to be used. It was a work for the laity, the preface explained, and contained 'plain thoughts, short and easy which may be understood without difficulty and read with less than a minute's expense'. It was to be resorted to after prayers in the morning when the owner should 'read the thoughts of that day but read them leisurely that you may understand them thoroughly'. Like Protestant readers, one was not to be content with a simple comprehension of the truth contained in the work but also to consider how it might be applied.[66] Clearly this was a text which was to be read privately and in a meditative mood, in the context of prayer and was to be absorbed slowly and fully. Weston had other books of a similar nature. *The devout prayers of St Bridget*, which was sold by Weston is based on the fifteen traditional prayers of St Bridget of Sweden, to be said in honour of the wounds of Christ, and was meant for personal meditative private prayer rather than for communal recital. This was an interiorised form of devotion that relied heavily on the response of the individual to the written or printed word rather than the communal assent to the meaning of the work or its performance in liturgy.

The world of the Catholic reader reflected in the stock of William Weston's bookshop was a multi-faceted one. It was a world of faith which concentrated on an individualised devotion inspired by meditation on the mysteries of Catholicism. It encouraged active, informed participation in the sacraments rather than the performance of communal rituals such as pilgrimage to one of the local holy wells around Dublin. It advanced Counter-Reformation ideas and devotions at the expense of traditional practice. In particular it demanded knowledge not simply that one was a Catholic but rather an understanding of why one had adopted that confessional position.

However, readers did not use books only for religious reasons. An insight into another world is provided by Richard Head's play about Dublin in the early 1660s, *Hic et ubique*, in which a landlady claimed to 'have read much'. On inquiry as to what she had read she replied 'In my youthful days the most part of the *Garland of good will* the *Seven wise masters* and there was not a godly ballad that 'scaped my hands'. She also claimed to have read works of grammar and 'multiplication'.[67] Schoolbooks, almanacs and popular romances all appear on bookseller's lists in the late seventeenth century. The cheap romance, the *Seven champions of Christendom*, for example, was owned not only by those at the bottom of the social order but in the 1650s by the godly Provost Winter of Trinity College, Dublin.[68] Readings of such popular works are ephemeral, often purely for entertainment, and hence almost impossible to recover. Attempts to control such readings do suggest something of that process. The presentation of St Patrick in the *Seven champions* is not that of a saint in the mould of a medieval hagiographical text. In its most developed form St Patrick redeems six Thracian ladies from satyrs before proceeding with the other champions to Greece, Portugal, Jerusalem and Egypt. He then returns to Ireland where he dies, after digging his own grave. However his character retained some of the miraculous and quasi-magical features which were associated with late medieval hagiography, the reading of which was popular among early modern Irish Catholics. Indeed, it seems that saints' lives and

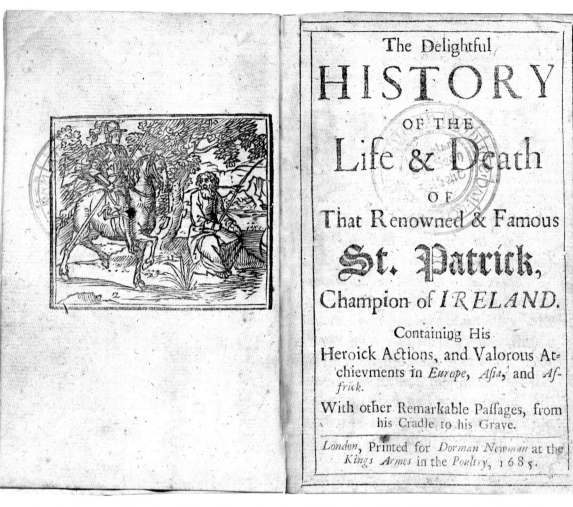

The Delightful
HISTORY
OF THE
Life & Death
OF
That Renowned & Famous
St. Patrick,
Champion of *IRELAND*.

Containing His
Heroick Actions, and Valorous At=
chievments in *Europe, Asia,* and *Af-
frick.*

With other Remarkable Paſſages, from
his Cradle to his Grave.

London, Printed for *Dorman Newman* at the
Kings Armes in the *Poultry,* 1685.

A chapbook extracted from the widely read *Seven champions of Christendom*. Although this was printed in London
it was clearly intended for the Irish market, to be sold by pedlars as well as booksellers.

(Dublin & Irish Collections: Gilbert Library. Dublin City Library & Archive)

chapbook stories may have silently elided into one another. Such miraculous stories would
not merely be tolerated but celebrated in the context of these popular histories. Yet they
were not acceptable to some in ecclesiastical authority who regarded these stories as mere
fables and felt that measures had to be taken to prevent them being read as devotional
works. That hagiography and histories were read in this way is suggested by a 1685 London
reprint for the Irish market of the part of the *Seven champions* dealing with St Patrick. In this
case it was prefaced by a short account of the traditional hagiographical story of St Patrick,
suggesting that both were to be read together as part of a seamless story.[69]

Popular romances and more practical books such as almanacs were part of everyday
life. One indication of this is the events surrounding a gathering in a house in Dublin in
November 1641. One man, George Hackett, 'drew a little book which the examinant

[Bartholomew Lennon] knewest was an almanac and there read the names of divers persons which the said Hackett said were the principal rebels'. Hackett, according to his own deposition, was able to sign his name while most of the others were not. He was clearly using a well-known object - the almanac - as a prop to convince others.[70] Moreover by the late seventeenth century such books began to be printed locally rather than imported and this meant they could be tailored to Dublin's taste. In one case, the three almanacs published in Dublin by John Bourke in the 1680s, it is possible to see something

An Exact Account of the principal High-ways and Fairs in the Kingdom of Ireland.

From Dublin to *Cork* along the Sea-fide, and fo to *Baltamore* 180 miles, thus;

From *Dublin* to *Brey* ten, Newcaftle 8, Wicklow 6, Arklow twelve, Glafcary twelve, Wexford twelve, Rofs fourteen, Waterford eight, Kilmactomas twelve, Dongarvan eight, Youghal 12, Corabby 18, Cork 10, Bandonbridg 10, Timoleague 8, Rofscarbery 8, Abbeyftrewry 8, Baltamore 4.

From Baltamore to Traley 47 miles, thus,

From Baltamore to Abbyftrewry 4, Afhtown 3, Balibagan 8, Glaneroty 12, Caftlelough 8, to Traley 12.

From Dublin to Gowran 42 miles, thus;

From Dublin to Naas 12, Kilcullan 6, Caftledarmot 9, Catherlotgh 5, Laughlin 5, Gowran 5.

From Gowran to Waterford 20 miles, thus;

From Gowran to Thomaftown 5, to Waterford 15.

From Gowran to Youghal 38 miles, thus;

From Gowran to Knocktougher 8, Carrick 8, Dungarvan 12, Youghal 10.

From Gowran to Cork 54 miles.

From Gowran to Bennets bridge 3, Kells 3, Colagh 4, Kilcafhel 6, Clonmel 6, Lifmore 12, Maftlehan 8, Cork 12.

From

The beginning and ending of the Terms, with their Returns, or Effoin days: Days of Exception, Returna Brevium, and days of *Appearance*, this year 1684.

	Return Bre:	App.
Hillary Term begins Jan. 23: *ends* Febr. 12:		
Return or Effoyn days, Exc. days, Return Bre: App.		
Octab: Hill: Jan: 21	21	22	23
Quind: Hill: Jan: 28	28	29	31
Craft: Purif: Febr: 4	4	5	6
Octab: Purif: Febr: 10	10	12	12
Eafter Term begins April 16. *ends* May 12			
Quind. Pafch: Apr: 14	15	16	16
Tref. Pafch: April 21	22	23	24
Menf: Pafch. Apr. 28	29	30	May 2
Quinq: Pafc. May 5	6	7	9
Craft: Afcen: May 9	10	10	12
Trinity Term begins May 30 *ends* June 18.			
Craft. Trin. May 26	27	28	30
Octab: Trin: June 2	3	4	5
Quind. Trin: June 9	10	10	12
Tres Trin: June 16	17	17	18
Michaelm: Term begins Octob: 23. *ends* Nov: 28.			
Tres Mich. Octob: 20	21	22	23
Menf; Mich; Octo; 27	27	29	30
Craft; Anim; Nov; 3	4	4	6
Craft; Mart; Nov; 12	13	14	15
Octab Mart; Nov; 19	20	21	22
Quind; Mart; Nov; 25	26	27	28

Note, that the firft and laft days of every Term, are the firft and laft days of Appearance.

Useful information from John Bourke's 1684 almanac.

(Dublin & Irish Collections: Gilbert Library. Dublin City Library & Archive)

Title page from John Bourke's 1684 almanac setting out the sort of material that a reader would expect to find in such a work.

(Dublin & Irish Collections: Gilbert Library.
Dublin City Library & Archive)

of the attempts of an author to make his work more appealing.[71] Little is known of Bourke himself. It is possible that he was related to Patrick Bourke, a 'teacher of mathematics', who petitioned Dublin Corporation in 1687 to set up a school to teach mathematics to the young and is probably the same 'Patrick Bourke, gent' who became a freeman of the city in 1688.[72] John Bourke issued his first almanac in 1683. In many ways it was a rather crude production, clearly copied from English models. Most of the content of the almanac was standard: lists of regnal years, tables for the conversion of money, a monthly calendar with weather prognostications, lists of routeways, and schedules of markets and fairs. Bourke's innovation was to use the page opposite the monthly calendar to print material which he thought might attract buyers. In the 1683 almanac he included a list of Irish lords deputy and lords lieutenant from 1169. This clearly was not attractive and in the following year he replaced this with medical and dietary advice for each month. This too seems not to have increased sales and in 1685 he included a history of Ireland from the coming of Christianity to 1172. This was apparently to be a history of Bourke's own devising drawing on a range of scholarly and popular works in English by James Ware and Peter Walsh to construct, in a traditional manner, a succession list of kings with comments on their reigns. In this case it may be that Bourke, sensing a change in attitudes to the world of Gaelic Ireland, as Protestants began to acquire copies of Keating's history of early Ireland and poets celebrated the period, was trying to cash in on popular sentiment.[73] No further almanacs by Bourke survive and it is possible that despite his manoeuverings he had failed to catch the mood of the market and was forced to suspend publication.

The popular tales of saints, monsters and the fabulous are a world away from the sober prose of Gilbert's *History of the city of Dublin*. Perhaps his Victorian mind might have been happier with the moral verses in Ambrose White's Dublin 1665

almanac, for instance, which urged readers to 'relieve the poor', entertain one's neighbours, be moderate in one's drinking and be faithful to one's wife.[74] But the fact that we can recapture something of the world of those who lived in seventeenth-century Dublin through their books is due in no small measure to the collecting habits of Sir John T. Gilbert for it is in his library that we have the best collection of those almanacs which open up that world. We should all be grateful that Gilbert's passion was caught in the animal depicted on his bookplate: a squirrel.

Sir John T. Gilbert's bookplate. The squirrel at the top reflects his acquisitive tendencies as far as books and manuscripts were concerned.
(Dublin & Irish Collections: Gilbert Library.
Dublin City Library & Archive)

Appendix 1

The books of Lady Alice Hamilton, 1638

It[em] One booke intitled a treatise of the lordshipp another entituled the strong helpe; another intituled Bifeilds Marrow of Divinitie and Dr Featleys handmaid to devot[i]on all valued 8s.

It[em] One new testament grecke translacion, the practise of pietie, one old English bible in 8° and one sermon booke intituled the incarnacon of Christ 8s.

It[em] Virgill in English poesie, one other booke called the safe way, one french dictionarie and one other french booke called Les Merueills de Liamoure divni 4s.

It[em] One little book called the arraignment of the tongue and the surveyors dialique 4s.

Source: Dublin City Archives, C1/J/2/4, p. 228.

Appendix 2

Some Dublin booksellers' advertisements

I. 1663   Books printed at the King's printing house and are to be sold by Samuel Dancer, Bookseller, in Castle Street, Dublin.

Dr Jeremy Taylors (lord bishop of Down and Connor) three sermons preached at Christ Church, Dublin, viz The righteouness evangelical described. The Christians compact over the body of sin, and faith working by love, Octav[o].

His funeral sermon at the funeral of the lord primate, 4°.

This present treatise on confirmation, 4°.

There will shortly be published his Treatise against popery, of the necessity of which no man can be ignorant.

Dr Lightbourne's sermon at Christ Church on 23 October, 4°.

A perfect collection of acts of the late parliament, to be sold together or severally, fol[io].

All sorts of proclamations.

Jacobi Waraei, equitis, Annales Henrici octavi, 8°.

The lord lieutenant's speech to the parliament.

The Church catechism at 1d for children, 8°.

Pompey, a tragedy, often acted in the new theatre in Dublin and written by a lady, 4°.

The counter-scuffle, 8°.

Poems by several persons of quality and refined wits, 4°.

The seven wise masters, 8°.

The acts of custom and excise with the Book of Rates to each of them annexed in a small pocket volume for the use of merchants and others.

A letter to a person of quality concerning the traitor Leckey, 4°.

The accidence.

Sententiae pueriles, 8°.

Acts of parliament made xv Caroli, fol[io].

Source: *A discourse of confirmation for the use of the clergy and instruction of the people of Ireland* (Dublin, 1663).

2. 1683   These books are printed for and sold by Robert Thornton at the Unicorn in Skinner Row

Absolom and Achitophel the first part.

Absolom and Achitophel the second part.

The medal, a satire against sedition by the author of Absolom and Achitophel.

The countess of Morton's daily exercise. A book of prayers and devotions.

Source: John Sheffield, Duke of Buckingham, *An essay upon poetry* (Dublin, 1683).

3. 1685   Printed for and sold by W. Winter at His Grace the Lord Primate's Head upon College Green.

Sir Richard Bolton's Rules for a Grand Juror &c, or articles given in charge to, and enquired of, by the Grand Jury in the General or Quarter Sessions of the Peace in 4°.

Rules and orders of the High Court of Chancery in Ireland in 8°.

Orders of keeping Court Leet and Court Baron in Ireland.

The interest of Ireland in its trade and wealth stated, in 2 parts by R. Lawrence, Esq; in 8°.

A judgement of the comet first generally visible to us in Dublin, Decemb[er] 13, 1680 by a person of quality, in 4°.

Foxes and firebrands, or a specimen of the danger and harmony of popery and separation in 2 parts 8°.

Penal bills for payment of money.

Bonds for payment of money, single or double.

Warrants for confession of judgements upon such bonds, single or double.

Bonds and warrants for counter securities, single or double.

Indentures for apprentices and bonds for the performance of the indentures.

Indentures for apprentices for foreign plantations, &c.

Gifts of the judges circuits.

Proceses for the several circuit, with ad testisicandums, &c.

Letters of attorney, with or without revocation.

Bonds of arbitration and General releases &c.

Most sorts of stationery ware to be sold viz quills or pens, writing paper of most sorts, paper books for merchants accounts, or otherwise, of several forms and sizes, ruled or plain. Music paper and music books folio, 4° or 8°. Sealing wax, hard or soft, sealing wafers, large or small, vials and standishes for ink and the best ink for records.

Primers, psalters, testaments, English, Greek or Latin: Acccidences, grammars, Lilly's Rules construed, Alvary's Prosodia & syntaxes, and most sorts of school books.

Parismus and Parismenos, in 2 parts.

Don Bellianis of Greece, in 3 parts.

Montelion, knight of the oracle.

The seven wise masters &c.

And most sort of histories to be sold as cheap as can be imported.

The statutes of Ireland complete.

Sir Richard Bolton's Justice of the peace; and most sorts of law books.

Articles of religion and cannons of the Church of Ireland.

Form of consecration of churches.

Bibles, Common prayers of all sorts and sizes, with or without cutts.

Books of private devotion and of divinity good choice.

The choice of the best collection of plays in this kingdom, viz Comedies, tragedies, tradgi-comedies, pastorals, masks & operas &c and a good choice of histories, novels and romances to be sold or lent at reasonable rates.

Books may be bound gilt or plain;

And money for old books.

Source: Michael [Boyle], *Rules and orders appointed to be used and observed in the High Court of Chancery in Ireland* (Dublin, 1685).

4. 1688   Books printed and sold by William Norman and Eliphal Dobson.

Bibles and Common Prayers in all volumes.

Book of Homilies.

Bolton's Statutes.

Bolton's justice of the peace.

Book of Rates.

Plurality of worlds.

Prayers and meditations.

Gawens Logics.

Morton's devotions.

Dr Lake's Officium Eucharisticum.

Dr Burnet's life of the Earl of Rochester.

Tillotson against transubstantion.

Bishop of Cork's sermons.

Silvius de Febribus.

Mullineux's Sciothericum telescopicum.

Discourse against purgatory.

Discourse against auricular confession.

The Interest of Ireland.

Source: Neal Carolan, *Motives of conversion to the Catholic faith as it is professed in the reformed Church of*

5. 1688   Books printed and sold by Will[iam] Weston, printer and stationer to His Excellency the Lord Deputy.

Abridgement of Christian doctrine with proofs of scripture.

The little vade mecum or continual companion of a devout Christian.

Belarmin's Christian doctrine.

Ledezma's Christian doctrine.

Jesus psalter.

Rosary of our B[lessed] Lady.

St Bridgets prayers.

The mysteries of the holy Mass.

Holy sacrifice of the Mass in English expounded.

The friar disciplined.

Small manuals.

Christian thoughts for every day in the month.

Nets for the fishers of men.

The maxims of eternity.

Prayers for the king in Latin and English.

The imposter posted or the author of the Protestant Resolution proved no Protestant of the Church of England.

New forms of meditations.

Source: Richard Hudleston, *Short and plain way to the faith and church* (Dublin, 1688).

6. 1695   Books printed by Richard Wilde and are to be sold at his shop in Cork Change, Dublin

1. The Psalter for school boys, of a very good paper and price.

2. The ABC, with the Church catechism.

3. The best New Year's gift, or an epitomy of the Bible: Dedicated to King William and Queen Mary.

4. A new almanac for the year of our Lord, 1695. Containing astrological judgements for the weather, rising and setting of the sun, change of the moon &cc. With an account of the highways and fairs: and particular directions for husbandry and for ordering of orchards and gardens by Sir Samuel Moreland, Knight.

With variety of other books upon all subjects.

Source: William Sherlock, *A sermon preached at the Temple Church, December 30 1694 upon the sad occasion of the death of our gracious queen* (Dublin, 1695).

Notes

1. Máire Kennedy, 'A passion for books: the Gilbert library' in Mary Clark, Yvonne Desmond and Nodlaig Hardiman (eds), *Sir John T, Gilbert, 1829–1898: historian, archivist and librarian* (Dublin, 1999), pp 59–78 and the catalogue of his books on pp 133–41.

2. Capel Molyneux, *An account of the family and descendants of Thomas Molyneux* (Evesham, 1820), p. 74.

3. *The Guardian: volume the first* (London, 1767), pp 257–8.

4. Trinity College, Dublin, MS 1490.

5. Marsh's Library, MS Z4.5.14, ff 273v–4v.

6. British Library, Add. MS 11,687, f. 125v, 127v; Dublin City Archives, C1/J/2/4, pp 200, 216, 221, 228, C1//J/2/1, pp 78; C1/J/2/2, pp 99, 107, 117.

7. Colm Lennon, *Richard Stanihurst: the Dubliner, 1547–1618* (Dublin, 1981), p. 28.

8. *Calendar of the Carew Manuscripts: vi Book of Howth* (London, 1873).

9. *Calendar of State Papers relating to Ireland, 1608–10*, (London, 1874), p. 192.

10. John Bale, *Index Britanniae scriptorum* ed. R.L. Poole (Oxford, 1902), pp 20, 472; J.C. Crosthwaite (ed.), *The book of obits and martyrology ... of Christ Church, Dublin* (Dublin, 1844), pp xxxii–xxiv.

11. J.L. Robinson, 'Churchwarden's accounts 1484–166, St Werburgh's church, Dublin' in *Journal of the Royal Society of Antiquaries of Ireland* xliv (1914), pp 138–9.

12. L.M. Oliver, 'A bookseller's account book' in *Harvard Library Bulletin* xiv (1965), pp 149–52.

13. D.B. Quinn, 'Edward Walsh's *The office and duety in fightyng for our country* (1545)' in *Irish Booklore* iii (1976-7), pp 28–31. Copies of this work were being imported into Dublin by James Dartas, Oliver, 'A bookseller's account book', p. 151.

14. Dublin City Archives, MR/35, pp 206, 207, 329, 662, 739; J.T. Gilbert and R. Gilbert (eds), *Calendar of ancient records of Dublin* (19 vols, Dublin 1889–1947), v, pp 192, 227, 258, 330, 444, 489; vi, pp 126, 176, 227.

15. Gilbert and Gilbert (eds), *Calendar of ancient records*, vi, p. 126.

16. Historical Manuscripts Commission, *Calendar of the manuscripts of the marquess of Ormond* (new series, 8 vols, London, 1902–20), v, p. 210.

17. British Library, Add. MS 21494, f. 2.

18. Historical Manuscripts Commission, *Calendar of Ormond MSS*, n.s. iv, p. 208.

19. John Rogers, *Ohel or Beth Shemesh* (London, 1653), p. 412(10).

20. Mary Pollard, *A dictionary of members of the Dublin book trade* (London, 2000), pp 465–6.

21. For example R.J. Hunter, 'John Franckton (d. 1620): printer, publisher and bookseller in Dublin' in Charles Benson and Siobhán Fitzpatrick (eds), *That woman! Studies in Irish bibliography: a festschrift for Mary 'Paul' Pollard* (Dublin, 2005), pp 1–26.

22. Mary Pollard, *Dublin's trade in books, 1550–1800* (Oxford, 1989), pp 6–11.

23. J.W. Phillips, *Printing and bookselling in Dublin, 1670–1800* (Dublin, 1998), p. 39.

24. British Library, Add. MS 41769, f. 35.

25. Raymond Gillespie, *Reading Ireland: print, reading and social change in early modern Ireland* (Manchester, 2005), Appendix, table 1.

26. Raymond Gillespie, 'Print and Protestant identity: William King's pamphlet wars, 1687–1697' in Vincent Carey and Ute Lotz-Heumann (eds), *Taking sides: colonial and confessional mentalities in early modern Ireland* (Dublin, 2003), pp 231–50.

27. Public Record Office, London, (now The National Archives, Kew), E190/1334/14, ff 15v, 18, 20v, 25v, 34v, 43.

28. R.J. Hunter, 'John Gwillam and the Dublin book trade in 1614' in *Long Room* no. 36 (1991), p. 17; Public Record Office, London, E190/1334/14, f. 16, 19v; Pollard, *Dictionary*, p. 548.

29. Dublin City Archives, C1/J/2/4, p. 212.

30. Public Record Office, London, E190/1336/12, ff 28v, 29; E190/1336/8, f. 10; E190/1336/18, f. 13. For more details on the early seventeenth-century trade, Gillespie, *Reading Ireland*, pp 55–74.

31. Pollard, *Dublin's trade in books*, p. 41.

32. Plantain-Moretus Museum, Antwerp, MS AR320, Groteboek A, 1681–1701 pp 88, 138; Ms AR400, Daybook, 1687–88, f. 34v.

33. For Gwillam described as such see Dublin City Archives, C1/J/2/3, p. 34 and for his bookselling activities see Pollard, *Dictionary*, p. 240.

34. As well as Gwillam there are, John Franckton, c. 1610 (Pollard, *Dictionary*, p. 225–6); William Wight, 1610 (Dublin City Archives, MR/15, p. 768, Pollard, *Dictionary*, p. 613); Humphrey Sadler, 1637 (Dublin City Archives, C1/J/2/4, pp 9, 11, 14, 14); Ralph Evans, 1637 (Dublin City Archives, C1/J/2/4, p. 14), Mr Morow, in Werburgh Street c. 1640 (Representative Church Body Library, P326/27/3/27); Thomas Richardson, 1652 (Dublin City Archives, C1/J/4/1, p. 16).

35. Olive C. Goodbody (ed.), 'Inventories of five Dublin Quaker merchants in the late seventeenth century' in *Irish Ancestor* x (1978), p. 43.

36. R.J. Hunter, 'Chester and the Irish book trade' in *Irish Economic and Social History* xv (1988), pp 90–1.

37. Public Record Office, London, E190/1336/3, ff 7, 9, 12; E190/1336/12, ff 13a, 15.

38 A. Stevenson, 'Shirley's publishers: the partnership of Cooke and Crooke' in *The Library* 4th ser. xxv (1945), pp 140–61.

39 For the emergence of this courtly society see Raymond Gillespie, 'Dublin, 1600–1700: a city and its hinterlands' in Peter Clark and Bernard Lepetit (eds), *Capital cities and their hinterlands in early modern Europe* (Aldershot, 1996), pp 85–7.

40 Trinity College, Dublin, MS 809, f. 266.

41 Phillips, *Printing and bookselling*, p. 28.

42 Public Record Office, London, E190/1360/1; E190/1359/1; E190/1357/4; E190/1355/4; E190/1353/9.

43 For Helsham see Pollard, *Dublin's trade in books*, pp 42–61.

44 Pollard, *Dublin's trade in books*, pp 57–8.

45 For a more detailed reconstruction of the trade see Gillespie, *Reading Ireland*, pp 80–90.

46 Bodleian Library, Oxford, Smith MS 52, ff 73, 112.

47 Patrick Thomas (ed.), *The collected works of Katherine Philips* (3 vols, Stump Cross, 1992), iii, pp 79, 97.

48 Mary Pollard, 'Printing costs c. 1620' in *Long Room* no. 10 (1974), pp 26, 28–9; Bodleian Library, Oxford, Carte MS 221, f. 152.

49 British Library, Sloane MS 1008, ff 226, 253v, 271.

50 Historical Manuscripts Commission, *Calendar of Ormond MSS*, n.s., v, p. 599; British Library, Sloane MS 1008, f. 301.

51 Michael [Boyle], *Rules and orders to be used and observed in the high court of chancery in Ireland* (Dublin, 1685), sigs A3–3v.

52 In Neal Carolan, *Motives of conversion to the catholic faith as it is practised in the reformed Church of England* (Dublin, 1688), p. 68.

53 Pollard, *Dublin's trade in books*, pp 60–1.

54 Molyneux, *Account of the family and descendants of Thomas Molyneux*, p. 7; Thomas's correspondence with William is edited in 'Sir Thomas Molyneux' in *Dublin University Magazine* xviii (July-December 1841), pp 314, 315, 318, 320, 476, 479, 607.

55 Elizabethanne Boran, 'The libraries of Luke Challoner and James Ussher, 1595–1608' in Helga Robinson-Hammerstein (ed.), *European universities in the age of Reformation and Counter Reformation* (Dublin, 1998), pp 109–15.

56 Raymond Gillespie, 'Borrowing books from Christ Church, c. 1608' in *Long Room* no. 43 (1998), pp 15–19.

57 Felim O'Brien, 'Robert Chamberlain OFM' in *Irish Ecclesiastical Record*, 5th ser., xl (July-Dec 1932), pp 277–9; Brian Mac Cuarta, 'Catholicism in the province of Armagh, 1603–41', unpublished Ph.D. thesis, Trinity College, Dublin, 2004, p. 210.

58 Dublin City Archives, C1/J/2/4, p. 228.

59 William Hamilton, *The exemplary life and character of James Bonnell late Accomptant General of Ireland* (London, 1703), pp 7–9.

60 James Barry, *A reviving cordial for a sin-sick, despairing soul in the time of temptation* (2nd ed.[?], Edinburgh, 1722), p. 23.

61 Pollard, *Dictionary*, p. 602.

62 Pollard, *Dictionary*, p. 602; Public Record Office, London, E190/1346/12, f 21v, 30v, 36, 40, 41v.

63 Hugh Fenning (ed.), 'The library of Bishop William Daton of Ossory, 1698' in *Collectanea Hibernica* no. 20 (1978), p. 41; P.J. Corish (ed.), 'Bishop Wadding's notebook' in *Archivium Hibernicum* xxix (1970), pp 63, 65.

64 Trinity College, Dublin, MS 1375.

65 Corish, 'Bishop Wadding's notebook', pp 88, 89, 90.

66 *Christian thoughts for every day of the month* (n.p., 1698), sigs A2-A3v.

67 Richard Head, *Hic et ubique or the humours of Dublin* (London, 1663), pp 20, 21. The reference to 'the brethren' appears to be to the Baptists.

68 Trinity College, Dublin, MS 807, f. 50.

69 *The history of the life and death of St Patrick* (London, 1685).

70 Trinity College, Dublin, MS 809, ff 180, 182, 184, 186, 190, 192, 196.

71 John Bourk, *Hiberniae Merlinus for the year of our Lord 1683* (Dublin, 1683); John Bourke, *Hiberniae Merlinus for the year of our Lord 1684* (Dublin, 1684); John Bourke, *Hiberniae Merlinus for the year of our Lord 1685* (Dublin, 1685).

72 Gilbert and Gilbert (eds), *Calendar of ancient records*, v, pp 461-2, 470.

73 Bernadette Cunningham, *The world of Geoffrey Keating* (Dublin, 2000), pp 190-2, 206–8, Bernadette Cunningham and Raymond Gillespie, 'Lost worlds: history and religion in the poetry of Dáibhí Ó Bruadair' in Pádraigín Riggs (ed.), *Dáibhí Ó Bruadair: his historical and literary context* (London, 2001), pp 37–41. The 1680 portrait of Sir Neil O'Neill of Killileagh in native Irish costume by Michael Wright now in the Tate Britain Gallery, London, may be another indication of this trend.

74 For a set of such verses from Ambrose White's almanac see Andrew Carpenter, *Verse in English from Tudor and Stuart Ireland* (Cork, 2003), pp 402–4.

SWIFT.

From the Original in the Possession of G. Faulkner

Mrs Harris, her pocket and her petition*

Some thoughts on Swift's Dublin Castle poems of 1699–1701

by **Andrew Carpenter**

✦❯─❯─❯─❯─❯─❯ ✦ ❮─❮─❮─❮─❮─❮─❮

Imagine that you are in a group of servants and retainers assembled in one of the reception rooms in Dublin Castle in 1701; the Lords Justices come in to the salon through the double doors after a session in the main audience chamber where they have heard petitions of various kinds from all over Ireland relating to disputes over land ownership, over debts, over marital rights and over trade. To your surprise, one of the chaplains, a youngish clergyman named Jonathan Swift (who has a reputation as something of a 'wit'), steps forward as the Lords Justices come into the room, and starts to read aloud what sounds initially like a formal 'Humble Petition' of the kind which has taken up the Lords Justices' morning. But as you listen, you soon realise that this is some kind of a joke, for the petition is in a running doggerel verse and the petitioner, one of your fellow-servants, Frances Harris, appears to be asking the Lords Justices for 'a share in next Sunday's collection' on the grounds that she has lost her pocket full of money. This is absurd: but it is clearly 'an event', so you lean forward to listen. And this is what you hear Dr Swift read out:*

*Gilbert Lecture, January 2006

TO THEIR EXCELLENCIES THE Lords Justices of IRELAND
The Humble Petition of Frances Harris,[a]
Who must Starve, and Die a Maid if it miscarries

Humbly Sheweth:
THAT I went to warm my self in Lady *Betty's*[b] Chamber,
    because I was cold,
And I had in a Purse, seven Pound, four Shillings and six Pence,
    besides Farthings, in Money, and Gold;

a The Justices at the time were the Earl of Berkeley (1649–1710) and Henri de Massue de Ruvigny, Earl of Galway (1648–1720).

b Lady Betty Berkeley (later Germain) (1680–1769), daughter of Lord Berkeley.

---

* Editor's note. Margin notes are used for the poem, while endnotes are used for the text of the chapter.

So because I had been buying things for my *Lady* last Night,
I was resolved to tell[c] my Money, to see if it was right:
Now you must know, because my Trunk has a very bad Lock,
Therefore all the Money, I have, which, *God* knows, is a very
    small Stock,

d A small bag or pouch for money,
normally carried outside the garments
at this time.

I keep in a Pocket[d] ty'd about my Middle, next my Smock.
So when I went to put up my Purse, as *God* would have it,
    my Smock was unript,
And, instead of putting it into my Pocket, down it slipt:

10 Then the Bell rung, and I went down to put my *Lady* to Bed,
And, *God* knows, I thought my Money was as safe as my
    Maidenhead.
So when I came up again, I found my Pocket feel very light,
But when I search'd, and miss'd my Purse, *Lord*! I thought I
    should have sunk outright:

Lord! Madam, says *Mary*,[e] how d'ye do? Indeed, says I, never
    worse;
But pray, *Mary*, can you tell what I have done with my Purse!
Lord help me, said *Mary*, I never stirr'd out of this Place!
Nay, said I, I had it in Lady *Betty's* Chamber, that's a plain Case.
So *Mary* got me to Bed, and cover'd me up warm,
However, she stole away my Garters, that I might do my self
    no Harm:

20 So I tumbl'd and toss'd all Night, as you may very well think,
But hardly ever set my Eyes together, or slept a Wink.
So I was a-dream'd, methought, that we went and search'd the
    Folks round,
And in a Corner of Mrs. *Dukes's*[f] Box, ty'd in a Rag, the Money
    was found.

f *Original note*: 'One of the footmen's
wives'.
g The Earl of Berkeley's valet.
h The old, deaf housekeeper.
i i.e. Lord Galway's.
j Original note: 'Drogheda, who with
the primate were to succeed the two
Earls'. Henry Hamilton Moore, Earl of
Drogheda (*c.* 1650–1714) and Narcissus
Marsh (1638–1713), Archbishop of
Armagh, succeeded as Lords Justices in
1701. The point of the line is that Lord
Galway's retainers would have to leave
Dublin Castle when they were replaced
by those of the incoming lord justice.

So next Morning we told *Whittle*,[g] and he fell a Swearing;
Then my Dame *Wadgar*[h] came, and she, you know, is thick of
    Hearing;
Dame, said I, as loud as I could bawl, do you know what a Loss
    I have had?
Nay, said she, my Lord *Collway's*[i] Folks are all very sad,
For my Lord *Dromedary*[j] comes a Tuesday without fail;
Pugh! said I, but that's not the Business that I ail.

30   Says *Cary*,[k] says he, I have been a Servant this Five and Twenty
      Years, come Spring,
  And in all the Places I liv'd, I never heard of such a Thing.
  Yes, says the *Steward*,[l] I remember when I was at my Lady
      Shrewsbury's,[m]
  Such a thing as this happen'd, just about the time of *Goosberries*.
  So I went to the Party[n] suspected, and I found her full of Grief;
  (Now you must know, of all Things in the World, I hate a Thief.)
  However, I was resolv'd to bring the Discourse slily about,
  Mrs. *Dukes*,[o] said I, here's an ugly Accident has happen'd out;
  'Tis not that I value the Money three Skips of a Louse,[p]
  But the Thing I stand upon, is the Credit of the House;
40   'Tis true, seven Pound, four Shillings, and six Pence, makes a
      great Hole in my Wages,
  Besides, as they say, Service is no Inheritance in these Ages.
  Now, Mrs. *Dukes*, you know, and every Body under-stands,
  That tho' 'tis hard to judge, yet Money can't go without Hands.
  The *Devil* take me, said she, (blessing her self,) if I ever saw't!
  So she roar'd like a *Bedlam*,[q] as tho' I had call'd her all to naught;
  So you know, what could I say to her any more,
  I e'en left her, and came away as wise as I was before.
  Well: But then they would have had me gone to the Cunning
      Man;[r]
  No, said I, 'tis the same Thing, the *Chaplain*[s] will be here anon.
50   So the *Chaplain* came in; now the Servants say, he is my
      Sweet-heart,
  Because he's always in my Chamber, and I always take his Part;
  So, as the *Devil* would have it, before I was aware, out I
      blunder'd,
  Parson, said I, can you cast a *Nativity*,[t] when a Body's plunder'd?
  (Now you must know, he hates to be call'd *Parson*, like the *Devil*.)
  Truly, says he, Mrs. *Nab*, it might become you to be more civil:
  If your Money be gone, as a Learned *Divine*[u] says, d' ye see,
  You are no *Text* for my Handling, so take that from me:
  I was never taken for a *Conjurer* before, I'd have you to know.
  Lord, said I, don't be angry, I'm sure I never thought you so;
60   You know, I honour the Cloth,[v] I design to be a *Parson's* Wife,
  I never took one in *Your Coat* for a *Conjurer* in all my Life.
  With that, he twisted his Girdle at me like a Rope, as who
      should say,
  Now you may go hang your self for me, and so went away.

k Clerk of the kitchen.

l A man named Ferris whom Swift called (in the *Journal to Stella*, 21 December, 1710) 'that beast'.

m The dowager Lady Shrewsbury, widow of the fourteenth earl; she died in 1702.

n person (a mock-legal term).

o *Original note*: 'A servant, one of the Footmen's Wives'.

p This is a proverbial saying, like others in the next two lines.

q An inmate of the lunatic asylum in London, the 'Bethlehem'; 'to call someone all to naught' meant to abuse them.

r The fortune-teller or someone able to discover the location of stolen goods.

s i.e. Swift himself, chaplain to Lord Berkeley at the time.

t draw up a prediction, cast a horoscope – like a fortune-teller.

u Some critics have identified this phrase as a reference to Dr John Bolton, who had just received a preferment (the Deanery of Derry) which Swift thought should have come to him.

v A reference to the distinctive clothes worn by the clergy. 'Your coat' in the next line also refers to clerical garb. 'design' = intend.

w Lord Berkeley. There is a note against the word '*Harry*': 'A Cant Word of my Lord and Lady to Mrs Harris'; i.e. their usual familiar name for her. cf. Swift's calling her 'Mrs Nab' (line 55).

x to come around, after being in a bad mood, to a pleasant one.

y This last paragraph, like the poem's title, is a parody of the language of official petitions.

z The offertory money collected at the church service – normally allocated to the poor.

aa An 'order' could be a written instruction to someone (in this case the chaplain) to pay money to someone else (in this case Mrs Harris).

bb 1) pray to God, as does a clergyman; 2) pray to a senior official, as does a petitioner.

Well; I thought I should have swoon'd; *Lord*, said I, what
    shall I do?
I have lost my *Money*, and shall lose my *True-Love* too.
Then my *Lord*[w] call'd me; *Harry*, said my *Lord*, don't cry,
I'll give something towards thy Loss; and says my *Lady*,
    so will I.
Oh but, said I, what if after all the Chaplain won't *come to*?[x]
For that, he said, (an't please your *Excellencies*) I must
    Petition You.

70 The Premises tenderly consider'd,[y] I desire your *Excellencies*
    Protection,
And that I may have a Share in next *Sunday's* Collection:[z]
And over and above, that I may have your *Excellencies* Letter,
With an Order for the *Chaplain* aforesaid; or instead of Him,
    a Better:[aa]
And then your poor *Petitioner*, both Night and Day,
Or the *Chaplain*, (for 'tis his *Trade*) as in Duty bound,
    shall ever *Pray*.[bb]

If we take the time to read this wonderful poem (normally known as 'Mrs Harris's Petition') carefully, it can suggest a lot about a cultural world of which we, otherwise, know precious little – that of Dublin Castle in the latter years of the seventeenth and early years of the eighteenth century. The poem is one of the earliest of Swift's occasional verses to survive: it was written in 1701 when he was domestic chaplain to Charles, second Earl of Berkeley, one of the Lords Justices who lived, with his entourage, in Dublin Castle. Swift knew the Berkeleys – particularly the earl's daughter Lady Betty Berkeley (Germain) very well. Though we do not have an actual description of the lifestyle of the Berkeley entourage in Dublin Castle itself (what I gave you just now is an imaginary reconstruction), we do have descriptions of the family, with Swift in attendance, at their castle in Gloucestershire at roughly the same time. These descriptions show us a relaxed, friendly household in which raillery (or teasing) was an everyday occurrence. For instance, in August 1702, when Swift was visiting Berkeley Castle for a month or so, the dowager countess (by this time a woman of advanced years) used to get the young chaplain to read to her every day. She was particularly fond of a book of Meditations written by the Hon Robert Boyle;[1] one day, the story goes – it was told by Swift's godson, Thomas Sheridan the younger, and there is every reason to believe it is a true story – Swift mischievously substituted a meditation of his own. 'Lady Berkeley, a little surprised at the oddity of the title, stopped him, repeating the words, "A Meditation on a Broomstick! Bless me, what a strange subject! But there is no knowing what useful lessons of instruction this wonderful man may draw from things apparently the most trivial. Pray let us hear what he says upon it." Swift then, 'with an inflexible gravity of countenance' (as Thomas Sheridan put it), 'proceeded to read a *Meditation on a broomstick*, in the same solemn tone which he had used in delivering the former. Lady Berkeley, not at all suspecting a trick, in the fullness of her prepossession, was every now and then, during the reading of it, expressing her admiration of this extraordinary man, who could draw such fine moral reflections from so contemptible a subject; with which, though Swift must have been inwardly not a little tickled, yet he preserved a most perfect composure of features, so that she had not the least room to suspect any deceit. Soon after, some company coming in, Swift pretended business, and withdrew, foreseeing what was to follow. Lady Berkeley, full of the subject, soon entered upon the praises of those heavenly Meditations of Mr. Boyle. "But," said she, "the doctor has just been reading one to me, which has surprised me more than all the rest." One of the company asked which of the Meditations she meant. She answered directly, in the simplicity of her heart, "I mean, that excellent Meditation on a Broom-stick." The company looked at each other with some surprise, and could scarce refrain from laughing. But they all agreed that they had never heard of such a Meditation before. "Upon my word," said my lady, "there it is, look into that book, and convince yourselves." One of them opened the book, and found it there indeed, but in Swift's handwriting; upon which a general burst of laughter ensued; and my lady, when the first surprise was over, enjoyed the joke as much as any of them. . . .'[2]

Swift is shown here, as in so many of his works – *A tale of a tub*, *The Drapier's letters*, *Gulliver's travels*, 'Mrs Harris's Petition' – delighting in his ability to parody not only the subject matter of text but also its style and tone, and delighting, also, in the effect his counterfeit has on an audience. When he first read 'Mrs Harris's Petition' aloud in Dublin Castle, to the audience I imagined just now, there would have been knowing laughs and winks at particular characterisations, phrases and ways of speaking parodied in the poem, and at echoes of in-house gossip. We can only guess at these now, but we can surely sense, from the richness of the text itself when it is spoken aloud, how much the author of the poem must have enjoyed his own performance: he was, for five minutes, in complete control of the household, exercising power over an audience – doing something which he always enjoyed.

There is a further example of Swift's role as writer in the Berkeley household in a sequence of two early poems written during his 1702 visit to Berkeley Castle. 'The doctor' (as he was generally known at this time in his life) was trying to write a poem describing a game of 'Traffic', a simple card-game in which even the less intelligent members of the Earl's household and family could play a part. The poem was proving rather difficult: notes which Swift supplied to George Faulkner for the Dublin 1735 printing of this poem explain the circumstances of its composition: Swift left down the unfinished manuscript in his study one night before he went to bed. To his surprise, when he looked at the manu-script the next morning, he found that a stanza had been added in the handwriting of Lady

Betty Berkeley herself. Tickled at what one might (to use an old-fashioned word) call the 'jape', Swift wrote another poem, this time about Lady Betty's bold intervention. This second poem carried, in early manuscripts and printed editions, the title: 'Lady B----- B------- finding in the Author's Room some Verses Unfinished, underwrit a Stanza of her own, with Railery upon him, which gave occasion to this Ballade'.[3] Swift is reported, in early footnotes, to have written out this second text 'in a counterfeit Hand, as if a third Person had done it'[4] waiting for it to be 'found' and to become the centre of amused attention. In this playful and permissive environment, Swift had imagined himself as a medieval friar: the first stanza of this second Berkeley Castle poem reads:

Once on a time, as old Stories reherse,
A Fryar would needs show his Talent in Latin;
But was sorely put to't in the midst of a Verse,
Because he could find no word to come pat in;
Then all in the Place
He left a void Space,
And so went to Bed in a desperate case.
When, behold the next morning, a wonderful Riddle,
He found it was strangely fill'd in the middle.

Let Censuring Criticks then think what they list on't,
Who would not write Verses with such an assistant.[5]

The comedy in the poem is partly due to its terrible double rhymes ('Latin' with 'pat in' and 'list on't' with 'assistant'), but it is also to do with the mock seriousness of its tone and the contrast between this elevated tone 'would needs show his talent' and the use of expressions from ordinary conversation 'put to it', 'come pat in'. His juxtaposition produces what we call 'bathos'. The humorous flattery of Lady Betty 'Who would not write Verses with such an assistant' is also telling: it bespeaks a friendly, bantering relationship crossing social and class boundaries. Though the poet remains outside the story – telling it rather than showing it – for the main stanzas, the poet's voice is the one which repeats the refrain 'Let Censuring Criticks then think what they list on't, / Who would not write Verses with such an assistant'; what we have is a piece in which the reader or listener is constantly jolted by changes of register, of vocabulary and of perspective – just as happens to us as we listen to 'Mrs Harris's Petition'.

Swift first became aware of the boundless possibilities of these comic techniques when he was a student at Trinity College in the 1680s. On the days of 'commencements' or graduation at the university, a student (the 'terrae filius') was allowed to interrupt the serious proceedings with a bawdy, comic speech parodying the academics on the stage and those receiving degrees, and mocking the university and its pretensions. The 'tripos' speeches (as they were called) of 1686, 1687 and 1688 (all of which Swift heard) are an ingenious and incongruous mélange of mock-serious scholarship, bawdy farce, personal invective and parody of individual academics. They were also texts written for performance, and performance within a strictly delineated circle – in this case, the circle of staff and students of Trinity College; the jokes are only intelligible to those living within the inner circle, i.e. within Trinity College – on this occasion. But, like all 'insider' jokes, they have a powerful effect.

I have argued elsewhere that Swift was heavily influenced by these Trinity 'tripos' speeches as, during the 1690s, he worked on the texts which were to appear in the volume entitled *A tale of a tub* in 1704.[6] As in the works in that volume, there are multiple voices in the poems I am considering here. 'Mrs Harris's Petition', in particular, exhibits Swift's exuberant delight at getting inside real or invented personae and making the reader or listener judge these speakers through their own words. In each case, we (as creative readers or listeners) find ourselves grasping, through our hearing of the language, syntax and tone, the mental state of each speaker so that we see how the world looks through the perspective glasses he or she is wearing; in other words, the speaker's language defines the distortions in his or her vision. Swift is here capitalising on one of the classic devices of satire – the invitation to recognise the folly of those who see the world in a way other than that of the reader. As we hear the world described like this, our own discrimination comes into play; we realise that the worlds these people are experiencing are worlds of egregious stupidity, of nightmare solipsism or that their minds are controlled by their own gentle but crazy hobby-horses: once we have tumbled to this, we, as intelligent readers, must keep ourselves apart from these worlds, seeing them as distorted, and laughing at the seriousness with which each speaker presents his warped visions to us. And the humour is heightened by the accuracy of Swift's portrayal of character through language and language usage – through the rushes, the pauses, the changes of register and vocabulary which characterise speakers in both *A tale of a tub* and 'Mrs Harris's Petition', for instance. As we read these texts aloud, we hear the authentic voices of characters – invented but recognisable to us. Swift has discovered how to reflect distorted visions through language as he would later do in *The Drapier's letters, A modest proposal* and, most famously in *Gulliver's travels.*

In my view, the first audience for the Berkeley Castle poems, for *A tale of a tub* and for 'Mrs Harris's Petition' was, in each case, a coterie or group, the members of which shared many common experiences which meant that they could see the full extent of Swift's joking. They were laughing 'with' Swift and with each other 'at' people they all recognised. The joke of the *Tale* has, of course, a strong visual element to it also – that is, that the book is a parodic version of the object we call a book and a parody of the contents of such an object – but the rhetorical structures in many parts of that text only take maximum effect when it is read aloud: anyone who experiments with the texts by reading them aloud will, I think, agree. In any case, we have concrete evidence that the young Swift not only enjoyed parodying serious or scholarly texts, but also that he enjoyed the effect his parody had on an audience. In the majority of Swift's poems (the non-satirical as well as the satirical), we see him revelling in his manipulation of the reader – for he himself (by his own definition) is a man of 'wit and taste' writing only for readers of 'wit and taste' who can see when they are being teased, and can enjoy the experience, whether they are members of a coterie or discriminating purchasers of books or pamphlets. Of course, he is also manipulating the vision we get of the caricatured or exaggerated persons in the text – Cassinus, Peter, Corinna, Lady Acheson or members of the Irish House of Commons; Swift controls how we see these people, and relishes that control. His extraordinary rhetorical powers are harnessed to the creation of visions through which we experience the nightmares or comic exaggerations of the 'mad' or foolish personae who (Swift pretends) wrote these texts. In fact, Swift's major works, poems and prose, are not unlike sermons – exercises from which an intelligent audience or congregation should learn discrimination, and from which we should all emerge as wiser human beings.

But Mrs Harris's petition is not such a serious piece of work: it is more a testing ground for the rhetorical devices and power-games Swift was later to use in more morally pointed pieces of writing. This poem is, essentially, a travesty or burlesque of a text and of an occasion and, indeed, of a social and political structure; it starts and ends as a parody of a formal petition read aloud as a genuine petition would have been to the Lord Justices of Ireland at a quasi-judicial hearing, and subsequently presented to them as a written document, formally laid out on the page. A true petition would be phrased throughout in legal language with its absurd circumlocutions and formalities – language Swift so often parodied and so heartily despised. It would also be careful about titles – and here, the title 'Mrs' is given to Frances Harris on the basis of her age and social position rather than as a reflection of her marital status. She was, in fact, an unmarried gentlewoman – presumably with no visible means of support outside the Berkeley household – who served the countess. The pompous language at the beginning (in which the words of the title flow into the first two words of the text) is given an unexpected dimension when we learn of Mrs Harris's threatened fate if her petition is not granted – i.e. that she will starve and die a maid – and there is a further twist in the word 'miscarries': I have heard it suggested that Mrs Harris was pregnant and that her appeal is to the Berkeleys for money and to Swift to marry her. But such an interpretation underrates what I have just been discussing – Swift's ability to step inside a persona and reflect, in the headlong rush of language which is this poem, the mindset of a distraught, panic-stricken, plain-minded senior servant. In this case, the comedy is heightened by the fact that the language of the true petition is soon abandoned and becomes, in places, the language of fantasy or wish-fulfilment. The reader who does not know the gossip of the Berkeley household is genuinely surprised and entertained to learn, from the voice of Mrs Harris, not only that she wants to marry a clergyman – a perfectly worthy and appropriate aspiration in itself – but that she has her eye on Swift.

One of the delights in the piece comes from the juxtaposition of the formal and informal speech. In the first place, a ceremonial petition to the Lords Justices containing phrases such as 'the Chaplain aforesaid', about something as unimportant as a lost purse is inherently comic; secondly, the unthinking use of particular, formal phrases – such as 'I resolv'd to bring the Discourse about' – is made to seem absurd when the reader sees it placed next to the demotic proverb about 'Three skips of a louse'; and the reader is entertained by double meanings throughout the poem – such as those around the words 'pray' and 'trade' in the lines: "And then your poor Petitioner, both Night and Day, / Or the Chaplain, (for 'tis his *Trade*) as in Duty bound, shall ever *Pray*." Just as the reader gets one register sorted out, Swift introduces another speaker or gets Mrs Harris's voice to skip to another register: the colloquial: 'I thought I should have swooned' is not far in the text from the formal 'I desire your Excellencies Protection'. Equally, we must be amused by the double meanings around the word 'tenderly' – on the one hand a legal term to do with tendering a plea in court, and on the other the standard word expressing, presumably, Mrs Harris's feelings towards the man she hopes to marry – though he certainly appears off-hand and dictatorial here.

These jumps of register and tone are unexpected and unprepared-for: when the poem was read aloud by Swift (for Mrs Harris herself would not [and perhaps could not] have read it aloud), one hears an educated, middle-class male voice (imitating the tone of a lawyer) speaking words put into the mouth of a minimally-educated, middle-class female, in a petition full of clichés, proverbs and solecisms. The joke is partly an oral / aural one. Swift was fascinated by people whose speech was peppered with homely clichés, and came back to play with cacozelia (as this rhetorical device is called) several times later in his writing life – particularly in *Polite Conversation* in which he ridiculed the inanity of the speech of people of fashion, and in *Irish Eloquence* in which he poked fun at the colourful, Hiberno-English used by Irish planters (such as those he would have met when visiting Thomas Sheridan in Co. Cavan). Cliché of word bespeaks cliché of mind. In addition, Swift loved to detect what we now call Malapropisms (rhetorical devices known, before Mrs Malaprop, as examples of 'soraismus'), as well as the absurdity of the language and mind-set of members of any institution which takes itself too seriously – of churchmen, professional writers, academics, musicians, Presbyterians, politicians, lawyers, doctors, publishers or booksellers. In this poem, he plays not only with legal terminologies but also with the language and tone of senior members of Lord Berkeley's household (who certainly took themselves seriously) – the housekeeper Dame Wadgar, Cary (clerk of the kitchen), and the steward (whose name was Ferris); he also gives us the voices of more junior servants – Mary (who wisely takes Mrs Harris's garters from her) and Mrs Dukes (who was, apparently one of the footmen's wives) – as well as those of Lord Berkeley and Lady Berkeley. In fact, the poem contains voices or grumpy sounds from at least nine members of the household – all of them, except that of Swift himself, English voices belonging to people English born and bred. And Swift enjoys playing with the different class registers (Mary calls Frances Harris 'Madam', the chaplain calls her 'Mrs Nab', and Lord Berkeley calls her 'Harry'), and milks to the full the entertainment value of words misheard and misunderstood. This leads to Dame Wadgar's memorable naming of the Earl of Drogheda as 'My Lord Dromedary', and of Lord Galway as 'My Lord Collway'.

One of the high points of the poem's hyperbole and caricature is in Swift's comic depiction of himself as the brusque, forthright and sharp-tongued chaplain. He is thoroughly unsympathetic in his dealings with Mrs Harris – nettled at her blurting out a remark which confuses the status of chaplain with that of a mere fortune-teller or street conjurer, and feeling no need to be even superficially polite to her. In addition, his name for her, 'Mrs Nab', seems a disparaging nickname – particularly as seventeenth-century cant meanings of the word included a fop, a fool, a cheater and a wheedler; what the chaplain actually says to Mrs Harris is also distinctly offhand – in contrast to the sympathetic treatment she gets from Lord and Lady Berkeley: 'It might become you to be more civil', he says to her: 'You are no *Text* for my Handling, so take that from me.' Swift must have felt completely confident of his place in the real-life household of Dublin Castle to portray himself as so unsympathetic in his dealings with a woman looking for help from him, but the exchange is particularly enjoyable as we learn that Mrs Harris has been flirting with, and has hopes to marry this tetchy parson. Swift's swinging of his girdle at her reminds us also that he had a particular, visible status in the household as he strode around in his cassock, while the reference to the Sunday collection reminds us that the money put into the collection plate in Anglican services would, at this time, have been distributed to the poor of the parish – among which group, Mrs Harris now numbers herself.

And then, of course, we have the form of the poem – lines of varying lengths (but usually with four main stresses) in ferociously rhyming couplets, the rhymes either embarrassingly predictable masculine ones (lock/stock/smock) or ticklishly ingenious feminine ones (Shrewsbury's/gooseberries, cunning man/anon). Clever rhyming tetrameters had become the standard form for comic verse in Swift's youth – most famously in Samuel Butler's *Hudibras*, but also in many Irish poems in English from the period of the Restoration. There are poems in this metre in the manuscript Whimsical Medley (1686–1722) in Trinity College,[7] for example, and the regular tetrameter was to become Swift's preferred verse form for satiric and comic verse for the rest of his life. But here (as in the later poem in the same form, 'Mary the Cookmaid's Letter')[8] Swift's language bursts the metrical form with enviable freedom and flexibility to reflect differing speaking voices with great skill and accuracy.

Few writers of the eighteenth century – and indeed, of any other age – have captured the bursting energy of the spoken word as well as did Swift. There is a confidence and an audaciousness which rushes us into the mind and actions of Mrs Harris *in medias res* with the breathless, hyperactive torrent of 'That I went…', 'And I had…', 'So, because I had been buying…' 'Now if you must know…' In this poem Swift is playing with the representation of the spoken voice precisely as he is in the texts he was writing at the same time; if there is only one such voice in the 'Meditation upon a Broomstick', there are at least five different authorial voices in *A tale of a tub* – each of them with its own intonation, its own vocabulary, its own way of forming sentences and of speaking them. Swift has inveigled himself into the personalities of each of the creatures he has created, reproducing their mindset in their voices. This is precisely, of course, what he was to do so effectively for the rest of his writing life. Only in his correspondence – and perhaps in the *Journal to Stella* – but even in those two places, not by any means all the time – can we hear the authentic voice of Jonathan Swift. Otherwise, the Dean impersonates others, speaking through their voices, using their vocabulary and capitalising on the craziness of their ways of seeing the world – their perspective glasses.

So what can we conclude about this poem: firstly, that it was written and designed to be read aloud by a male voice in the domestic circle of the Berkeley family in Dublin Castle. Secondly, that this was a community in which Swift, confident of his place in the household, felt free to tease, to parody, to satirise and to mimic anyone below the Lord Justice and his mother: even Lady Betty was open to ridicule. It is safe to assume, also, that the poems which have survived were not the only ones written in this place at this time – by Swift or, maybe, by others too. What we have now is what was available when the Swift canon was provisionally established by George Faulkner and others in 1730s – but much else was circulating in manuscript and has since disappeared. (Manuscripts were in constant demand for the lighting of fires and pipes, for the lining of pie dishes and for certain lowlier uses; only a fraction of what was circulating in the seventeenth and eighteenth centuries has come down to us). In the third place, Swift had learned how to manipulate public performance of verse and prose in this domestic and limited context and how to get laughs: poems were 'performed' in Dublin Castle in the early eighteenth century – as we know they had been in the Restoration period. Swift enjoyed the power which the performance of such texts bestowed on him – he relished it, he sought it. Finally, these Dublin poems show the same self-confidence and control of language and tone as *A Tale of a Tub*, which Swift was probably still revising (with the other early prose texts) at the time of his residence in Dublin Castle. In fact, the works show the same mind at work – one bursting with brio and self-confidence, one blessed with an impressive mastery of rhetorical devices and an iconoclastic sense of fun. But let none of this commentary distract us from the delight of this poem. As I have said elsewhere, this is the finest poem in English to come out of Early Modern Ireland.[9] We should celebrate and enjoy it as such.

Notes

1 Robert Boyle, *Occasional reflections upon several subjects...* (London, 1665).

2 Thomas Sheridan, *The life of the Rev. Dr. Jonathan Swift, Dean of St. Patrick's Dublin* (2nd ed. London, 1787) pp 37–9.

3 *Miscellanies in prose and verse* (London, 1711), p. 361.

4 *The works of the Reverend Dr Jonathan Swift volume* VIII (Dublin, 1772), p. 221.

5 *The poems of Jonathan Swift* ed. Harold Williams (3 vols, Oxford, 1958), I, 76–7.

6 Andrew Carpenter, "*A tale of a tub* as an Irish text", *Swift Studies* 20 (2005), pp 30–40

7 TCD Ms. 879.

8 Swift's *Poems* ed. Williams, III, 985–7.

9 Andrew Carpenter, *Verse in English from Tudor and Stuart Ireland* (Cork, 2003) p.18.

Through streets broad and narrow*

Dublin's trams

by Michael Corcoran

Getting Around Cities: The First Trams

As cities grew in size during the nineteenth century, the provision of public transport systems became increasingly important. The horse-drawn bus was introduced from France to London in 1829 and Dublin had similar services within a few years.

*Gilbert Lecture, January 2007

Nineteenth century Dublin was a compact city, the canals and circular roads constituting most of its boundary. Outside this cordon, nine independent townships were established between 1834 and 1879. Kingstown was the first, calling itself the Premier Township and was served by Ireland's first railway. The Dublin and Kingstown Railway offered one of the world's first suburban passenger services.

Carlisle Bridge in the 1870s with DTC tram No. 9 heading for Nelson Pillar. The bridge was widened and renamed in 1880

Horse buses were boxlike and uncomfortable, the poor road surfaces of the time aggravating a very uncomfortable ride. In contrast, early tramroads and railways had vehicles running on smooth rails, carrying more passengers in greater comfort and affording an easier draught for the horses. In 1832, John Stephenson, a New York-based Irish coach-maker built a vehicle that ran on rails in the street. Improved and developed, Stephenson's pioneering work led to the widespread introduction of street tramways around the world.

While some Dublin suburbs and townships had railway or horse bus services, there were widespread hopes of a tramway network that would give easier access to all parts of the city. In 1867, the City of Dublin Tramways Company's proposed service from Kingsbridge (Heuston) Station to Earlsfort Terrace via the South Quays, D'Olier Street, Brunswick (Pearse) Street, Westland Row, Upper Merrion Street and St. Stephen's Green was aborted because of the type of rail to be used.

The Dublin Tramways Company

In 1871, the rights of the City of Dublin Tramways Company were acquired by the Dublin Tramways Company, which obtained its first empowering Act in 1871. The DTC's first line connected the city with Rathmines, the prosperous township established in 1847 and already served by horse buses, which were acquired by the DTC. The Managing Director of the Dublin Tramways Company was the enthusiastic William Barrington of Glasnevin, who passionately promoted tramways, proposed traffic regulation, expressed concern for the poor and for horse welfare.

Dublin's first trams ran on 1st February 1872 between College Green and Rathgar via Dawson Street, Harcourt Street and Rathmines, with a journey time of twenty minutes. The line was later extended to Terenure and Nelson Pillar, a total distance of 3 1/2 miles. The four cars that provided the service on the first day carried 2,055 passengers who received souvenir tickets showing an image of a tram and a portrait of Queen Victoria. Two additional cars were expected imminently.

The gauge of the Terenure line and all subsequent tramways in Dublin City was the same as that of Irish railways – five feet and three inches (1600 mm). This was later reduced fractionally, enabling railway vehicles to run on their wheel flanges in the grooves of the rails. The DTC's first depot was at Terenure, opposite St. Joseph's Church, and which today houses an electrical firm.

During the 1840s, a central longitudinal seat along horse bus roofs increased seating capacity, the passengers sitting back to back on what came to be called the knifeboard seat. Access was by a ladder, with railings along the vehicle sides to prevent passengers from falling off. In time, the ladder evolved into a spiral staircase from a platform on which the conductor stood and which also eased access to the lower deck.

There has always been interchange of developments between vehicle types and so double-deck knifeboard trams came to be. Trams, double-ended vehicles with which the horses were brought round to the opposite end of the vehicle at termini, had a platform and staircase at each end. When women began to travel on the upper decks, decency

DUTC horse tram No. 50 in Baggot Street bound
for Donnybrook.
This tram was scrapped on 25th July 1887

A model of horse tram (No. 3 number notional)
made by Spa Road craftsmen.
Model restored by Dublin Bus in 1987

boards were fixed to the railings to preserve female modesty and these boards soon
displayed lucrative advertising.

The DTC's first trams, supplied by the Metropolitan Railway and Carriage Company,
were described as 42-seaters, twenty downstairs (inside) and 22 upstairs (outside). These
trams were probably 46-seaters, a capacity common on horse-drawn double-deckers. The
discrepancy arose from deciding how much space should be allowed to each passenger.
The minimum laid down was sixteen inches but Dublin Corporation, using its supervisory
powers, increased this to eighteen inches in January 1873.

The two horses that pulled each tram were changed at intervals during the day and a
stud of ten animals, a standard often not reached, was the ideal usually stipulated for each
car. There were also trace horses that were attached to the normal team to pull trams up
steep inclines and these were in the care of trace boys stationed at the bottom of each
incline. The stables for the horses occupied a considerable space at the depots and the
animals had the services of farriers and a veterinary surgeon.

At first, a flat fare of three pence was charged on the Terenure trams but a one penny
tariff for passengers travelling a shorter journey was introduced following public agitation.

Reduced fares were offered for "inferior carriages", often meaning seats on the outside (top) of double-deckers. This arrangement was intended primarily for artisans, mechanics and daily labourers who could afford to ride. Fares were to remain controversial throughout the history of the Dublin tramways and, despite the difficulty of making adjustments for currency changes and inflation, were not dissimilar to what is normal today.

On 3rd June 1872, the DTC opened its second route, the one originally proposed in 1867 from Kingsbridge to Earlsfort Terrace. It became known as the Three Stations line, serving Kingsbridge, Westland Row (Pearse) and (from Earlsfort Terrace by Hatch Street), Harcourt Street. The fare from either terminus to Carlisle (O'Connell) Bridge was two pence, or three pence all the way. The depot for this line was at Victoria Quay, on the site of the present Guinness Brewery garage.

Across the Grand Canal lay the southeastern township of Pembroke, established in 1863. It included the village of Sandymount which became an increasingly attractive residential area in the 1870s. While the railway to Kingstown (Dun Laoghaire) served part of Sandymount, a tramway was a more convenient mode of transport and so the DTC built its third line, Nelson Pillar-Sandymount, which opened officially on 1st October 1873. It shared the tracks of the Three Stations route between D'Olier Street and Lower Merrion Street, where it turned along Merrion Square North, Lower Mount Street and on to Northumberland Road. It turned again past Beggar's Bush, going on by Bath Avenue to Tritonville Road and Sandymount Road. A one-way system brought the outgoing track through Seafort Avenue on to Beach Road towards the terminus at the Martello Tower. Incoming cars left Beach Road at Newgrove Avenue, travelling by Sandymount Green to resume two-way running at Sandymount Road. The depot for this line was at Gilford Road.

Donnybrook was another developing Pembroke suburb in the 1870s that was served by the Dublin Tramways Company with a line opened in March 1873. Starting from Sackville Street, the Donnybrook trams shared the Terenure track as far as Dawson Street, then went by way of Nassau Street to Merrion Square North along which they used the Sandymount rails. They branched right along Merrion Square East and up Lower Fitzwilliam Street, turning left into Baggot Street, and right again into Waterloo Road. Turning left on to Morehampton Road and through Donnybrook village the line terminated just beyond the Dodder at Donnybrook Church. Opposite the church, a depot was built on part of the site now occupied by the (newer) Donnybrook Garage No. 2 of Dublin Bus.

Although the smaller and less affluent north side developed more slowly than the south side, Clontarf, Drumcondra and Glasnevin became attractive middle class residential areas in the 1870s. Clontarf village lay at the end of Vernon Avenue, with some large houses in the area and incipient ribbon development along the main road. There were Town Commissioners in office from 1869, when new roads were being developed. Clontarf had a horse bus service, taken over by the Dublin Tramways Company shortly before the opening of its new line on 31st May 1873. Clontarf trams operated from Nelson Pillar via North Earl Street and Talbot Street, Amiens Street and Fairview, with a three penny fare. At 4.1

miles the Clontarf line was the DTC's longest, served by a depot where Clontarf Bus Garage is today.

The last line opened by the DTC had its terminus on Bachelor's Walk and ran to Parkgate Street. Known as the North Quays line, it opened on 16th April 1874. Its trams were housed in the Victoria Quay depot. Two months before the North Quays line opened the DTC, operating sixteen route miles, had 70 trams and 435 horses, well short of the ideal ten animals per car. In 1875, the DTC purchased the six cars of the short-lived Cork Tramways and put them to work on the Terenure line. Improvements made by the DTC to its trackage included a line through Lower Abbey Street and Gardiner Street, connecting with the Clontarf line at Talbot Street.

The North Dublin Street Tramways Co.

Following disagreements with his fellow directors, William Barrington left the DTC and established the North Dublin Street Tramways Company to construct lines authorised but not built by the DTC. He also believed in extending tramways to the less affluent areas of the city, the DTC being described (in 1878) as an institution, "making excellent returns to the proprietors, and proving of great convenience to passengers of the genteel and well-to-do classes." On 10th December 1876, the NDST opened a line from Sackville Street via North Frederick Street and Berkeley Road to North Circular Road, which it traversed to the Phoenix Park gate. At Dunphy's (now Doyle's) Corner, a branch or second line diverged into Phibsborough Road, going along the Prospect and Botanic Roads to Glasnevin (Botanic Avenue).

The third NDST line had a temporary city terminus at Grattan (Capel Street) Bridge, from where its trams ran via Capel and Dorset Streets to Drumcondra, the route ending at Botanic Avenue. In operation by 1877, the NDST trams contributed notably to the development of Drumcondra, which became a Township in 1878. The Drumcondra line also represented Barrington's philosophy in serving working people, as did the last NDST line, to Inchicore.

Beyond the city boundary at South Circular Road was the Township of New Kilmainham, established in 1868 and with its population overwhelmingly made up of tradesmen. The Inchicore line, which was in full operation by July 1877, had its city terminus at College Green and went to Inchicore via Dame Street, Thomas Street, Mount Brown and Kilmainham, the terminus being at Tyrconnell Road just beyond the Black Lion public house. The line from Drumcondra was extended across Grattan Bridge, up Parliament Street and along the Inchicore tracks to the College Green terminus. The contractor who built these lines was William Martin Murphy.

The NDST, which strived for economy that led to corners being cut, operated some one-man single-deckers. On these cars, the passengers dropped their fares into a transparent box beside the driver. The NDST 's northside routes were served by a large depot at Dalymount on the North Circular Road, while the Inchicore trams had a depot at Goldenbridge.

The Dublin Central Tramways Company

The Dublin Central Tramways Company, incorporated in 1878, shared the College Green terminus of the North Dublin. William Martin Murphy, who later became a director, built and equipped this company's six mile system of three routes.

The first DCT line, fully operational by May 1879, ran via South George's Street, Camden Street and Charlotte Street (now closed) to Ranelagh. Turning into Charleston Road at the Triangle, the line continued through Charleston Road and Belgrave Avenue to Palmerston Park. From the Ranelagh Triangle, also called the Angle, a branch extended to Clonskea. At Kelly's Corner, the Central's longest route branched into Harrington Street from Camden Street. At Leonard's Corner it turned off for Rathfarnham, going via Harold's Cross and Terenure.

By June 1879, the entire DCT system was in operation with a fleet of 22 trams, including some single-deckers for the Clonskea branch. The company had two depots – at Clonskea and Terenure, where Cormac Terrace now stands.

Working on the Trams

In an era of harsh working conditions, working on the trams was regarded as good employment. Being a driver involved standing on the open front platform in all weathers and although slightly less exposed, the conductor fared little better. Everything had to be done according to each company's Rule Book, usually based on a standard text that was suitably modified to suit particular local circumstances.

The Rule Books usually contained a contract for every employee, all emphasising the employer's rights and the employee's duties and responsibilities. Drivers were expected to attend regularly ten minutes before starting, in uniform, and with badge, whip and whistle. They were required to examine their horses and report if one of them was unfit for work.

Conductors were to be present fifteen minutes before starting time. They had to brush the cushions, polish the windows and brass-work and see that the lamps were in good order. Both drivers and conductors were to look out for potential passengers, encouraging them to travel.

There were explicit instructions for depot staff, particularly those looking after the horses. However, most of the staff loved the animals in their care, which many people believed received better attention than the humans who looked after them.

Long working hours, days off and dining facilities were constant causes of disputes and the plight of the men was often raised by people like Sir George Owens, a tramway shareholder who was also a doctor and city councillor. Drivers and conductors usually had to consume their meals between journeys at Nelson Pillar or outer termini, family members often bringing the food to their fathers, husbands or sons. These conditions persisted long into the electric era.

The Dublin United Tramways Company

All three Dublin tramway companies were small and mergers had been mooted as far back as 1877. They finally combined to form the Dublin United Tramways Company in July

1880. The new entity took charge of 32 route miles and 137 tramcars: 82 from the DTC, 25 from the North Dublin and 30 from the Central. William Anderson, formerly Manager of the DTC, became Secretary and Manager of the DUTC, with R. S. Tresillian of the North Dublin as his assistant. William Martin Murphy was one of the directors.

Right to the end of the horse era, the DUTC continued to integrate and improve the formerly separate systems. New connections were installed and some routes were extended from College Green to the Pillar – and vice-versa. Only one new line was opened; that to Dolphin's Barn, opened in 1896 and which continued along the South Circular Road from the Rathfarnham line at Leonard's Corner.

The DUTC exploited every opportunity to increase revenue. Advertising on the cars was an obvious source, and a lucrative parcels service was inaugurated in 1883. A penny fare introduced early in 1884 was so successful that 69,942 passengers were carried on Whit Monday, 2nd June. The company was proud of its efforts and in 1886 could point to the service on the Rathmines line. The buses that operated the route prior to the trams ran every 13 minutes and could carry 31 passengers, while the trams had a three-minute frequency and could accommodate 41 passengers.

One of the DUTC's greatest achievements was the establishment, in 1882, of the tramcar works at Spa Road, Inchicore. Previously trams were imported, but with a few exceptions, new vehicles were henceforth built at Spa Road. William Martin Murphy, who believed in the industrialisation of Ireland, would not import anything that could be made within the country and practised this principle throughout his life. The works, which later built buses, achieved an outstanding reputation for craftsmanship and remained in production until 1978. The first tramcar built at Spa Road in 1882 was No. 138. By 1889, trams with a central aisle between double seats, known as garden seats, outside (on top) were being turned out.

Serving Blackrock, Kingstown, Dalkey

On 19th March 1879, the Dublin Southern District Tramways Company connected Kingstown and Dalkey. The line, which was of 4' 0" gauge, had its Kingstown terminus at the bottom of Royal Marine Road. The company's second line, on the 5' 3" gauge, ran to Blackrock from the junction of Northumberland Road and Haddington Road, where its terminus adjoined the DUTC line to Sandymount. The DSDT had two depots, at Ballsbridge (Shelbourne Road), and Dalkey.

In August 1885, the Blackrock and Kingstown Tramways Company opened a line between the two townships. This concern, which had its depot at Newtown Avenue, Blackrock, ran on the 5' 3" gauge.

Steam: Lucan and Blessington

There were two steam tramways in the Dublin area. The first was the Dublin and Lucan, whose 3' 0" gauge from Conyngham Road to Palmerstown began to operate in June 1881. The complete line to Lucan was ceremonially opened on 17th February 1883.

The 5'3" gauge Dublin and Blessington Steam Tramway, which had its Dublin terminus at Terenure, opened on 1st August 1888, an extension to scenic Poulaphouca following in 1895. The D & B carried freight as well as passengers.

While steam had advantages, its appeal to urban tramway operators was limited. The Dublin Tramways Company tested a steam locomotive, *Pioneer*, on the Donnybrook line in July 1877. The Southern District company went further in 1881 with two Kitson locomotives on the Blackrock line. All the tests were technically successful, but powerful opposition was mounted by the horse lobby and speed restrictions also militated against steam traction in urban areas.

The Electric Tram

The electric tram was invented in 1879 by Werner von Siemens. Following a gestation period, one of the earliest electric lines in the world opened in 1883 between the Giant's Causeway and Portrush. Early electric trams suffered from dangerous and unreliable methods of current collection which were eliminated with the perfection of the overhead sprung trolley by Frank Sprague in the USA in 1887. An unstoppable challenge to horse traction was now imminent.

Clifton Robinson at the controls of No. 2
on opening of electric services.
Kingstown 16th May 1896

Travelling by horse tram from Nelson Pillar to Dalkey was only for masochists, involving three changes of car, but changes of a more revolutionary nature began in 1892. Imperial Tramways, which owned the Southern Districts Company, appointed J. Clifton Robinson, a gifted engineer and businessman, as Managing Director. In August 1893 he bought out the Blackrock and Kingstown and immediately prepared to unite and electrify the entire line from Haddington Road to Dalkey.

A generating station capable of driving fifty trams was built at Shelbourne Road, with substations at Blackrock and Dalkey. The overhead wiring was supported by elegant poles, a diminishing number of which are still in use as lamp standards. An initial fleet of twenty 54-seater motor trams and twenty 46-seater trailers, all built by Milnes of Birkenhead, was purchased.

DUTC horse tram 170 and electric car No. 31 at Annesley Bridge, c. November 1897

Electric trams began running between Haddington Road and Dalkey on 16th May 1896 and were immediately successful. Robinson now proposed to extend his line into the city in direct competition with the Dublin United Tramways Company. The DUTC was already planning electrification but was being stymied by Dublin Corporation, which opposed overhead wiring in the city. In 1896, the DUTC was operating about 162 horse trams over 33 route miles. The highest fleet number carried by a horse tram was 188.

While photographs of important events such as the start of the Dalkey electric service have exact dates, many other old pictures are inaccurately captioned. But the trams and other vehicles in these pictures, while of little or no interest to most historians and writers, invariably set the period, sometimes very narrowly, of old streetscapes. Vehicle history, already recorded, locates many Dublin scenes within tight timeframes.

The DUTC (1896) Ltd.: Electrification

William Martin Murphy, Chairman of the DUTC, tackled the company's challenges in a typically forthright manner. He bought out the Southern Districts Company in September 1896 and set up the Dublin United Tramways Company (1896) Ltd., which obtained the necessary powers to operate electric trams. For legal reasons the DSDT remained in existence until 1905. William Anderson became Managing Director of the new DUTC, with R. S. Tresillian as Secretary. The General Manager was Charles W. Gordon.

The first section of the DUTC system to be electrified was the outer part of the Dollymount line. Clontarf depot was extended and modified and a steam-powered generating station capable of driving 25 trams was installed. Its 112-foot red brick chimney was for many years a prominent landmark. A fleet of twelve Milnes-bodied trams, distinguished by having five windows at each side, was purchased for the Clontarf electrification. They took the numbers 21–32, immediately following numbers 1–20 of the former Southern District cars.

On 11th November 1897 electric cars began operating as far as Annesley Bridge, which was the boundary between Clontarf and the city. Negotiations with the Corporation were successfully concluded shortly afterwards and the first electric trams in public service to the city centre reached Nelson Pillar on 20th March 1898.

Once the initial obstacles were overcome, the DUTC pressed ahead with electrifying and extending its system. Having sufficient power was a problem so plans were

Trams in Upper Sackville Street 1899. Turreted building is DUTC head office

drawn up for a large generating station at Ringsend. Equally critical in the electrification programme was the availability of new trams.

Trams for the electrification programme came from three sources: new vehicles built at Spa Road or from outside builders; and converted horse trams: 86 of these vehicles were rebuilt and were easily distinguishable by having seven windows between the bulkheads as opposed to four or five on cars built as electrics. One former horse car, No. 84, was destroyed by fire in August 1899.

The Dalkey electrics reached Nelson Pillar on 12th July 1896, initially via Westland Row and Great Brunswick Street, but via Nassau Street from October. Following a fatal accident at Merrion Square in November 1898 the use of trailers was discontinued and all thirty of these vehicles were rebuilt as motor trams by mid-1900.

By the beginning of 1898 there were around 90 electric trams, the operation of which taxed the capacity of the Ballsbridge and Clontarf generating stations, which between them could energise 75 cars, very severely.

The DUTC experienced great frustration, frequently expressed, at the delays in equipping the Ringsend power station. Several routes that were already wired up were still operated with horse trams. The new Kenilworth Road-Ballsbridge route, which had been built in sections, opened with horse cars on 22nd August 1898, as did also the reconstructed North Quays line, on 1st November. This route had been closed since 1896 to facilitate the laying of a main drainage interceptor sewer.

Morale was boosted, however, when the Phoenix Park line through Phibsboro went electric on 22nd November. This was joined, on 23rd January 1899, with the Donnybrook line, giving the city its first cross-town service. But no further conversions could take place until the Ringsend power station became operational on 28th August 1899.

Conversions now followed very rapidly, the Nelson Pillar-Terenure line going electric on 28th August – the day Ringsend opened – and all the lines, with one short exception, were changed over by early 1900.

Radial services from the city centre went electric as follows: College Green-Inchicore, 4th September 1899, O'Connell Bridge-Parkgate Street, 18th October; Nelson Pillar-Palmerston Park, 24th October; Nelson Pillar-Clonskea via Appian Way and Leeson Street, 1st December; College Green-Drumcondra via Capel Street, 5th January 1900. The Kingsbridge-Hatch Street line saw its first electric cars on 16th January 1900.

Two important cross-city services resulted from amalgamating four previously radial lines. The entire route from Drumcondra to Rathfarnham via Rutland (Parnell) Square and Harold's Cross, afterwards regarded as the backbone of the cross-city system, was electrified on 9th November 1899. The Dolphin's Barn-Glasnevin line changed over on 4th December 1899 and was extended from Botanic Avenue to the corner of Ballymun Road.

Two new routes were opened in 1900. On 4th July a service was inaugurated between Sandymount Tower and Grand Canal Dock; it was extended via Great Brunswick Street to Nelson Pillar on 18th March 1901. Another new service began on 1st October between

Ballybough and Parkgate Street, going via Parnell Street and Capel Street to join the North Quays at Grattan Bridge.

The remaining horse service referred to earlier was the line to Sandymount via Bath Avenue, animal traction being latterly confined to the section between Haddington Road and Irishtown Road. This was due to the low railway bridge at Bath Avenue, under which double-deck horse trams could just about squeeze, but electrics could not. The solution was single-deckers, Dublin's only such electric vehicles, which replaced horse traction on 14th January 1901 with a full service from Nelson Pillar to Sandymount Tower.

From its earliest days, Ringsend power station was continuously improved and was soon able to energise 300 trams. On its completion, generating plant was removed from Ballsbridge and Clontarf, which became sub-stations operating the outer ends of the Dalkey and Howth lines in February 1901.

The DUTC electrification gave Dublin one of the world's finest tramway systems, which became a model to be copied in other cities. Even greater developments were to follow, but three other electric tramways owned by different companies opened in the Dublin area by 1901.

Among the many disputes between the DUTC and Dublin Corporation was that of way leaves. From the beginning of horse tramways, the companies had to maintain the road-way between the rails and for eighteen inches on either side. An additional burden placed on the DUTC from the time of electrification was a fixed annual payment to the local authority for each mile of tramway. Interpretation battles continued until 1925.

The Dublin and Lucan Electric Railway

When faced with the need for renewal in 1897, the Dublin and Lucan Steam Tramway Company decided to change over to electric traction. The line was rebuilt, its gauge widened by six inches to 3' 6". The line re-opened on 8th March 1900 and was extended to Dodsboro (the Spa Hotel) in 1912. This was a partial revival of an extension of the steam line to Leixlip, abandoned some years previously.

The Dublin and Lucan Electric Railway, as the line was now known, had its generating station at Fonthill in a building which still exists; its Dublin depot was where Conyngham Road bus garage now stands. The D & LER had eight-wheeled (bogie) cars seating 62 and 66 passengers. These were Dublin's first eight-wheeled trams.

Dublin and Lucan bogie car No. 14, 1900

Clontarf & Hill of Howth Tramroad Co.

This company's name suggests that it operated over the Hill of Howth. Instead, the Clontarf and Hill of Howth Tramroad Company built a line from Dollymount to the East Pier at Howth. Originally intended to serve Killester and Raheny, it eventually materialised as an end-on junction to the DUTC Dollymount line.

The Clontarf and Hill of Howth Company opened its line on 26th July 1900. It had a complicated relationship with the DUTC, which provided traction current and other services. In the early years crews changed at Dollymount, known as the junction but by 1907 the entire line to Howth was managed and operated by the DUTC.

The Clontarf and Hill of Howth Company purchased twelve bogie open-top trams numbered 301–312, the highest DUTC fleet number for some years being 293. There was a small depot at Blackbanks capable of holding twelve trams but Clontarf was where the Howth vehicles were housed.

Hill of Howth tram No. 1 at Howth Station in early 1900s

Dublin – Howth line No. 301 at Howth Station,
Hill of Howth car on bridge

The Hill of Howth Tramway

During the 1890s the Hill of Howth became increasingly attractive as a place to live or as a tourist destination. Sutton and Howth stations are less than two miles apart on the railway but more than five by road across the hill. In 1897, the Great Northern Railway obtained the Act which authorised the construction of the legendary Hill of Howth Tramway.

The Sutton and Howth Electric Tramway ran from a terminus now occupied by the car park at Sutton Station. At Sutton Cross, it crossed the

Dublin-Howth line on the level. It went via Carrickbrack Road to the Summit station, three and a quarter miles from Sutton. The descent to Howth was less than two miles, the trams crossing Harbour Road on a bridge, and terminated in the railway station yard. The line was single throughout with passing loops and a simple signalling system.

Power for the trams came from a generating station at Sutton in the red brick building that later became a paint factory. The depot was where the Sutton sewage pumping station now stands. The tramway opened in two sections: Sutton to the Summit on 7th June 1901 and from the Summit to Howth on 1st August.

The Hill of Howth Tramway had ten bogie passenger cars: Nos. 1–8 supplied by Brush in 1901 and Nos. 9 and 10, built by Milnes in 1902. There was also an all-purpose engineering and goods car, probably built in 1903 and numbered 11.

DUTC Growth and Development

In the early years of the twentieth century, Dublin faced many challenges. The municipal boundary was extended in 1901, bringing the former Clontarf, Drumcondra and Kilmainham townships into the city. There was a grave housing deficit, with thousands living in terrible conditions that would prevail for several more years. Unemployment was rife and, despite the herculean efforts of Sir Charles Cameron, the City Medical Officer, health and nutrition were major concerns.

Building development continued in the more genteel areas, which was where the vast majority of the DUTC's passengers lived. The trams were well patronised and there were prospects of attracting extra passengers from several suburbs. As a result, two lines were extended, a new link provided in the city centre and a completely new route opened in the first six years of the new century.

From horse days, Drumcondra trams terminated at Botanic Avenue. There was already some new building around Home Farm Road and the 1901 city boundary extension would encourage more. This led the DUTC to build the Whitehall Extension, bringing the tracks to a new terminus just beyond the junction of the Swords road (at that time a country road) and Griffith Avenue, which was more than twenty years into the future. The terminus, and later the area, was named after a house called Whitehall, which was just north of the present Garda station. The extension opened for traffic on 7th September 1903 and was originally single track with passing loops at Ormond Road and Wellpark Avenue.

A new route was opened on 27th January 1905 with a branch that left the Terenure line at Rathmines for Dartry. The new line went by way of Upper Rathmines Road and Highfield Road into

D.U.T.C. TRAMWAY SERVICES

No.	Route		No.	Route	
1	NELSON PILLAR - RINGSEND		16	WHITEHALL - TERENURE	
2	NELSON PR. - SANDYMOUNT GN.		17	DRUMCONDRA - RATHFARNHAM	
3	NELSON PR. - SANDYMOUNT TOWER		18	KENILWORTH RD. - LANSDOWNE RD.	
4	NELSON PR. - SANDYMOUNT VIA BATH AVE.		19	RIALTO - GLASNEVIN	
5	PHOENIX PARK · PEMBROKE NELSON PILLAR		20		
6	NELSON PILLAR - BLACKROCK		21	INCHICORE · COLLEGE GN. · WISTLAND RW.	
7	NELSON PR. - DUN LAOGHAIRE		22	KINGSBRIDGE - HATCH ST. - RATHMINES	
8	NELSON PILLAR - DALKEY		23	PARKGATE ST. - BALLYBOUGH	
9	PHOENIX PARK - MERRION SQ. - DONNYBROOK		24	O'CONNELL BDGS. - PARKGATE ST.	
10	PHOENIX PK. - ST. STEPHEN'S GN. - DONNYBROOK		25	O'CONNELL BDGS. - LUCAN	
11	CLONSKEA - DRUMCONDRA		26	O'CONNELL BDGS. - CHAPELIZOD	
12	NELSON PR. - PALMERSTON PARK		28	JAMES'S ST. - ST. LAWRENCE RD. (LATER NELSON PR. - FAIRVIEW)	
13	FAIRVIEW - WESTLAND ROW VIA ABBEY ST.		29	NELSON PR. - CASTLE AVENUE	
13			30	NELSON PR. - DOLLYMOUNT (ST. LAWRENCE ROAD - 30A)	
14	NELSON PILLAR · DARTRY GLASNEVIN		31	NELSON PILLAR - HOWTH	
15	NELSON PR. - TERENURE RATHMINES		–	COLLEGE GN. - CAPEL ST. - WHITEHALL	

Symbols as used from 1903 to 1918

No. 154, one of 50 trams imported from the USA in 1899 at Dartry terminus

Dartry Road to its terminus near Orwell Park. The Palmerston Park rails were extended to join with the new route at Highfield Road, affording the Palmerston Park trams access to the new Dartry depot, now the offices of a consulting engineering company.

The Dolphin's Barn line was extended westwards to Rialto on 20th May 1905, the new terminus lying just short of the former canal bridge that now spans the Luas tramway to Tallaght.

On 14th May 1906 a new service began between Phoenix Park and Donnybrook. Instead of following the existing route serving Nassau Street, Merrion Square Lower Baggot Street, the new alternative was by Dawson Street, Merrion Row and over new tracks in Baggot Street to rejoin the existing route at Fitzwilliam Street.

The network now totalled 54 route miles, mostly double track. Various changes were made to the layout throughout the system to improve the service, e.g. a short spur in Palace Street to accommodate a terminus for Dublin Castle and the laying of tracks in Anglesea Road to cater for major shows at the RDS.

The Staff and Their Passengers

The staff of the DUTC was noted for efficiency and courtesy. To distinguish them from their predecessors on the horse trams, the skilled drivers of electric cars were known as motor-men. Conductors also had more responsibility, especially in relation to the correct wiring and roping of the trolley.

Motormen and conductors were smartly dressed, uniforms at that time being seen as an emolument. Kepi style caps were worn, but conductors and inspectors changed to strawboater hats during the summer months. In later years, army type service caps were worn the year round, with detachable white covers in summer. The elaborate enamel cap badge showed the wearer's title. Motormen and conductors displayed licence badges.

Until World War I, passengers were given coloured geographical tickets. There were dedicated issues for each line and the values were colour coded, e.g. three pence was pink, four pence was green. The geographicals listed the stage points, but the standard issue that replaced them on all routes from 1918 had the stage numbers printed down each side of the ticket. There were returns, season and special event tickets. The conductor's Bell punch rang to indicate that the ticket was holed at the appropriate stage point. Collecting tickets was a popular childhood activity and the innumerable issues and styles of tickets have been the subject of serious study by many people.

Although there were well marked stopping places, conductors were allowed latitude in outlying or lonely places, especially in bad weather or after dark. Special consideration was shown to the elderly or infirm and to women with children.

The DUTC favoured men from the country in filling vacancies, but the sons of existing or deceased staff members also received preferential treatment. Cottages were built adjacent to the depots and were much appreciated by staff lucky to qualify for them. Tramwaymen were held in high esteem by the travelling public, but the terms and physical conditions under which they worked were little changed from the horse days and the company did everything possible to thwart unionisation.

Behind the front line staff there were great numbers of workers whose very existence was unknown to most people outside the company. Among many others in that invisible community were fitters, electricians, bodymakers, painters, overhead linesmen and power station engineers. Then there were administrators, managers, storemen – even today, the support staff in any large transport company is virtually invisible.

First Generation Electrics

Most first generation electric trams were generically similar in appearance, with open platforms and staircases. In 1901, the DUTC fleet of 293 four-wheeled cars included 156 from outside builders, 52 built at Spa Road and 85 former horse cars. But even by then, major advances in Dublin tramcar design and construction had taken place. On No. 191, new from Spa Road in December 1899, the canopies were extended over the platforms, which also had vestibules or windscreens. This set the standard for most subsequent cars and many of the older vehicles were rebuilt to this pattern, which usually increased the seating capacity by four.

The design of the vestibules became a distinguishing feature of Dublin's trams, the rubbing strake or moulding along the sides of the cars extending all the way around the

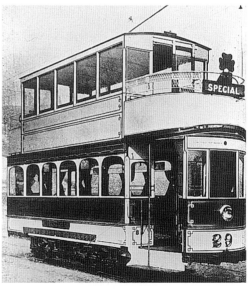

No. 29 of 1897 rebuilt as Dublin's first top covered tram, it left Spa Road in October 1904.
Note Dalkey Shamrock

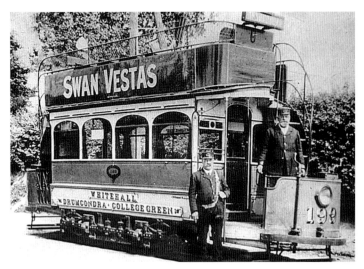

No. 199, a former trailer, at Whitehall
soon after the extension opened in 1903

dash or vestibule structure, with the headlamp in the upper panel and the fleet number below. There was a further advance in October 1904 with No. 29, a rebuilt 1897 Clontarf car. It not only received vestibules but also had a covered upper deck with an open balcony at each end. On later cars, the roof was extended out over the balcony.

In the horse era, trams on the various lines were painted in different liveries, enabling people who were illiterate to identify their car. The Southern District electrics were green, but Prussian blue and ivory was the livery adopted by the DUTC. However, the background colour of the removable destination boards on the sides of the trams continued the horse tram tradition and at first large boards above the platforms of open-fronted cars proclaimed the destination.

Backlit roller destination blinds, always known in Dublin as scrolls, were first used in 1903, with a symbol special to each route surmounting the box. There were squares, circles, shamrocks, lozenges, triangles and other shapes. At night, identification was further simplified by two coloured bullseye lights above the scroll, the combination varying according to the route. A coloured table showing the symbol for each line appeared in the timetable.

Another feature of the trams was the exterior advertising, most of it on enamelled plates screwed to the upper deck panelling. The coloured plates were highly artistic, some surviving to the end of the tramway era, by which time there were also many paper posters. A study of tram advertising in old photographs provides a fascinating perspective on social and commercial history.

A particular tram from this period deserves special mention. Aloof from its more ordinary fellows, this was the Directors' Tram, built at Spa Road in 1901 and intended for the use of the Directors and their guests. An open top four-wheeler, it had internal window pillars carved as classical columns, carved hinged tables and a drinks cabinet. There were carved armchairs, special lampshades and twelve coloured etchings of Dublin scenes in the ventilator windows.

The Directors' Car had splendid upper deck wrought iron railings. It never had a fleet number and was the only Dublin tram to carry the city arms, the Three Castles, on its sides instead of the company garter. Mounted on a Dublin-made truck, this unique vehicle, rarely used after 1913, survived until 1949 through the efforts of Charles Ross, a foreman at Ballsbridge depot. To transport what the Customs House is to architecture, the transcendent Directors' Car still exists in a very sad state.

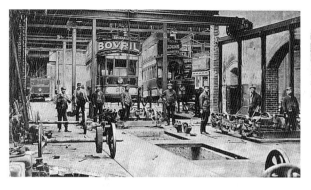

Above: A freight train at Ringsend. The locomotive is a former passenger car.

Left: Nos. 32 and 65 undergoing overhaul at Ballsbridge in early electric days. The bodies have been lifted from the trucks

Freight and Refuse

The parcels express service, instituted in 1883 and further developed on the electric system, was a useful source of revenue. In 1909, it was joined by a freight service, by which large loads, such as sand, gravel, building materials or coal could be delivered in wagon loads to any part of the system. When they were retired from passenger service, some old trams were rebuilt as locomotives to haul the goods wagons.

There was intensive exchange of traffic between the DUTC and the Blessington steam tramway at Terenure, dairy, farm produce and quarried materials coming in and various heavy items going out. There were also cattle wagons which were electrically hauled to and from the Dublin Cattle Market on the North Circular Road. The Blessington management at one time considered electrifying their line as far as Jobstown, but instead tried petrol-electric traction, unsuccessfully.

Another activity centred on the reclamation of the foul sloblands where Fairview Park is today. From 1907, all the city refuse was brought to an incinerator at Stanley Street, the ashes and other debris being loaded into wagons owned by Dublin Corporation. There were three electric locomotives and at night, when normal passenger traffic had ceased on the tramways, trains of wagons were hauled down Queen Street to the North Quays line and via Lower Abbey Street to Fairview. This service operated until about 1927.

A large permanent way yard, which contained track, poles, wiring and all the items needed to maintain the tramway system, was developed beside the Ringsend generating station. This operated until 1929, after which the whole operation was transferred to Donnybrook. The newer (No. 2) Dublin Bus garage now occupies the site of the Ringsend Permanent Way Yard.

The Golden Age

The Golden age of Dublin's Tramways was the decade that preceded World War I. A constantly improving service with ever better cars were the most obvious features of the system, with special facilities that attracted passengers on to the longer lines. During this period, DUTC men Tierney and Malone invented the automatic point, a device later adopted on most tramway systems. This enabled a tram to select its route at a junction without the need to change the points manually.

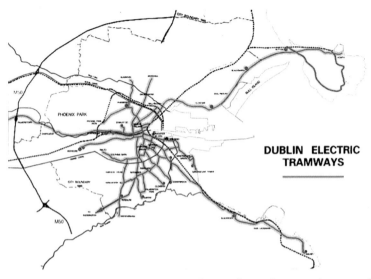

DUBLIN ELECTRIC TRAMWAYS

Map of tramways in the Dublin area. The M50 is marked as a reference boundary

A major step forward was the introduction of eight-wheeled (bogie) cars on the Dalkey line in 1906. Nine of these were imported incomplete and finished at Spa Road, but the first to be built entirely at Spa Road, No. 313, set a new standard in craftsmanship. Up to 1912, a further twenty-nine of these vehicles were built at Spa Road for the Dalkey line and it was these trams that made DUTC craftsmen and the vehicles they built so famous. DUTC maintenance standards were very high and systematic replacement of older cars began in 1909. When a tram was withdrawn its fleet number went to its replacement, resulting in cars of the same type having a scatter of numbers. The highest fleet number was 330 and non-passenger cars were numbered in a separate series. A new depot was built at Blackrock c. 1906, housing the majority of the Dalkey trams, some of which were based at Shelbourne Road and Dalkey.

The Dalkey bogie cars were known as Windjammers to the tramwaymen. The sight of one of these brightly illuminated giants swaying majestically was surely what inspired AE to write:

Mine eyes behold new majesties; my spirit greets
The trams, the high-built glittering galleons of the streets.

Before World War I, morning and evening, special limited stop trams operated on the Howth and Dalkey lines. The Dalkey expresses, which were especially famous, overtook ordinary trams at Ballsbridge and Booterstown, where the stopping cars changed lines to let the expresses pass. The express trams could run for up to four miles without a stop, something inconceivable today. Three Dalkey trams specifically allocated to this duty were Nos. 79, 85 and 183.

Trouble and Strife

At its zenith, the Dublin tramways suffered its first major blow in August 1913. During the next ten years the Dublin trams would be centre stage in a series of events unique in the history of transport.

Low wages, harsh conditions and long hours without any job security were but four of the many burdens borne by tramway staff, who were forbidden to join James Larkin's Irish Transport and General Workers' Union. During June and July 1913 many of the tramwaymen joined the Union, as did workers in the *Irish Independent*, the newspaper owned by William Martin Murphy. Murphy, who was the leader of the employers' organisation, sought promises from his employees that they would resign from the union and not join it in the future.

The remains of No. 308, blown up at the corner of Earl Street and Sackville Street, Easter week 1916

Forty *Independent* employees were dismissed on 15th August, followed by a hundred tramwaymen a few days later. The situation worsened rapidly, a dramatic event taking place on 26th August. The Dublin Horse Show began on that day, and at ten o'clock that morning, motormen and conductors walked off their trams, leaving them where they had stopped. Disputes now broke out everywhere and within a week 25,000 people were either on strike or locked out.

Demonstrations degenerated into serious disturbances in which 50 policemen and 500 civilians were injured; two subsequently died. The plight of the workers and their families got steadily worse until the lockout ended on 19th January 1914. The employers' victory over the humiliated workers, however, was a pyrrhic one because people now realised their own worth and the age of deference was all but over. Many people joined the Irish Citizens Army, formed to protect workers' rights and destined for future fame.

During the uneasy months of early 1914, a spectacular accident occurred at Merrion Square. Just before 9.30 on the evening of Sunday 1st February, balcony bogie car No. 295, with Motorman Downes and Conductor Kavanagh and 22 passengers was outbound on the Dalkey line. The points opposite Holles Street malfunctioned and the tram overturned. Twenty-two people were injured and one of the six more seriously hurt later died. This accident was a unique occurrence, the DUTC having a good safety record.

During the Howth gun running on Sunday 26th July a large party of police and soldiers called to Clontarf Depot, demanding transport to Howth to thwart the Irish Volunteers. The Depot Inspector was Patrick Clifford, who would not allow four-wheeled trams to proceed beyond Dollymount and was unable to provide crews for any bogie cars that might have been available. Nor could he assist them to get in touch with Dublin Castle, the telephone having mysteriously gone dead. By the time matters were resolved the Volunteers had long left Howth with the arms and ammunition.

War broke out in August 1914 and Murphy, who supported John Redmond's Irish Party and Home Rule, endorsed the British Army's recruitment campaign. Festooned with posters and flags, tram No. 242 toured the city encouraging men to sign up. Until its replacement in 1922, tramway staff called this tram the Recruiting Car.

When the Easter Rebellion or Rising began on Monday 24th April 1916 the trams were operating normally, services not being suspended until the afternoon. During the terrible days that followed, one DUTC employee was killed. James Hogan was a carter who worked out of the Nelson Lane (now Earl Place) stables. One of two men who came in to look after the terrified horses during the fighting, he ventured out twice on Thursday (27th) to get milk. On his second outing he was shot down in North Earl Street, an unsung hero needlessly killed.

There was considerable damage to the overhead equipment in the city centre and two trams were totally destroyed. Howth line car No. 308 was blown up at the junction of North Earl Street and Sackville Street. No. 72, an unvestibuled former horse car, was burned out at Usher's Quay. No. 18 and another unidentified car appear in a photograph of St. Stephen's Green where they formed part of a barricade.

War conditions affected the DUTC in several ways, the supply of coal for the generating station being a particular worry. Costs rose as did fares and there were some service cutbacks. The most serious of these was the withdrawal of some services in 1918. A short-lived cross-town route that ran from Fairview to Rathmines was closed, as was the one from College Green via Capel Street to Drumcondra on 21st March. It re-opened briefly in 1922, and its disappearance resulted in the first permanent track closure, reducing the efficacy of the centre city network.

A more progressive event in 1918 was the replacement of the symbols by route numbers. These were probably introduced gradually and the system adopted was very simple. Starting in the southeast at Ringsend, numbers were allocated in the order of the termini going round clockwise until 31 was reached at Howth; there was an allowance for possible extensions. Fifteen of the numbers are still displayed on buses working over the tram routes that originally had them.

The years 1920–1922 were traumatic for the DUTC and its employees. Curfews, raids, threats and a generally dangerous atmosphere made life very unpleasant. An example was cited by Joe Greally, who was collecting fares on the upper deck of a tram in South George's Street in 1920. A revolver was thrown into his cash bag by a passenger when a Black and Tan patrol stopped the tram. Joe resourcefully hid the gun in the destination box and later, failing to identify the coward who had endangered him to own up, turned the weapon in as lost property.

Major Changes

Several DUTC management changes took place in the second decade of the twentieth century. The first major loss was the death, on 31st August 1910, of William Anderson at the age of 70. He was well liked by the staff and more than 330 uniformed tramwaymen, including 30 inspectors, marched in his funeral procession. Charles W. Gordon, the General Manager, was killed in a riding accident on 27th May 1915. Two days later Richard Tresillian, the company Secretary, also died. The loss of such an experienced and resolute management team appeared complete with death in June 1919 of William Martin Murphy.

None of the DUTC directors was as forceful or focussed as Murphy, but the appointment in 1916 of George Marshall Harriss as General Manager was inspirational. He was a decisive personality capable of motivating dithering directors and bringing the tramway system through difficult times. Harriss was an outstanding electrical engineer and skilled administrator who would serve the company well for eighteen eventful years.

The DUTC was again at the centre of hostilities during the civil war in 1922, when staff were threatened and terrorised by both sides. Many fine buildings, starting with the Four Courts, were destroyed when hostilities broke out and on 5th July the entire east side of Upper Sackville Street was devastated. Included in the conflagration was the DUTC head office, No. 9 at the corner of Cathedral Street. With it went an irreplaceable historical archive including a comprehensive photographic collection.

Renewing the Fleet

On a more positive note, tramcar building had resumed at Spa Road in 1917 with a replacement for No. 72, one of the cars lost in 1916. In 1918, an intensive programme, which was to continue in three stages until 1936, got under way. During the first stage, which lasted until 1922, 31 new open-top four wheelers were built and 90 were reconstructed. Forty new balcony cars were also turned out and the second stage followed on from these.

Balcony trams were unable to pass under some bridges and this led, in 1922, to the construction of a new lower style of car. No. 8, completed in October 1922, was the first of 33 similar trams, the last emerging in 1924. A further development followed with the commissioning in August 1924 of No. 111, the first totally enclosed Standard Saloon, 57 similar cars being built up to 1929. These were the all-weather trams so often called for by passengers enduring the elements on open-top or even balcony vehicles.

A problem arose with the four-wheeled balcony cars, those built before 1922 being taller than the new ones. Because the fleet numbers were random, an accident involving a tall balcony car and a bridge was

Top: No. 129, a standard balcony car built in 1923, at James's Street, and below, rebuilt as a standard saloon, seen in St Stephen's Green in 1948

always possible – and this happened at Westland Row in 1925. To avoid any further incidents, it was decided to have all 33 standard balcony cars fitted with Standard Saloon tops, bringing the total of these trams with excellent route availability to 91.

The upper and lower deck structures of Dublin trams were built separately, facilitating transfers. As they were removed, the surplus balcony tops were fitted to open-top cars, and fifteen extra top covers were built up to 1931, increasing the number of four-wheeled balcony trams to 87; 178 of 282 four-wheeled trams were now top covered.

The Dalkey Windjammers, always seen as a somewhat separate fleet, also evolved further after 1917. The last four, built in 1924, incorporated several features of the standard four-wheeled balcony cars and the next two Dalkey cars, 224 (1925) and 218 (1926) were totally enclosed Bogie Standards. They were also the last new Dalkey trams with transverse rather than longitudinal seats downstairs.

Buses – Lucan Closure and Resurgence

By 1922, the DUTC and its staff had come through a devastating period of upheaval: the 1913 labour dispute, World War I, the 1916 Rising, the War of Independence and the Civil War all had their effects. Now growing numbers of constantly improving motor lorries and buses were becoming a serious threat to the railways and tramways. Incipient traffic congestion also influenced matters, leading the DUTC to end its commercial freight service on 1st July 1927.

The Dublin and Lucan Electric Railway was now very weak and in urgent need of renewal. It also experienced, from 1923, intense competition from the Tower Bus Company. Early in 1925, while negotiations for a possible DUTC takeover were in progress, the D&LER went bankrupt, all services except a mail contract ceasing on 29th January. Many people were left without a service.

At that time, the DUTC was seeking powers, which were not included in its 1905 Act, to operate buses. Negotiations with the Dublin City Commissioners, who had replaced the elected councillors in 1924, led to the DUTC agreeing to take over the Dublin and Lucan. The company got its bus operating powers and the first DUTC bus ran from Eden Quay to Killester on 9th July 1925. The long running wayleaves dispute was also resolved.

Under the provisions of the Dublin United Tramways Company (Lucan Electric Railway) Act of 1927, the DUTC took over the Lucan line, reconstruction beginning in September. The tramway was relaid to the 5' 3" gauge, with several extra loops or passing places and a modern signalling system. The new terminus was at Lucan village and the line was connected to the North Quays tracks at Parkgate Street: Lucan trams could now operate from O'Connell Bridge.

Trams on the new route 25 began operating in May 1928: to Chapelizod on 14th and all the way to Lucan on 27th. Twenty minutes were allowed for the journey to Chapelizod, forty for the entire nine miles to Lucan. The reconstructed line attracted good numbers of passengers, especially at holiday periods.

Conyngham Road Depot was rebuilt and a new bus garage later opened at its western end. Fonthill power station became a substation, fed from Ringsend by a high tension cable. Power to local customers previously supplied from Fonthill was maintained until the Electricity Supply Board took over. Some service vehicles were based at Fonthill.

Nine new Bogie Standard trams were built at Spa Road for the Lucan line and were joined by the two built in 1925–26. This least numerous class in the DUTC later acquired a curious twelfth hybrid member (No. 313) that presaged the entry of the Dublin tram into a completely new age.

A New Age: Buses and Luxury Trams

The DUTC, which had so far closed only one section of route, was faced with severe bus competition in the late 1920s. The General Manager, George Marshall Harriss, was dedicated to maintaining and improving the tramway system and foresaw extensions when traffic levels would justify them. He also appreciated that trams and buses should complement each other in a modern system of transport. The bus fleet therefore expanded rapidly, numbering about 100 vehicles by 1932. DUTC buses were built at Spa Road from 1925 onwards. The buses shared the Prussian blue and ivory livery of the trams, but both types of vehicle received a new colour scheme of French grey and white in 1929.

The South Quays tram line (Route 22), which was paralleled by the one on the north side of the Liffey, was closed on 30th March 1929. The single-deck Route 4, Nelson Pillar to Sandymount via Bath Avenue, was replaced by a bus service on 31st July 1932.

While opinions varied, four-wheeled trams were generally expected to have a working life of about twenty-five years. But eight-wheelers, if properly maintained, could last much longer and the DUTC therefore considered converting some of the early Dalkey Windjammers into saloons. No. 313, the 1906 Spa Road prototype, was successfully rebuilt in 1929 but its styling belonged to a different era and could not compete with the sleek buses coming into service around that time. The tram badly needed a new image.

In the 1930s, many tramway systems throughout these islands needed renewal. Track, overhead and trams would have to be replaced at great cost and too often the decision was abandonment, buses being seen as an attractive alternative to the trams. In Britain and Ireland, only about a dozen tramway systems invested in new trams in the 1930s, and the

Luxury trams nos. 9, 135 and 26 at Terenure c.1947

Bogie luxury car No. 326, second last new tram,
it left Spa Road Works in October 1936, Blackrock, 1949

DUTC was the only company-owned one to do so. The 57 new trams built between 1931 and 1936 were very different from No. 313, the 1929 rebuild.

Bogie Luxury tram No. 280, the first of twenty eight-wheelers built up to 1936, entered service on the Dalkey line in April 1931. While the body design owed much to contemporary bus styling, it also exhibited features that placed it firmly in the evolution of the Dublin tram. Curved lines, half-drop windows and chrome or stainless steel in place of traditional brass, made this vehicle stand out. Inside, reversible seats with backs and cushions in moquette, recessed lights and white ceilings put this timeless design well ahead of its time. Seating capacity was 74.

Later in 1931, No. 131 was the first of 37 four-wheeled Luxury 60-seaters. Although allocated to various routes around the city, a preponderance of the Luxury cars served routes along which lived people with cars and whom the DUTC was anxious to entice on to the trams. Fifteen of the bogie cars were allocated to the Dalkey line, while five went to Clontarf to work the basic winter service on the Howth line.

The Howth open-top fleet, increased from 12 to 15 trams, carried large numbers of day trippers during the summer. The three extra Howth cars were older double-deckers that had been cut down to single-deck for the Bath Avenue service and were now open-toppers.

A unique vehicle allocated to Clontarf was No. 80, known as the Storm Car. Originally a horse tram, it had its motors mounted high above the axles. It was able to operate along the sea front between Clontarf railway bridge and the Bull Wall during floods caused by high tides that inundated the roadway prior to work on the Clontarf Promenade in 1936.

Monopoly – Beginning of the End

Around 1930, bus competition was an increasingly serious problem for the railways and the DUTC. The Dublin and Blessington Steam Tramway, which had attracted heavy leisure traffic in times past was in serious trouble in the 1920s. Its freight traffic had transferred almost exclusively to lorries and the Poulaphouca extension closed in 1928. The company tried rail buses and a railcar but they were ineffective and the line from Terenure to Blessington succumbed to competition from Paragon buses on 31st December 1932.

A series of early 1930s enactments which imposed tightening conditions on all road transport operators culminated in powers for the statutory companies to compulsorily buy out their competitors. As a result, twenty-five private bus undertakings were acquired by the DUTC between 1933 and 1936, more than 260 vehicles being taken over.

The largest, best organised and most powerful of the acquired companies was the

General Omnibus Company, taken over in November 1934. This was akin to a reverse takeover, with officials from the General filling senior posts in the DUTC. It happened that George Marshall Harriss, who was on sick leave at that time, was about to retire as General Manager of the DUTC and he was replaced by A. P. Reynolds of the General. With the retirement of Harriss, the future of the tramway system became very dubious.

A new livery of Audley green and cream was applied to the trams from the end of 1935. The first car to wear this colour scheme was Luxury bogie car 300 of the Howth (31) line.

Reynolds, an accountant and convinced busman, wasted little time in persuading the DUTC directorate that buses were flexible, economical to operate and more modern than the trams. At that time, the highly successful and constantly improved Leyland Titan, originally introduced in 1927, was setting new standards in double-deck bus design, with its thrifty diesel engine and metal-framed bodywork. Aggressive advertising by Leyland took advantage of the view that all trams were obsolete and that buses could provide a better service. While Reynolds's plans to replace the Dublin trams were already being formulated, the last Luxury car, No. 327, left Spa Road on 17th October 1936. By that time, only 39 open-top four-wheeled trams remained and these had been effectively withdrawn. In any case, less than 270 cars were required to fulfil timetabled services.

Despite their days being numbered, several four-wheeled balcony trams were overhauled a few months before being withdrawn. A premature withdrawal was No. 76, the victim of Dublin's second instance of a tram overturning, on 1st November 1937. On Washerwoman's Hill in Glasnevin it ran out of control and failed to negotiate the right hand bend half way down. There were no serious injuries but the tram was written off.

Following the arrival of two prototypes in 1937, the construction of metal-framed 56 seater R class Leyland Titans began at Spa Road. The first closure under the replacement programme took place in February 1938 when Rialto (19) trams were cut back to Dolphin's Barn. The first services to be withdrawn completely were Ballybough-Parkgate Street (23) and O'Connell Bridge-Parkgate Street (24), on 16th April 1938. Dollymount (30) followed on 31st May.

Just before the beginning of the changeover to buses, the trams were carrying 88.5 million passengers per year, while the buses accounted for 65.3 million.

On 1st January 1939, buses took over from trams on Route 12 (Palmerston Park), which was extended as a cross-town service to Cabra. During 1939, two important cross-town routes were closed: Glasnevin-Dolphin's Barn (19) on 5th March and Whitehall-Terenure and Rathfarnham (16, 17) on 30th April. At the same time, the Whitehall-Nelson Pillar section of the No 11 route to Clonskea also ceased, its southern section closing on 2nd July.

The College Green-Inchicore line finished on 4th February 1940, cutting off the Spa Road Works from the remainder of the system. The last tram to be overhauled at Spa Road, No. 110, had left the Works on 6th January 1939. After that, all overhaul work on trams was carried out at Ballsbridge. For more than 20 years from 1939 Patrick Colman, the meticulous paint shop foreman at Spa Road, recorded the identity and departure date for every vehicle that left the works.

Route 25, O'Connell Bridge-Lucan, closed on 12th April 1940. The Bogie Standard trams which operated this line were transferred to the Dalkey route where they replaced some of the older balcony cars dating from 1906–1910.

Sandymount services (2, 3) were withdrawn in stages, final closure taking place on 26th March 1940. The southern section of Route 9 (Donnybrook-Phoenix Park via Dawson Street) and all of Route 10 (Donnybrook-Phoenix Park via Merrion Square) closed on 2nd June 1940. The northern part of Route 9 was replaced by buses four days later. The final closure of the year was on 1st December when trams were withdrawn from the Kenilworth Road-Lansdowne Road (18) route.

By this time, about 220 trams had been replaced by an equal number of Leyland Titans. On 29th March 1941 Motorman Dick Ward brought the last Howth (31) tram, No. 294, in to Nelson Pillar. On this occasion, no replacement buses were required as Howth was already served by Great Northern Railway buses running through Killester and Raheny. Reflecting the change in the company's operations, its title was changed to the Dublin United Transport Company in 1941 and the Winged Wheel symbol, known as the Flying Snail, replaced the garter belt on vehicles.

It was originally intended to complete the changeover to buses by 1944, but worsening wartime shortages of vehicles, materials and fuel prevented this. Only three tram routes now remained – the Dalkey (8) with its short workings to Blackrock (6) and Dun Laoghaire (7); and the shorter lines via Rathmines to Dartry (14) and Terenure (15). As these would now have to operate indefinitely ninety trams were overhauled at Ballsbridge and continued to provide excellent service. A much propagated myth has persisted that the former DUTC system and its trams were rickety and worn out but nothing could be further from the truth. Maintenance on rolling stock, track and overhead was, as always, to the highest standard.

For most people, the war years were a time of misery with shortages, rationing and an all-pervading atmosphere of gloom. Bus services were continuously cut back, last buses eventually leaving the city centre at 9.30 p.m. A drought in 1944 caused a shortage of electricity and on 1st April last tram departures were cut back to 9.30 p.m. Worse followed two months later when the trams were withdrawn completely and replacement buses had to be filched from every possible source, including as far away as Cork. The trams were restored to service, amid much public satisfaction, on 22nd October.

Córas Iompair Éireann

The state of public transport throughout the country became so grave in 1944 that the Government decided to amalgamate the DUTC and the Great Southern Railways. There was bitter public reaction and a nasty general election following which the scheme went ahead. Córas Iompair Éireann came into being on 1st January 1945 with A. P. Reynolds as Chairman and the DUTC operations, with 113 trams and 364 buses, became the Dublin City Services of CIE.

CIE met with some initial success, leading to a reduction in fares in March 1946. This

No. 308, the car destroyed in 1916 was replaced in 1920. This vehicle at Donnybrook awaiting the breakers in 1941

saw the tariff from Nelson Pillar to Terenure reduced to three pence, the same as it had been in 1872. Unfortunately, rising costs and wages, industrial disputes and political chicanery began to effect a sharp deterioration in the company's performance. Inevitable fare rises, culminating early in 1949 with the withdrawal of the sacrosanct one penny fare introduced in 1884, caused great disquiet.

Following a change of government in 1948, Reynolds was replaced as Chairman of CIE by T. C. Courtney who held office beyond the final demise of the trams. Since 1946, CIE had been turning out new buses to restore existing services and replace thirsty worn-out petrol-engined vehicles, hoping in time to reach a stage when it could replace the remaining trams.

Early in 1948 a Leyland offer of a hundred complete Titan double-deckers was grasped by CIE. Existing bus routes were strengthened with these Bolton class buses, of which there were enough by the autumn to replace the Dartry and Terenure trams. The last trams on these lines ran on 31st October, when Motorman Tom O'Brien and Conductor Tom O'Shaughnessy crewed No. 57 to Terenure. It was followed shortly into the depot by No. 291, the last Dartry car, with Motorman Tom Cahill and Conductor Paddy Butler.

In 1949 Leyland, which had to export as much of its output as possible to earn overseas money for Britain, made a further 50 Titans of the Capetown class available to CIE. It was originally intended that the last trams would run on Saturday 2nd July but due to trade union negotiations the closure was deferred for one week. In the early hours of Sunday 10th July, the last car to carry passengers on the Dalkey line, No. 252, staggered into Blackrock depot, severely vandalised.

Trams replaced in the earlier stages of conversion to buses were all scrapped but the bodies of the trams from the Dartry, Terenure and Dalkey lines were sold off and survivors can still be found around the countryside. A few lengths of track lie covered over in the streets and some traction poles are still used as lamp standards.

The last Dublin tram, No. 252 enters Blackrock depot in the early hours of Sunday 10th July 1949, badly vandalised

Farewell and Hail: Hill of Howth and Luas Trams

The GNR Hill of Howth Tramway outlived the Dalkey line by ten years. Its fate was sealed when CIE, then in a stringent cost-cutting phase, took over all GNR services and assets in the Republic on 1st October 1958. This was the last tramway anywhere to operate only open-top trams and its tourist potential was, sadly, not exploited.

During the Spring of 1959, the eight serviceable Hill of Howth trams – Nos. 5 and 8 had been cannibalised – could barely cope with the great numbers of people they carried. On 31st May, Tom Redmond drove the last tram from Howth to Sutton. He was followed from the Summit by No. 9 which, crewed by Christy Hanway and Alf O'Reilly, closed Ireland's first tramway era. Strangely, the three buses that replaced the Hill of Howth trams were from the batch that had taken over from the Dalkey cars a decade earlier.

Five Dublin trams and one from the Hill of Howth survive in the care of the National Transport Museum. Two of them provide a direct link between the DUTC and Luas systems. Highlighting the reintroduction of trams to Dublin, restored open-fronted car 224 and Bogie Standard 253 have appeared at several venues. No. 224, with several retired tramwaymen aboard, was at St. Stephen's Green for the opening of the Sandyford Luas line at the end of June 2004 and No. 253 was stationed at Collins Barracks for the start of the Tallaght service in September. Few tramway systems served any city as well as Dublin's first one did and the most frequently asked question from people who enjoy the Luas trams and encounter the survivors from 60 years ago is why did they ever get rid of them?

Hill of Howth
nos. 7 and 10
at the summit
in the mid 1950s

Notes on contributors

DOUGLAS BENNETT is a lecturer, writer and broadcaster. A member of the Institute of Professional Auctioneers and Valuers from 1980 to 2005, he has written widely on antiques, especially Irish silver, and on aspects of Dublin's cultural history. He is the author of *Irish Georgian silver* (1972), *Collecting Irish silver 1637–1900* (1984), *The Company of Goldsmiths of Dublin 1637–1987* (1987) and *The encyclopedia of Dublin* (1991, new ed. 2005).

JOHN BRADLEY studied archaeology and history at University College Dublin. He is senior lecturer in the Department of History at the National University of Ireland, Maynooth.

NICHOLAS CAROLAN is Director of the Irish Traditional Music Archive, Dublin. From Drogheda, Co. Louth, he is a lecturer and writer on traditional music, and is best known as presenter of the RTÉ archival television series *Come West along the Road*.

ANDREW CARPENTER is Emeritus Professor of English at University College Dublin and a member of the Royal Irish Academy. He has edited many texts from seventeenth- and eighteenth-century Ireland and was founding editor of the journal *Eighteenth-Century Ireland/Iris an dá chultúr*. His most significant publications in recent years are two anthologies, *Verse in English from eighteenth-century Ireland* (1998) and *Verse in English from Tudor and Stuart Ireland* (2003).

HOWARD B. CLARKE retired from full-time teaching at University College Dublin in 2005, but continues to give his course on medieval Dublin to MA students. He remains one of the editors of the *Irish historic towns atlas* of the Royal Irish Academy and is the author of the first fascicle for Dublin in that series (no.11). He is also chairman of The Medieval Trust, the parent body of Dublinia Ltd.

MICHAEL CORCORAN worked with Dublin City Council for 48 years as a draughtsman in the Planning and Drainage sections. He is president and founding member of the National Transport Museum in Howth. He gives lectures on aspects of transport in Dublin city and is the author of *Through streets broad and narrow: a history of Dublin trams* (2000), *Our good health: a history of Dublin's water and drainage* (2005), and, with Gary Manahan, of *Winged wheel: a history of CIE buses 1945–1987* (1996).

ALAN J. FLETCHER is Professor of Medieval and Renaissance Language and Literature at University College Dublin. He is a member of the Royal Irish Academy. He is the author of *Drama, performance, and polity in pre-Cromwellian Ireland* (2000), and *Drama and the performing arts in pre-Cromwellian Ireland: a repertory of sources and documents from the earliest times until c. 1642* (2000).

RAYMOND GILLESPIE is a professor of history in the National University of Ireland, Maynooth. He has written extensively on early modern Ireland and is the author of *Reading Ireland: print, reading and social change in early modern Ireland* (Manchester, 2005) and editor, with Andrew Hadfield, of *The Oxford history of the Irish book: iii the Irish book in English, 1550–1800* (Oxford, 2006).

RUTH McMANUS lectures in the Geography Department at St. Patrick's College, Drumcondra, and with the Open University. She is the author of *Dublin 1910–1940: shaping the city and suburbs* (2002) and *Crampton built* (2008), as well as articles on different aspects of urban geography, suburban history, population, heritage, tourism and geography education. She is particularly interested in the nature of the urban landscape and much of her work focuses on the physical and social development of everyday spaces.

JACINTA PRUNTY is a lecturer in the Department of Modern History, National University of Ireland, Maynooth, and a Holy Faith sister. She has published and lectured on the slum geography and social history of her native city of Dublin, and the role of church charities in relieving poverty. Her books include *Dublin slums, 1800-1925, a study in urban geography* (Dublin, 1998 & 2000); *Margaret Aylward 1810-1889, lady of charity, sister of faith* (Dublin, 1999), and *Maps and mapping for local history* (Dublin, 2004). She is currently working (with Paul Walsh, archaeologist), on the Galway city fascicle of the *Irish historic towns atlas*, Royal Irish Academy.

Index

TRACK LISTING FOR CD, INSIDE BACK COVER

1 'By Memory Inspired', Barry Gleeson, 2003
2 'The Carmagnole', Tim Dennehy, 1993
3 'Let Erin Remember', or `The Little Red Fox', No 1 Army Band, n.d. [late 1920s]
4 'Arbour Hill', Joan McDermott, 2003
5 'Emmet's Speech from the Dock', Mícheál Mac Liammóir, n.d. [c. 1957]
6 'Oh! Breathe Not His Name' (air: The Brown Maid), Jane Cassidy, n.d. [c. 1995]
7 'When He Who Adores Thee' (air: The Foxe's Sleep), Margaret Burke-Sheridan, 1944
8 'She is Far from the Land' (air: Open the Door), John McCormack, 1911
9 'My Emmet's No More', Barry Gleeson, 2003
10 'Emmet's Farewell to His Love', Maggie McGee, 1993
11 'Bold Robert Emmet', Barry Gleeson, 2003
12 'Young Emmet', Abbey Tavern group, Howth, Co. Dublin, n.d. [1960s]
13 'The Three Flowers', Barry Gleeson, 2003

For further details on CD track list see p130.